Praise for TLC at Work

"*TLC at Work* brings the MBTI® tool to life. Understanding how behavior patterns shape performance can help you, as a manager or a performer, begin to move beyond labels to bring out the best in yourself and others while respecting the diversity around you."

Darnell Lattal, Ph.D., president, Aubrey Daniels International

"*TLC at Work* uses personality type within a competency framework to help coaches define and develop measurable behaviors. This valuable resource shows professional coaches how to create a practical plan for developing competencies in themselves and others."

Laura Whitworth, cofounder, The Coaches Training Institute; coauthor, *Co-Active Coaching*

"Bravo! I'm convinced the secret to success is one of tailor fitting coaching and development programs based on individual type. Donna Dunning has captured this winning strategy by utilizing personality type."

Thomas F. Duncan III, manager, human resources, ConocoPhillips; principal consultant, DuncanResearch.com

TLC at Work

.

TLC
at Work

Training, Leading, Coaching
All Types for Star Performance

DONNA DUNNING

Davies-Black Publishing
Palo Alto, California

Published by Davies-Black Publishing, a division of CPP, Inc., 3803 East Bayshore Road, Palo Alto, CA 94303; 800-624-1765.

Special discounts on bulk quantities of Davies-Black books are available to corporations, professional associations, and other organizations. For details, contact the Director of Marketing and Sales at Davies-Black Publishing: 650-691-9123; fax 650-623-9271.

Visit the Davies-Black Publishing web site at www.daviesblack.com.

08 07 06 05 04   10 9 8 7 6 5 4 3 2 1
Printed in the United States of America

Library of Congress Cataloging-in-Publication Data
Dunning, Donna
    TLC at work : training, leading, coaching all types for star performance /
    Donna Dunning.— 1st ed.
      p. cm.
    Includes bibliographical references and index.
    ISBN 0-89106-192-4 (pbk.)
    1. Career development. 2. Leadership. 3. Motivation (Psychology) I. Title.
HF5549.5.C35D86 2004
658.3′124—dc22

                                    2003028303

FIRST EDITION
First printing 2004

To everyone who is striving to enhance
the development of others

Contents

Part 1: Competencies for Developing Others

Chapter 1: Building Relationships

Chapter 2: Facilitating Development

Part 2: Workplace Competencies

Chapter 3: Self-Responsibility

Chaper 4: Communication

Chapter 5: Mindfulness

Chapter 6: Productivity

Chapter 7: Proactivity

Introduction

TLC at Work presents a practical approach for developing workplace competencies. It is designed as a resource for trainers, leaders, coaches, and human resources professionals, and for people who recognize a need to build their performance at work. You can use this book to define, describe, and clarify specific areas of performance key to workplace success. You will learn an effective process for assessing performance gaps and facilitating development in others or in yourself.

In Part One of the book, I provide the groundwork for establishing working relationships and facilitating development of people in the workplace. These are the two competencies people in developmental roles must master to be effective helpers. I call them the *TLC competencies* (for "training, leading, and coaching," of course), and present them in the context of specific behaviors and practical development tips designed to be useful to anyone in a helping role.

In Part Two, I define five basic *workplace competencies,* describing specific, measurable behaviors necessary for high performance. In each chapter, you'll find practical tips and strategies to facilitate the development of one of these five competencies—a combination of how-to and what-to-develop that will give you all the tools you need. At the end, a closing summary captures the key points for ready reference.

You may be working in or with an organization that uses a competency model for human resources functions such as recruiting, evaluating performance, compensation, and learning based on a different list of competencies. Many comprehensive lists—including literally hundreds of specific competencies arranged in countless configurations and levels—have been published, and many organizations have created customized systems to identify, measure, and develop competencies. You can still use this book, as it does not compete with established competency systems. Its intent is to supplement rather than replace.

My focus here is on the basic competencies that form a universal starting point. No one can function within even the simplest competency- and performance-based development model without the ability to take personal responsibility, communicate effectively, learn and think, achieve results, and plan ahead.

As an analogy, compare your existing competency-based performance system to a typical high school or university curriculum, which shows what students need to know and do to pass and therefore qualify to move to another level. This book, in contrast, can be compared to the basic elementary school curriculum—the skills in arithmetic, reading, writing, spelling, and learning that the students were expected to have developed before high school. Without these basic skills, it is difficult to learn and perform well in any advanced course.

The competencies described in this book are as important to individual development as basic literacy, numeracy, and study skills are to academic success. Once students know how to read, write, calculate, and learn, they can succeed in a wide variety of courses. Likewise, once people demonstrate the competencies in this book, they will be able to work independently and effectively. If they have performance gaps, they will know *how* to develop themselves and how to choose *what* they need to work on. The basic competencies provide an approach that allows people to develop and succeed in a wide range of work roles.

This book can help those in both traditional and nontraditional types of work. These days many people find themselves working without the resources of an organization to facilitate their development. If you are in this situation, you may need to act as your own development coach. This can be a difficult process, since self-development requires awareness facilitated by feedback. Self-development may require you to challenge your assumptions and change habitual behaviors. If you are working through this process on your own, you may well find that the insights provided here will be enough to go on with. However, recruiting a supportive individual to work with you in the process may still prove helpful. Many private coaches work with individuals inside and outside organizations to help them develop their potential.

In recognition of the changing nature of the workforce, I have tried to minimize the use of terminology reflecting the traditional employment relationship. For example, I generally refer to the person being helped as a *worker, individual,* or *client* rather than as an *employee.* This frames the book as a twenty-first-century resource, one that reflects current realities and is inclusive for all types of workers, and that looks toward the new paradigm of *work* as opposed to the nineteenth- and twentieth-century concept of *jobs.*

A ROAD MAP FOR THE BOOK

Part One introduces the TLC competencies that enable people in helping roles to build relationships and enhance development. It lays the groundwork for establishing a working relationship built on mutual respect.

Chapter 1 begins by defining and describing the essential step of establishing credibility and trust. It contains information to help build a working relationship with clients. No one-size-fits-all development program is likely to work well every time. This is a challenge for human resources professionals, trainers, leaders, and coaches. As organizations strive to maintain a competitive advantage, it is especially important for those in development roles to customize their strategies to accommodate individual differences. To be effective in their work, people in development roles must understand and coach different clients in different ways.

Because of the importance of individual differences, Chapter 1 also contains a comprehensive guide focused on personality type to help you understand your individual style and accommodate the style of others. This book focuses on personality type as measured by the *Myers-Briggs Type Indicator*® (MBTI®) assessment, which has in-depth, empirical data and support materials. Many people find the MBTI language somewhat abstract, so—to make the theory more accessible—the book incorporates a jargon-free, user-friendly way to understand, share, and apply personality type concepts.

Chapter 2 presents a practical approach to facilitating development. It describes ways to help others by identifying specific development outcomes, roadblocks, and strategies, and it also shows you how to create, coach, and monitor an effective development plan.

Part Two addresses the basic question, What competencies do twenty-first-century workers need?

Five workplace competencies are key to success in all types of work. By using observable and measurable behaviors, the chapters in Part Two provide a clear picture of what effective individual performance looks like. Development then becomes a concrete process focused on accomplishing a specific, positive outcome to increase individual effectiveness. This process is practical rather than theoretical and is designed to make specific, concrete interventions to improve performance in an observable, measurable way. When people demonstrate the five competencies described here, they will be self-directed, mindful, and able to communicate, learn, and adapt.

Workplace Competency 1: Self-Responsibility

Chapter 3 introduces the basic competency of self-responsibility. That is, effective workers are personally accountable and responsible for the consequences of their actions. People who take responsibility for their actions and the resulting consequences will be able to direct themselves, adjust their behavior, and take initiative. Self-responsible workers will show up ready and willing to work and will take ownership of their successes and mistakes. This allows them to adjust and improve their performance. When people are ready and willing to work, they will be realistically optimistic, energetic, and alert and will work independently toward their goals. When people take ownership of the results of their work, they will demonstrate personal accountability and maximize their personal assets.

Workplace Competency 2: Communication

Chapter 4 underscores the basic truths that effective communication is as essential to success at work as everywhere else in life and that effective communicators listen carefully. People who listen carefully encourage others to express differing perspectives. They clarify and act on communications and incorporate feedback. Effective communicators are also able to share information in a clear, focused manner. They customize their messages, give useful, positive, and constructive feedback, and resolve issues before they spiral into problems.

Workplace Competency 3: Mindfulness

Chapter 5 takes up the complex topic of mindfulness. Mindfulness involves awareness of, reflection on, and adjustment of behaviors and strategies. Workers who are mindful think about and evaluate what they are learning and doing. Mindful workers know how to learn and are able to access and use new information. They critique sources of information and transfer what they learn to new situations. Mindful workers systematically solve problems and make informed decisions. They are aware of different modes of thinking and they consciously switch thinking modes when it is appropriate to do so.

Workplace Competency 4: Productivity

Chapter 6 gets to the bottom line: the point of work is to produce something. Productive workers focus on obtaining results. They prioritize, plan, and organize time and tasks. Rather than give up easily, they persist on the tasks at hand. This allows productive workers to achieve exceptional results. A productive worker achieves a high standard, continuously improves the way work is done, and exceeds performance expectations.

Workplace Competency 5: Proactivity

Chapter 7 addresses the need to keep looking ahead. Proactive workers anticipate and adapt. They look for patterns in the world around them and prepare for changes. Proactive people are open-minded and actively gather diverse perspectives. This allows them to see things in many different ways. When functioning proactively, workers can create original ways to improve situations and to capitalize on opportunities. People who are proactive develop and promote themselves to achieve career and life goals. By fulfilling career and life goals, they position themselves for success.

USING TLC AT WORK

TLC at Work will help you develop your personal TLC and workplace competencies. It will provide you with all the tools you need to enhance the performance of others.

As a trainer, leader, or coach, you can use this book as a comprehensive resource for dealing with virtually any employee performance difficulty. You can also use it with your clients as a tool for assessing and developing specific workplace competencies.

Acknowledgments

I'd like to thank the trainers, leaders, and coaches who contributed their stories as well as my clients and colleagues who shared their personal development experiences. Thanks to all the wonderful people at Davies-Black/CPP, Inc., for their support and encouragement. And special thanks to Paul, Kelly, and Eric.

About the Author

Donna Dunning is director of Dunning Unlimited, a learning, career development, and work performance consulting firm. An award-winning psychologist, educator, and certified human resources professional, she has more than twenty years of experience providing assessment and out-placement services, facilitating workshops, and consulting in the area of employee development. Dunning is a member of the APT MBTI® International Training Faculty and author of *What's Your Type of Career?*

Competencies for Developing Others

Two competencies—building relationships and facilitating development—will enhance your effectiveness in your role as a practitioner. If you don't take the time to build a relationship based on credibility, trust, and respect with those you are helping, chances are your clients will not be comfortable sharing personal information with you and taking the risks necessary to improve themselves. Chapter 1 focuses on what you need to do to build such relationships. But establishing a relationship isn't enough for success; it must be linked to the implementation of a well-planned development process. Chapter 2 presents strategies and techniques that will help you implement a successful development plan.

A Gap Analysis near the beginning of each chapter will help you assess each competency and its components. This simple instrument presents a pair of statements on a continuum that defines each component. The left side of the continuum describes an area for improvement; the right side describes a positive demonstration of the component. You can use this Gap Analysis to target general areas for improvement within each practitioner competency for yourself and the workplace competencies for your clients. As a next step, you can translate any of the individual components into specific behaviors to address by finding a more detailed description of that component in the corresponding section of the chapter.

1

Within each section you will find a Detect & Describe box for each component assessed by the Gap Analysis. This tool allows you to clearly define specific positive behaviors as desired outcomes within each of the components. On the left of the Detect & Describe box is a list of behaviors seen when the component is not being demonstrated. The right side lists desired behaviors. By completing the Detect & Describe boxes you will be able to more clearly define specific desired outcomes, gaps, and behaviors for development. Familiarize yourself with these two levels of behaviors by skimming the chapters. Overviewing the chapters will provide a clearer context to help you accurately complete the Gap Analysis and Detect & Describe boxes.

Another important tool in Chapter 2 is a Development Plan worksheet that is useful in two ways. You can use it to map your own development as you become familiar with the steps in developing a plan. Later, you can use it as a guide in developing a plan collaboratively with each client.

Chapter 1
Building Relationships

Few people willingly share weaknesses or try new behaviors if they are uncomfortable with the person trying to help them. This means that, before you can help others improve their performance, those you wish to help must see you as a credible, interested, trustworthy, and sincere professional.

The relationship-building competency has two components. The first part of the chapter focuses on establishing credibility, rapport, and trust with others. The second part of the chapter considers ways to acknowledge, appreciate, and accommodate individual differences. Note the list of the components of relationship building in the order in which they will be covered in the chapter.

The following Gap Analysis addresses broad areas of behavior and will help you assess your relationship-building performance. Completing the analysis will help you identify specific components of the competency to focus on as you read the chapter. Before completing this tool you may find it helpful to scan the chapter content. This will privide a context for your assessment and will help you familiarize yourself with the specific behaviors considered within the five broad areas included in the Gap Analysis.

COMPONENTS OF RELATIONSHIP BUILDING

Establish Credibility, Rapport, and Trust
- Role-model ongoing self-development
- Use a professional approach when helping others

Acknowledge, Appreciate, and Accommodate Individual Differences
- Consider personal situations
- Acknowledge and appreciate different personalities
- Adjust interventions to accommodate different preferences

GAP ANALYSIS
Building Relationships

The pairs of statements that follow represent the endpoints of a continuum of possible performance in building relationships. To assess your current level, place an X on each line at the location that best describes the approach you use now.

Establish Credibility, Rapport, and Trust

Not engaged in self-development $\longleftrightarrow$ Role-model ongoing self-development

Not using a professional approach when helping others $\longleftrightarrow$ Use a professional approach when helping others

Acknowledge, Appreciate, and Accommodate Individual Differences

Do not consider personal situations $\longleftrightarrow$ Consider personal situations

Do not acknowledge differences in personality $\longleftrightarrow$ Acknowledge and appreciate different personalities

Do not customize interventions $\longleftrightarrow$ Adjust interventions to accommodate different preferences

Take time to reflect on building relationships. Use the space below to write down any specific information or insights you have regarding your ability to apply this competency. You may want to ask leaders, colleagues, or clients to fill out the Gap Analysis to provide you with an external assessment to compare with your self-assessment. Before you leave the Gap Analysis with someone, take a few minutes to discuss the meaning of each element so they will understand the kind of behavior you want to review.

_____

_____

_____

ESTABLISH CREDIBILITY, RAPPORT, AND TRUST

When you need assistance, you look for someone who is knowledgeable, an expert in the area in which you are seeking help. Your clients have the same needs; they need to know you are someone with the expertise to help them. One of the best ways to establish this credibility is to demonstrate what you know. However, even the most skilled experts tend to lose business if they are not willing to build rapport and trust with their clients. This is especially true in the helping professions, whose practitioners expect people to share their weaknesses and take personal risks. Thus you will need to both establish yourself as a competent, skilled, and sincere role model and establish rapport and trust with your potential clients by being professional and genuine in your approach.

Role-Model Ongoing Self-Development

If you intend to help others, you first need to be seen as someone who knows what they are doing. Certificates and degrees on the wall may provide you with some initial credibility. These indicate that you have taken time to learn, at least in theory, something about how to coach, lead, train, or support others. However, the credentials themselves will not be enough to convince potential clients you are the person who is able to help them. They will also need to see that you are a credible resource in areas of professional development.

The Detect & Describe box on the following page provides a checklist of specific behaviors people engage in when modeling ongoing self-development. If you engage in the negative behaviors on the left you will be able to replace them with the positive behaviors on the right after working through the material in this chapter. Clients will respect you more when they see you demonstrating self-development.

The first thing potential clients will look for is how effective you are in your own work performance. People tend to be most convinced of your ability to help them when they see you perform your roles effectively. When you are beginning to establish a working relationship focused on helping someone else, be sure to demonstrate your ability to practice what you teach. People tend to place little confidence in someone who says one thing and then does something else: Effective coaches "walk their talk."

DETECT & DESCRIBE
Role-Model Ongoing Self-Development

. . . .

Don't see high performance

Evidence of failure to engage in self-development:

○ Advocating one thing but doing something different

○ Displaying ignorance of the basic competencies necessary for top performance

○ Maintaining rather than improving personal work performance

○ Remaining stagnant in personal work roles

Do see high performance

Evidence of self-development sufficient to serve as role model:

○ Practicing the principles advocated in day-to-day work

○ Knowing and applying the basic work competencies

○ Striving to enhance personal work performance

○ Learning and developing at all times

Walking your talk means you are engaged in the same process that you are advocating. It means you are actively working toward self-improvement. You see your own strengths and areas for development and are consciously working toward being the best you can be. This may sound somewhat idealistic, but why would you expect others to develop themselves if you are not undergoing a similar process with positive results?

For example, how can you expect to teach someone to demonstrate self-responsibility if you blame others for your problems? Workers are not likely to believe that timeliness is important if the coach shows up late for coaching sessions. Any discrepancy between what you do and what you advocate can seriously undermine your credibility. The most effective trainers, leaders, and coaches are willing to be taught, led by others, and coached. They are effective when working with others partially because they value and are already actively involved in enhancing their own performance. In the following example, a training facilitator describes the ongoing self-development journey of another trainer she was coaching. Notice how she has coached the trainer to engage in and model his own learning.

TRAINING THE TRAINER

I worked with a young forklift driver who was promoted to a training position because of his skill and leadership abilities. His challenge was to teach older drivers on new, highly computerized, equipment. The trainer not only needed to learn the specific content training skills, he also needed to find ways to overcome the resistance and fears of the older drivers. Through experiential training using role playing, case studies, and discussion, the trainer's personal development was enhanced. He has become more confident dealing with older employees in his leadership position. He not only teaches new skills but also makes a concentrated effort to develop mutual trust between himself and his trainees. He reports success and appreciation for the personal skills he has learned.

Role modeling also extends to being aware of and actively engaging in learning the basic competencies for workplace success. By honing your performance in all five basic competency areas you will enhance your credibility. Effective coaches will model the five basic workplace competencies of *self-responsibility, communication, mindfulness, productivity,* and *proactivity.* If you do not demonstrate self-responsibility, others will not be motivated to take ownership of their actions. If you do not demonstrate effective communication, you will not be able to build the relationships necessary for helping others. Communication is especially key for establishing rapport. (Read through the discussion of communication in Chapter 4 to ensure you are an excellent model of listening carefully and sharing information.) Coaches, perhaps more than most individuals, require effective communication to understand the perspective of others, give and receive feedback, share messages, and resolve issues. Likewise, mindfulness is indispensable when coaches are helping others assess themselves and challenging unproductive behaviors. Productivity will be important to model while helping others set and follow through with a development plan. Demonstrating proactivity will show the benefits of looking to the future, creating and capitalizing on opportunities. When others see you doing this, they are likelier to understand the importance of self-development and promotion.

To determine your knowledge and preparedness in the area of professional development, first assess yourself on the five basic workplace competencies (covered in Chapters 3 through 7). As a prerequisite to helping others, you might consider developing your workplace competencies by completing the development process offered in this book. This can be especially beneficial if you have someone who can help you assess and enhance your work performance. If you work within an organization or are networked with others, you may want to partner with a colleague to gain familiarity with the approach. Once you're familiar with the basic concepts presented here, respond to the Gap Analysis and work through the Detect & Describe boxes in all the competency chapters. This process not only will help you become acquainted with the approach and competencies, it also will enhance your self-development.

When you are learning and developing, you are establishing credibility with others. At the same time, you are becoming more skilled in your area of expertise. Others will see the positive results of your actions and will hopefully see your effective performance as something they would like to emulate. This doesn't mean you need to demonstrate perfection in the area of workplace performance, of course. (Who could be perfect, anyway?) As a matter of fact, showing that you, the expert, are still willing to improve and engage in development can be inspiring to others. When you openly admit your areas of weakness and work toward your own goals, you provide a development role model. This may help others feel less inhibited about exploring their blind spots and taking new risks to improve their performance.

As well as demonstrating basic work performance competencies, effective helpers also focus on developing competencies that directly enhance their ability to work with others. They develop the TLC competencies covered in this chapter and the next chapter. This orientation toward advocating for and demonstrating ongoing self-development establishes credibility and sets the stage for developing relationships based on rapport and trust.

Use a Professional Approach When Helping Others

As well as being a role model for the process of self-development, an effective helper also acts in a genuine and professional manner. Others will note your authenticity and professionalism. This will create an environment where potential clients will begin to sense you are trustworthy.

DETECT & DESCRIBE
Use a Professional Approach When Helping Others

Don't see high performance

Evidence that someone is not using a professional approach:

○ Neglecting to learn about or focus on the ethical principles of helping others

○ Sharing information without respect for confidentiality

○ Seeking input from others without considering confidentiality issues

○ Neglecting to discuss and agree with clients on how information is to be shared

○ Using self-disclosure inappropriately

○ Behaving in an artificial or nonauthentic manner

○ Tightly controlling the amount of information and skills that is shared

○ Trying to help people in areas beyond current expertise

○ Trying new methods without considering possible effects on others

Do see high performance

Evidence that someone is using a professional approach:

○ Following the ethical guidelines of professional organizations and associations

○ Ensuring that clients have as much confidentiality as possible

○ Using discretion when involving others in the development process

○ Clearly explaining to all people involved how information will be shared

○ Using self-disclosure appropriately

○ Behaving in a genuine and authentic manner

○ Freely transferring skills and knowledge to others

○ Working only within current areas of expertise

○ Using tried methods and carefully considering how new methods will affect others

If you are certified as a human resources professional or a coach, or hold some other type of professional designation, you are probably bound by your association's set of principles or a code of ethics. These guidelines have been created to help you conduct your work in a professional way. Make sure you are familiar with and operate conscientiously within these standards. When you adhere to your principles and demonstrate ethical interactions, you will begin to develop relationships based on trust.

Many ethical considerations arise when someone sets out to help others. The next sections will focus on some of the key considerations for working ethically with others to develop workplace competencies.

Confidentiality

Confidentiality is an important consideration, especially in an organizational setting. Within many organizations, workers who are being assisted in their performance tend to lose or gain status as a result. Their status plummets in organizations where people are asked to create a performance improvement plan only when experiencing performance problems. Their status rises in organizations where selected high-performers are fast-tracked or given coaching assistance as a perk. Although both situations can lead to confidentiality issues, the first type can be especially sensitive. In all cases, you are not likely to establish trust with your client unless you address confidentiality.

The initial confidentiality concern is related to the simple fact that someone is receiving assistance in the development process. Clients may not want others to be aware that they are involved in a development process or receiving any type of assistance to enhance their performance. The best practice is to ensure that your helping service is as invisible as possible. People should be able to access support for development without its becoming common knowledge. This can sometimes be difficult to implement. You might want to ask yourself the following questions to assess how confidential your services are.

- How do your clients contact you?

- How do you contact your clients?

- Where do you meet?

- When do you meet?

- Who needs to know about the meetings?

The next concern regards the information that is shared with you by the client during your meetings. Someone who is unsure how you will be using the information is apt to be uncomfortable sharing personal experiences. This is especially true when focusing on topics such as weaknesses, areas of growth, mistakes made, and conflicts with others. This personal information can put a client at a serious disadvantage in the workplace if it is brought to others' attention or used in an evaluative rather than a developmental context. Organizations often have integrated systems of recruitment, development, training, compensation, and performance evaluation. These integrated systems have advantages, since human resources functions can become more aligned and effective. However, they may not create the ideal confidentiality conditions to promote development. In favorable situations, you may be able to ensure that the information generated in the coaching sessions is used solely for the purpose of individual improvement.

If the performance improvement process was initiated as a result of a problem, your client may be facing serious consequences if the performance doesn't improve. In such situations, you may not be able to offer complete confidentiality. In fact, the efforts and results from the development process may be used as input to a decision-making process affecting compensation or employment. In these cases, the process and consequences need to be made clear. The client needs to know how the information you are gathering will be used and to agree on exactly what, when, how, and with whom information will be shared. Do this first thing in your helping process to avoid any potential misunderstanding. Use information only for the agreed purposes. As you read the following questions, assess where and how information regarding individual development is used in your organization. Make a clear communication plan as a result of your answers, so everyone is aware of what will be shared.

- Where do you store information related to clients' development?

- Who has access to this information?

- Do you report back to anyone about your clients' competencies and progress?

- What information do you share about your clients' competencies and progress?

- How is the information about progress going to be used?

When you are helping someone develop, you may want to seek input from others. It is often helpful to have others involved in an individual development plan. The client may benefit from feedback from others. You may want to initiate a conflict resolution process as part of a development plan. You may know someone within or outside the organization that you want to involve to act as a trainer, mentor, or evaluator of the client's plan. Decide about these external resources carefully. Avoid bringing in an external resource, especially one within the organization, until you have discussed and approved this with the client. Coach any others you bring into the process about the importance of confidentiality. Additional people you plan to use as resources should demonstrate the TLC competencies.

If you are careful to consider all these aspects of confidentiality, explain and agree on specifics about how information is shared, and then walk your talk, you are likely to be able to establish a working relationship based on trust. Without these conditions, no one is likely to feel comfortable confiding in you. Also remember that confidentiality has a limit. For example, you will be obliged to share information that others confide if it demonstrates intent to do harm to themselves or others. If you are facing thorny confidentiality issues, you may want to consult with another professional helper such as a psychologist.

If you work with individuals as a consultant or as a private coach, you will need to address confidentiality issues in a slightly different way. You are considering the needs of two distinct clients, the organization that is paying you and the person who is receiving your coaching. The organization may want information about the individual's progress and the individual may not want some information shared. You must be clear, up front, about exactly what information will be shared and with whom. Both parties must be aware of and agree on what and how information will be shared. I suggest preparing a form that summarizes how and what information will be shared and having all involved parties sign it; that is the most prudent way to deal with this situation.

Self-Disclosure and Authenticity

Self-disclosure is a tool that can be used by helping professionals to establish rapport. When using this tool, you share a personal example or experience in an effort to develop rapport by demonstrating that you have experienced a similar situation. Self-disclosure can also show others that you are not perfect and have had to deal with issues yourself. You may be able to give an example of how you worked through a weakness or managed a problem or issue. This story can model the process you are teaching and can be an example of a positive outcome. Used appropriately, self-disclosure can be a useful tool when you are sharing a process and establishing a helping relationship.

However, too much self-disclosure can be detrimental to a helping relationship. Some clients may not want to hear about and focus on your personal experiences. Some may find your self-disclosures inappropriate. Others may find the self-disclosures detract from your credibility. Be careful not to reverse the roles so the person you are supposed to be helping ends up with a major role of supporting and encouraging you. Also make sure you refrain from sharing excessive doubts with and expressing all your frustrations to someone who is struggling to implement the development process.

When you are helping people develop, your responsibility is to take the lead. You must be positive and supportive. If you are not in a position to carry out this responsibility, you may need to work through some of your own issues before assuming the helping role. Self-disclosure may not be an issue if you will be engaged in a mutually supporting relationship where it is appropriate for both or all parties to help and be helped. However, in most situations a clear distinction between what is appropriate and inappropriate disclosure needs to be addressed.

Authenticity refers to presenting yourself in a genuine way. Clients will be aware of attempts on your part to present yourself in an overly favorable or artificial manner. This is another balance point to consider carefully. You are a unique individual and others will tend to know immediately when you are pretending to be something that isn't genuine. Your interactions will reflect your style and your immediate situation. Although you will strive to accommodate others, make sure you are authentic in your interactions.

For instance, if you are feeling extremely frustrated one day, it might be better to admit to it rather than try to mask it. Without turning the focus on yourself, you can succinctly explain that you are frustrated and that you will work toward getting yourself back on track. Take ownership of your feelings and be careful not to blame situations or people for how you are feeling. This simple, honest self-expression will be much more appropriate than efforts to hide your emotion. As with any form of self-disclosure, promptly return the focus to the person you are helping. Of course, you will disclose your feelings only in a situation where you know the emotion is bound to affect your interaction. In most cases you will be able to exhibit self-control and tune out distracting emotions. The key is to be genuine in your interactions so that others will be able to understand and trust who you are and how you respond.

A QUESTION OF BALANCE
Self-Expression and Self-Control

Self-expression and self-control are both important tools for a helper to use when developing rapport with clients. Think about which end of the continuum can be more of a problem for you and focus on having a balance in this area.

Self-expression allows the client to see and understand who you are and what is important to you. Although some may argue that your life is not the client's business, many clients will need to get to know who you are and what you believe in before they will be willing to trust you. It is often appropriate to express your beliefs about the importance of self-development. Personal examples of your own experiences, when shared wisely, can be inspiring to the client. Of course, too much or inappropriate self-expression can turn the focus away from the client and confuse the helping relationship. As well, it is usually unhelpful to express things in an overly negative way; this undercuts your ability to act as a role model.

Self-control is also important in a helping relationship. For example, sometimes clients act in ways that undermine your intentions. In such situations, you will want to explore this with them, but you need to be careful to control how you express your thoughts and feelings. In a similar way, it may be tempting to develop rapport with clients by running down their organization, systems, bosses, and so on. This may help develop morale in the short-term, but does not lead to the type of self-responsible outcomes you are seeking. Too much self-control, however, can make you seem overly detached or mechanical. Others will not be able to get a sense of who you really are.

Collaborative Mind-Set

A professional helper must have a mind-set focused on transferring information and expertise rather than on controlling it. People with a collaborative mind-set do not want to control the information and competencies they possess. Rather, they are focused on transferring as much of their knowledge and skills as possible to the people they are helping. You are a resource and a source of information you are willing to share. As well, you see your clients as sources of valuable information and you respect their contribution to the process. This is not a top-down process where you fill the client's mind with the right stuff. It is a process of ongoing growth and development for everyone involved.

A collaborative mind-set is also based on an equal distribution of power between the client and the helper. This is not always totally possible. For example, when setting a development plan, you may need to set a consequence that a client will disagree with. You can engage in dialogue and explain your position, but no matter what you may discuss, the consequence is not negotiable. However, in most other situations, it is possible to set up the helping relationship so both parties are able to share their opinions and influence the steps that are taken. If you are too directive or controlling in this type of process, you may meet significant resistance. You also deprive your client of the opportunity to take personal responsibility. Sometimes it is difficult to avoid the impulse to give advice. Here is an example of a helper who is carefully considering how to be more collaborative and less directive with her clients.

GET OUT OF THE DRIVER'S SEAT

Resisting the impulse to give advice or suggest how to solve the problem was a challenge for me when working with clients. I needed to focus on letting clients identify the problem and having them suggest ways to resolve it. Then I could gently ask questions to ensure they had the result they wanted and the path to get there. Previously I would have jumped right in with a solution, which meant I lost the opportunity to let the other person think things through and find a solution. To develop this approach I constantly reminded myself before and during a meeting to listen empathically and resist trying to solve a problem for someone. It took a lot of practice and self-reminders.

When working with a client, assess your willingness or ability to work with a collaborative mind-set. Be aware that your attitudes about how to carry out the helping process will affect the level of trust and respect you are developing with the client.

Areas of Expertise

As a helping professional you will be exposed to situations where people are experiencing difficulties that are outside of your expertise. To name just a few, these difficulties might include addictions, abusive relationships, learning disabilities, health problems, or mental health issues. In these cases it is important to show concern and know your limitations. Don't try to diagnose or solve the problem yourself unless you have been trained to do so.

Here are some cues that might lead you to suspect work behaviors are related to personal issues or difficulties:

- Increased work absences

- Changes in typical behavior

- Reduced productivity or quality of work

- Variable work pace

- Missed deadlines

- Mood swings

- Emotional outbursts

As a trainer, leader, or coach in an organization, you are not expected to have the resources or the mandate to diagnose or address these issues. If you suspect or learn of problems that you are unable to deal with, it is essential to recommend seeing a professional skilled in the area that needs to be addressed. If clients are willing to define such issues and deal with them, you might want to have them focus on that before addressing work performance. Be sure to give your clients as many chances and as much encouragement as possible to access professional help. If you work within an organization, you may have an assistance program you can use as a referral source. If not, you will need to develop a referral list. Many communities have a community services guide that lists service providers in the area. However, even if someone does not choose to face or resolve personal issues, it is still appropriate to expect high workplace performance. Discuss the performance issues with the client and clarify expectations. This doesn't mean you have to stop working with clients who want to improve their work performance if you find they have additional problems. It may be possible to continue development work. This is a judgment call that you, in collaboration with the person you are helping, will need to make. However, offer help only within your areas of expertise; address other issues with the client and encourage efforts to find additional help in those areas.

If you work on your own as a coach, it will be especially important to take the time to establish a network of contacts for referral. Confidentiality will be an especially important issue in this regard. Have the people you are working with contact the referral sources and arrange funding themselves whenever possible. If they want you to help them in this regard, make sure you clearly establish and agree on who will hear from you and what information you will share. If you are unsure of how to proceed in any of these ethical areas, you may want to consult with a health or legal professional.

When you have taken the steps to develop and model work competencies and have acted in a professional manner toward others, you are well on the way to developing a relationship based on trust. As a next step, consider the needs, situation, and preferences of each individual you are helping.

ACKNOWLEDGE, APPRECIATE, AND ACCOMMODATE INDIVIDUAL DIFFERENCES

Every person you help is unique, facing a different situation and bringing a unique set of preferences to the table. As you work with clients, consider their personal needs. These needs will affect how and what someone wants to and chooses to focus on during the development process. Whether you are working one-on-one or in a group, it is important to explore these differences.

You have your own situation and preferences. As well as exploring your clients' individuality, consider how your situation and preferences influence your work with clients. Your individuality can predispose you to certain biases and ways of interacting. Understanding, acknowledging, and appreciating your individual preferences as well as those of your clients can help create relationships based on mutual respect.

Consider Personal Situations

Everyone has a unique set of experiences and characteristics that influence the way they respond and do their work. Considering these will help you work with a client in a more holistic way.

DETECT & DESCRIBE
Consider Personal Situations

Don't see high performance

Evidence of failure to consider situational differences:

- ○ Failing to take time to understand or assess the client's personal situation
- ○ Ignoring situational factors when addressing work performance
- ○ Being overly objective or subjective
- ○ Lacking knowledge of potential referrals for dealing with a client's personal problems

Do see high performance

Evidence of considering personal situations:

- ○ Taking time to understand an individual's personal situation
- ○ Watching for and addressing situational factors affecting performance
- ○ Balancing objectivity and subjectivity
- ○ Maintaining a network of referrals to facilitate dealing with a client's personal problems

Once you have proven to be a trustworthy helper, you can turn your focus to the process of helping clients develop workplace competencies. With everyone you work with, take time to understand what personal factors are influencing the way they approach their work. No two clients will react the same way or have the same needs. Personal factors greatly affect an individual's ability to perform work roles. Here are some factors you may want to take into consideration. In certain circumstances, each may play a role in work performance.

- Addictions
- Additional roles and responsibilities
- Age
- Attitudes
- Beliefs
- Community involvement
- Criminal record
- Domestic obligations
- Educational background
- Energy level
- Experience
- Financial situation
- Gender
- Intelligence
- Interests
- Learning difficulties
- Marital status

- Mental health
- Minority status
- Motivation
- Physical health
- Physical limitations
- Recreational interests and activities

- Relationships
- Religious practices
- Self-esteem
- Skills
- Values
- Work roles

You can probably think of a situation when one or more of these factors directly affected a worker's performance. Several of these factors will emerge as important to only a specific situation. Perhaps an individual has a number of absences because of family, physical health, or addiction problems. Perhaps someone, whether male or female, in a nontraditional role is frustrated and distracted by the way others treat him or her at the work site. Workers often have certain attitudes and beliefs that affect the way they carry out their work. Many of these factors will be considered in the workplace competency chapters. For example, Chapter 3 will discuss energy level, attitudes, and beliefs as they affect self-responsibility. Chapter 7 will look at career development and will directly consider career and life goals in the context of proactivity.

It would probably not be helpful to create a checklist or assessment to go through these factors one by one. As a helping professional, you need to keep all these factors in mind as you begin to work with someone. You can use cues such as increased work absences, changes in typical behavior, reduced productivity, reduced quality of work, missed deadlines, mood swings, or emotional outbursts to help you assess the possibility that personal factors are influencing work performance.

As you develop trust in the working relationship, the client may begin to tell you about some of these personal factors. Listen carefully and, when appropriate, be sure to include strategies to manage specific factors in your plan. For example, if gender or racial differences are creating problems because of attitudes of coworkers, you may need to customize your intervention to address them. Ignoring situational factors can create a scenario where your best-planned interventions are ineffective. As mentioned earlier in the chapter, someone whose serious personal problems are damaging performance may not be willing, ready, or able to work through a development process. You may need to refer such an individual for outside assistance.

A QUESTION OF BALANCE
Objectivity and Subjectivity

Looking at situational factors affecting performance reflects a subjective, holistic approach to the development process. On one hand, you need to see each worker as a unique individual operating under unique conditions. Successful coaching can require attention to the whole person and exploration of factors outside the work setting that may be affecting performance in the work setting. On the other hand, it can be argued that these factors are best left out of the work setting and should be seen as beyond the scope of work performance and that objective measures of work performance should be equally applied to all workers. If personal situations are addressed and accommodated, inequalities can emerge in performance expectations.

Further compounding this issue is the fact that workers as well as helpers will have very different opinions as to how much of personal life relates to work life or should be explored when assessing and developing the ability to perform at work. As a professional helping others develop, you will find it important to see and respect both objective and subjective perspectives when helping others. Note your own biases toward one or the other and ensure you are able to accommodate those who have a different perspective. Consider both subjective and objective factors carefully when creating a development plan.

Getting to know a person's situation can help develop rapport. You may find common topics of interest to discuss. You can also think of examples and activities that reflect your client's personal situation and interests. For example, if your client is a baseball fan, you might want to use baseball analogies or stories to illustrate a point—but only if you yourself are fond enough of baseball to get them right. Your client will know if you are faking an interest, and may well reject your help entirely in that case.

At this point, it is time to introduce the Development Plan form—(see page 52). I refer to this form repeatedly throughout this chapter and Chapter 2. It provides a working document for you to fill out as you move through the development process. The first part of the plan focuses on the individual considerations discussed here. When you are helping clients work through their plan, think about what individual considerations need to be dealt with to enhance the effectiveness of the plan.

If someone is willing to define personal issues and deal with them, it may be possible to allow some additional time to manage these problems before initiating a development plan. You may choose to set a specific time frame to deal with these problems. This might entail a broad range of activities for the client: visit a medical doctor to clarify and deal with a health problem, hire domestic assistance, carry out some necessary financial changes. Referrals may need to be made and followed through on, and appointments monitored. Encourage your client to access additional professional help throughout the process. However, keep in mind that personal issues can become excuses for poor performance rather than roadblocks to be overcome. Whether or not the client chooses to face or resolve personal issues, it is still appropriate to expect performance improvement. It is important to set time lines and clarify expectations of progress to be made on work and personal issues.

Acknowledge and Appreciate Different Personalities

Not only do all individuals have different personal circumstances, they also have different preferences in the way they approach work. By becoming aware of these preferences, you can begin to understand, acknowledge, and appreciate different work approaches. One of the most effective ways of looking at differences is to assess an individual's innate personality type. This knowledge can help you customize development plans to maximize their effectiveness. The personality type framework in this book uses as a starting point the insights and writings of Carl Jung. Jung's approach looks at the ways individuals prefer to gather information and make decisions. Personality type also shows how people prefer to orient themselves and deal with the world around them. It is essential to recognize that there are no good or bad personality types. Instead, high-work performers are to be found in all types, each with characteristic preferences in the way they approach work.

In the past several decades, thousands of studies have been conducted in the area of personality type. The research literature includes a wealth of information on how personality type affects career choices and

DETECT & DESCRIBE
Acknowledge and Appreciate Different Personalities

Don't see high performance	**Do see high performance**
Evidence of failure to acknowledge differences in personality preferences:	Evidence of acknowledgment and appreciation of personality preferences:
○ Failing to acknowledge different ways of working	○ Acknowledging different ways of working
○ Criticizing different ways of working	○ Appreciating the strengths of different ways of working
○ Using negative labels to describe different personality types	○ Avoiding using negative labels to describe different personality types
○ Treating some people with less respect	○ Treating all people with respect

work preferences. Understanding personality type thus provides a useful tool for identifying how people prefer to do their work and the type of work they prefer to do.

Personality type is a nonjudgmental tool that looks at the strengths and gifts of individuals. This is a refreshing change from many other personality tools, which compare the so-called normal and abnormal. This tool has many practical applications in the competency development process. Understanding personality type allows development professionals to quickly assess potential strengths and blind spots for their clients. As well, personality type information provides clues to how each client will prefer to move through the development process. Personality type can also assist development professionals in the exploration of their own biases and preferences in how they carry out helping activities.

Jung's theory of personality type has been elaborated and popularized through the work of Katharine Cook Briggs and Isabel Briggs Myers. This mother-and-daughter team created the *Myers-Briggs Type Indicator®* (MBTI®) personality inventory, an assessment tool for identifying personality type, which has thrived through more than sixty years of research and development. The MBTI instrument can be administered and interpreted only by a trained individual. If you are interested in using this tool, the Association for Psychological Type (APT) can refer you to an MBTI specialist in your area.

Even if you are not employing the full personality assessment tool, however, you will find the mind-set and terminology useful. The boxed text on pages 24 through 27 will give you a quick overview of personality type theory. First you will need to define the characteristic ways you and your client prefer to function and orient yourselves to the world. These ways of functioning and orienting are grouped into four pairs. You will naturally prefer one element of each pair over the other. By choosing one preference from each pair, you can discover a four-letter personality type, one of sixteen personality types. Read through the preference pairs to identify your personality type, and check the circle that best applies to you.

Note that it is essential not to use personality type to categorize, label, or limit yourself or others. The descriptions given here are general, so not all statements will apply to you or any other individual. For instance, the preferences you express and develop are greatly influenced by your current situation and experiences. You may have ignored your natural disposition and learned the skills and attributes of an opposing preference in your pursuit of success. And you may be at a point in your life where you need to or choose to develop preferences you haven't used much in the past. The characteristics and descriptors of personality type theory are provided as a guide to your self-assessment and understanding.

Each of the letter combinations forms a distinct personality type. Four elements have sixteen possible combinations, which means sixteen different personality types. Your four-letter personality type is more than the sum of your four preferences. Each of the sixteen combinations of letters represents a way of relating to the world that is different from the others. However, although all sixteen types are distinct, it is possible to make personality type a bit simpler to apply by placing the sixteen types into closely related pairs. These pairs of personality types share a characteristic approach to work, resulting in eight characteristic ways of working. The pairs of personality types can be combined because both have the same most trusted, comfortable, and developed preference. For example, the ESTP and ESFP personality types both approach the world in a practical, flexible, external, here-and-now way and are called Responders.

Everyone can carry out a wide range of work activities and see aspects of himself or herself in more than one of the eight ways of working. However, research demonstrates that one of these eight approaches will be most preferred, or core. This core preference will define your characteristic approach to work. The other approaches will be used in support of and will be secondary to your preferred approach. As you develop skills

EXTRAVERSION & INTROVERSION

This preference pair describes alternative ways of orienting to the world. Extraversion (E) is an external, action orientation and Introversion (I) is an internal, reflective orientation.

E: EXTRAVERSION *"Let's talk this over."*

People disposed toward Extraversion tend to share the following characteristic behaviors and preferences:

- Focus energy and process information externally by talking and taking action
- Dislike complicated procedures and working on one thing for a long time, especially when alone
- Learn and work best when able to share, discuss, and process information with others
- Ask questions and think out loud during activities or while working through a decision
- Understand the world best by acting on it or talking about it

I: INTROVERSION *"I need to think about this."*

People disposed toward Introversion tend to share the following characteristic behaviors and preferences:

- Focus energy and process information internally, through reflection and introspection
- Prefer quiet places to work and can work on one thing for a long time
- Learn and work best by having time to relate, understand, and process information on their own
- Tend to think before speaking or acting, and may be uncomfortable when asked to perform or respond on demand
- Downplay their strengths externally, with the result that their abilities can often be underestimated

Everyone uses Extraversion and Introversion to carry out day-to-day activities. However, one of the two will be more natural and comfortable. Check the preference that seems to reflect your personality:

    ○ **E: Extraversion**   ○ **I: Introversion**

SENSING & INTUITION

Sensing and Intuition are two ways to take in information. Sensing (S) indicates a preference for more practical attention to specific facts and details. Intuition (N) indicates a preference for more abstract attention to general patterns and possibilities.

S: SENSING   *"Just the facts, please."*

People disposed toward Sensing as a way to take in information tend to share the following characteristic behaviors and preferences:

- Focus on individual facts and details before seeing underlying patterns or whole concepts
- Take most interest in the facts as they are known now
- Prefer information and tasks that are organized and presented in an orderly, sequential, format
- Work at a steady pace
- Become impatient or frustrated with complicated or future-oriented tasks that may take a long time to complete
- Like having the senses engaged at work

N: INTUITION   *"I can see it all now."*

People disposed toward Intuition as a way of taking in information tend to share the following characteristic behaviors and preferences:

- Focus on what facts mean and how they fit together, paying more attention to implications, possibilities, and relationships between concepts than to facts and details alone
- Become bored or impatient with details and take more interest in understanding the big picture
- Like solving problems and developing new skills; apt to be easily bored with routines and sequential tasks
- Jump around between ideas and tasks at work and in learning activities; likely to have bursts of energy rather than stamina

Everyone uses Sensing and Intuition to carry out day-to-day activities. However, one of the two will be more natural and comfortable. Check the preference that seems to reflect your personality:

○ **S: Sensing**   ○ **N: Intuition**

THINKING & FEELING

Thinking and Feeling describe information processing and decision-making preferences. An individual with a preference for Thinking (T) would focus more on logic and analysis. An individual preferring Feeling (F) would focus more on personal values and effects.

T: THINKING   *"Is this logical?"*

People disposed toward Thinking as a way to make decisions and process information tend to share the following characteristic behaviors and preferences:

- Focus on logic and analysis
- Deal best with objective data and cause-and-effect relationships
- Consider the pros and cons of ideas, information, and opinions
- Understand emotions and feelings best when they are introduced as facts and details to consider in decision making and problem solving
- Prefer calm, objective interactions

F: FEELING   *"Will anybody be hurt?"*

People disposed toward Feeling as a way to make decisions and process information tend to share the following characteristic behaviors and preferences:

- Take more interest in the effects of information on people than in things or ideas themselves
- Need feedback from other people and work best in an environment that provides support and encouragement
- View the atmosphere at work as being as important as the work itself
- Make subjective decisions; often good at understanding and appreciating the values of others
- Find objective, logical reasoning harsh; may feel criticized by others who function in a logical, analytical mode

Everyone uses Thinking and Feeling to carry out their day-to-day activities. However, one of the two will be more natural and comfortable. Check the preference that seems to reflect your personality:

○ T: Thinking   ○ F: Feeling

JUDGING & PERCEIVING

Judging and Perceiving describe two ways of orienting to and dealing with the external world. An individual with a preference for Judging (J) would tend to be decisive and prefer structure and control. An individual with a preference for Perceiving (P) would tend to keep options open as much as possible and to prefer spontaneity and flexibility.

J: JUDGING   *"Just do something."*

People disposed toward Judging tend to share the following characteristic behaviors and preferences:

- Make decisions as soon as possible to have closure
- Plan and organize the world
- Tolerate routines and structure comfortably
- Like roles and expectations to be clear and definite
- Find change and ambiguity uncomfortable
- Complete tasks and move on
- Take an organized approach and have a plan

P: PERCEIVING   *"Let's wait and see."*

People disposed toward Perceiving tend to share the following characteristic behaviors and preferences:

- Defer judgment and gather more information
- Act spontaneously and leave things to the last minute, often choosing not to plan or organize tasks or time
- Prefer starting projects to following through with projects
- Stay flexible and adaptable
- Become frustrated by rules, routines, and closure
- Focus on exploring and seeking new information; embrace change

Everyone uses Judging and Perceiving to carry out their day-to-day activities. However, one of the two will be more natural and comfortable. Check the preference that seems to reflect your personality:

○ J: Judging   ○ P: Perceiving

List the four letters you have chosen as your personality type here:

__ __ __ __

and experience, you will learn to access and use all of these approaches to facilitate your success. Nonetheless, by understanding your first and most trusted approach, you can see how the other approaches will flow and develop from what you are initially likely to do best.

Take the time to read through the eight descriptions of core preferences that follow, as they will help you understand the variety of types of individuals you will be dealing with as you engage in helping others develop. The remainder of the book will refer to these eight ways of working and the underlying personality preference pairs. By keeping personality type in mind, you will be able to customize both the process and the content of your interventions.

To confirm your natural way of working, focus on what approach seems most natural and comfortable. Remember—you use all of the preferences at times, but one of each pair is more natural. For example, everyone uses Thinking and Feeling to make decisions, looking at the logical consequences as well as considering the needs of the people involved in the situation. One of the two will be most salient and take the forefront for an individual when a decision is being made. The situation will have a dramatic influence on this choice. A judge will need to use a highly logical approach to make a decision and a parent may need to be more subjective and personal, no matter what their natural preference might be. By being aware of and deliberately applying both elements in a preference pair, you can achieve balance.

If you found it difficult to choose between elements in a preference pair, one of them is likely tapping into parts of your personality type you use for balance. You will find it helpful to read through the eight descriptions with this in mind. For example, if you are unsure about your preference for Thinking or Feeling and you are sure the other three are ENJ, then you can compare the ENTJ (Expeditor) and ENFJ (Contributor) descriptions to see which one is more accurate. You may also find it helpful to observe and think about how you react and interact in different situations. Ask people close to you how they see you in terms of these preferences. But be careful not to rely too heavily on what other people see and how you are currently acting. In many situations you must be able to operate using or showing preferences other than the ones you would naturally choose.

Another way to confirm your preferences is to go back to the list of personality type preference pair descriptors. Review the four preferences you have chosen to make sure they are the correct ones for you. Or, you might want to complete a personality type indicator with someone qualified to administer and interpret the results to help you confirm both your personality type and your natural way of working.

Four Extraverted Ways of Working

People with Extraverted ways of working are most comfortable and at their best when they are interacting with the world around them. The primary approach of such people involves doing, talking, taking action, and trying things. There are four Extraverted approaches.

RESPONDERS: ACT AND ADAPT

PERSONALITY TYPES: ESTP AND ESFP

Responders react immediately to the environment around them by taking action. They are observant and quick to see problems and opportunities. They tend to be spontaneous and prefer responding to things that are happening right away. They like to take practical actions that don't require a lot of pondering. Responders enjoy improvising, changing, and maneuvering. They are good at fixing things or getting something done right now. They often enjoy handling emergencies or solving practical problems.

Everyone uses this approach while observing and responding to the immediate environment. For example, as you hammer a nail you note whether the nail is bent and adjust the direction and strength of the next blow accordingly. Responders go beyond the general tendency to use this approach; they prefer and are drawn to activities that focus on direct observation and action. They are in tune with and focused on the world of actions and reactions.

Responders come in two types, balancing their ability to react quickly with a secondary approach that allows them to slow down and evaluate information and make decisions. Logical Responders (ESTP) balance their approach of immediate action with an internal focus on logical reasoning. Thus they are analytic as well as practical. Logical Responders like to jump into and solve problems. These Responders tend to be competitive, take risks, and want just the straight facts.Compassionate Responders (ESFP) balance their approach of immediate action with an internal focus on personal values. The resulting combination leads to an awareness of people's immediate needs and a playful, considerate disposition. These Responders tend to be sensitive and personal in their approach.

EXPLORERS: INNOVATE AND INITIATE

PERSONALITY TYPES: ENTP AND ENFP

Explorers are constantly scanning the environment looking for associations and patterns. They naturally link ideas together and see connections. They like to focus on what could be rather than what is. They see many possibilities in everything they can sense, experience, and imagine. Explorers are enthusiastically and outwardly focused on the future and like to initiate change. They see every situation as an opportunity to try something different. They are drawn to work that requires them to anticipate the future and create new ideas.

Everyone uses this approach when imagining a new way of doing something. While everyone to some extent sees potential in things, Explorers prefer and are drawn to activities that provide them with the opportunity to find and use patterns to create new possibilities.

Explorers come in two types, balancing their ability to see many possibilities with an approach that allows them to evaluate information and make decisions. Logical Explorers (ENTP) balance their approach of innovation and initiation with an internal focus on logic and analysis. They are independent, assertive, and questioning and like to debate both sides of an argument. They want to work with those who are competent, objective, and matter-of-fact. Compassionate Explorers (ENFP) balance their approach of innovation and initiation with an internal focus on values. They enjoy developing human potential and making personal connections. They can be strongly affected by a lack of morale or by conflict in their environment and thrive on support and praise.

EXPEDITORS: DIRECT AND DECIDE

PERSONALITY TYPES: ESTJ AND ENTJ

Expeditors like to use logical analysis. They critique situations and spot flaws. They are organized and efficient, priding themselves on getting the most accomplished in the least time. Expeditors like to solve problems, make decisions, complete tasks efficiently, and be clearly in charge. They are likely to quickly analyze a situation, take control, and mobilize people to get the job done.

Everyone uses this approach at times to describe flaws, list pros and cons, or organize tasks. While everyone is to some extent logical and analytical, Expeditors prefer and are drawn to activities requiring analysis and active organization of people and resources to complete tasks.

Expeditors come in two types, using analysis and decisiveness as their preferred approach to situations but balancing their decisive nature with an effective way of taking in information. Practical Expeditors (ESTJ) use concrete facts and immediate goals as inputs for their decisions and analysis. They prefer to work with facts and details and solve immediate and tangible problems. They use a matter-of-fact, results-oriented approach and work well with practical applications and a step-by-step sequence. Insightful Expeditors (ENTJ) focus on connections, patterns, and possibilities to help guide their decisive nature. They take a strategic approach and are stimulated by knowledge, complexity, theories, and abstract ideas. They enjoy making long-term goals and completing challenging projects.

CONTRIBUTORS: COMMUNICATE AND COOPERATE

PERSONALITY TYPES: ESFJ AND ENFJ

Contributors focus on personal relationships, values, opinions, and interactions. They actively strive to connect with others, create harmony, and cooperate. Contributors want to make sure that everyone is happy and involved. They are especially interested in organizing and coordinating events, processes, and activities to meet the needs of everyone involved. Contributors naturally appreciate others and want to be appreciated themselves for their uniqueness and their effort.

Everyone uses this approach when remembering a birthday, celebrating successes, engaging in social or family traditions, and sharing losses. While everyone is focused to some extent on connecting with others, Contributors prefer and are drawn to activities that allow them to actively communicate and cooperate with others.

Contributors come in two types, using a personal, subjective decision-making approach to situations but balancing their decisive nature with an effective way of taking in new information. Practical Contributors (ESFJ) are focused on the here and now. They pay attention to details and are observant. They are helpful and like to focus on practical aspects of situations. They like to build on their experiences and appreciate personal stories and real-world examples. Insightful Contributors (ENFJ) see potential for growth and development in others and often act as mentors. They enjoy learning about theory and abstract ideas. They like opportunities to generate new ideas and interpret or respond to ideas they are being exposed to.

Four Introverted Ways of Working

People with Introverted approaches are most comfortable and at their best when they can take time to think things through. They like to reflect on or interpret their experiences and plan their actions. People with Introverted approaches are sometimes seen as cautious, hard to get to know, or reserved. They are often quiet and not likely to blow their own horn. Because of this, the casual observer will not easily see the best side of people with Introverted preferences and may underestimate their skills and strengths.

Because those with Introverted preferences tend to use their most trusted approach internally, you often see them doing activities that are characteristic of someone with a different approach. For example, a Responder (using an Extraverted approach) and an Analyzer (with an Introverted approach) both prefer to immediately react to and solve problems. To the casual observer, they seem to have the same natural approach. However, the Analyzer is actually focused more on an internal analysis of the situation while taking action. The first, natural, most preferred approach of an Analyzer is an internal logical assessment focused on understanding and critiquing the situation. The Extraverted Responder, in contrast, is focused more on the external, practical aspects of the situation. For the Responder, analysis is at most a secondary focus. It is important to recognize that these two individuals are using different natural approaches to deal with the same situation.

ASSIMILATORS: SPECIALIZE AND STABILIZE

PERSONALITY TYPES: ISTJ AND ISFJ

Assimilators like to take in detailed information and then spend time integrating that information with past experiences and knowledge. They like to have a comprehensive understanding of the facts. Assimilators are able to draw on this rich accumulation of facts and experiences to make decisions and take action. As they approach a situation or solve a problem, they take time to reflect on past experiences; they remember and use strategies that worked well in the past.

Everyone uses this approach of recalling detailed information. You are using this approach when you are able to list extensive details about your favorite type of car, music, or vacation. While everyone retains and classifies experiences to some extent, Assimilators use this approach as their primary way of understanding and dealing with the world. They are strongly focused on collecting and organizing facts and experiences.

Assimilators come in two types, working within the internal world, reflecting on and categorizing experience, but balancing this internal focus by making decisions and acting in the world around them. Logical Assimilators (ISTJ) are outwardly decisive and analytical. They are task oriented and focused on carrying out obligations and meeting goals. They critique information and want materials and tasks to be presented in an orderly, logical manner. They look for competence in those around them.Compassionate Assimilators (ISFJ) balance their internal focus on facts and experiences with an external focus on people and values. They like to create and work within a positive, supportive, and harmonious environment. They dislike debates and impersonal analysis.

VISIONARIES: INTERPRET AND IMPLEMENT
PERSONALITY TYPES: INTJ AND INFJ

Visionaries like to take time to think about and find meaning in data, ideas, and experiences. They create and revise rich mental models that help them understand and interpret their experiences. Visionaries are future-oriented. They like to look at possibilities and often make complex plans for changing systems or improving processes.

Everyone uses this approach when studying and comparing theoretical models or interpreting data and ideas.
While everyone seeks to understand and relate experiences to theories and mental models to some extent, Visionaries use this approach as their primary way of interpreting the world.

Visionaries come in two types, working within the internal world, reflecting on and categorizing experiences, but balancing this internal focus by making decisions and acting in the world around them. Logical Visionaries (INTJ) trust and naturally use logical analysis to help them sort through ideas to find the most expedient way of solving a problem or improving a system. They may challenge authority and existing points of view and will seek competent coworkers, teachers, and leaders. Compassionate Visionaries (INFJ) focus on creating and implementing projects or other activities that will help people. Using a personal and caring approach, they like a supportive work environment that allows them to exchange ideas and develop a personal connection.

ANALYZERS: EXAMINE AND EVALUATE

PERSONALITY TYPES: ISTP AND INTP

Analyzers like to take time to analyze information and make logical decisions. When presented with a problem or a task, they immediately begin to think the situation through by collecting information, asking themselves questions, and looking for the best course of action. They like to relate principles of science, technology, or other areas of expertise to problem solving and they like to find ways to try their ideas and test their conclusions. An Analyzer enjoys trying things to see what will happen.

Everyone uses this approach when thinking about problems or making logical decisions. While everyone seeks to make logical sense of the world to some extent, Analyzers use this approach as their primary way of interpreting the world.

Analyzers come in two types, working within the internal world of reflection and analysis, but balancing this internal focus by taking in new information and acting in the world around them. Practical Analyzers (ISTP) like to troubleshoot and solve problems. They enjoy dealing with immediate situations and are most engaged when analyzing the details and specifics of a concrete problem. They are hands-on workers and like to be active. Insightful Analyzers (INTP) are naturally attracted to opportunities to independently analyze and solve complex problems. They enjoy working with theoretical ideas and seek knowledge and insights that help them objectively understand the world around them.

ENHANCERS: CARE AND CONNECT

PERSONALITY TYPES: ISFP AND INFP

Enhancers create personal relationships to situations. They are thoughtful and tend to focus on how others feel as well as on the effects situations and circumstances have on others. Enhancers are careful to accommodate other people and often put others' needs ahead of their own. They take time to assess and evaluate situations by relating them to personal and human values.

Everyone uses this approach when choosing what pictures to put into a scrapbook for a friend or deciding how to customize a recipe to suit the tastes of a specific group. While everyone seeks to understand and relate experiences to values to some extent, Enhancers use this approach as their primary way of interpreting the world.

Enhancers come in two types, working within the internal world of reflection and analysis and using their values to organize and evaluate their external world, but balancing this internal focus by taking in new information and acting in the world around them. Practical Enhancers (ISFP) naturally enjoy and find ways to connect to and be in harmony with the moment. They are kind and considerate and appreciate the people and things around them. They enjoy hands-on, practical work and can be impatient with abstract theory. Insightful Enhancers (INFP) appreciate people, ideas, and possibilities. They work to help others achieve their goals. They are quietly supportive of others and appreciate and seek positive feedback themselves. They are idealistic and individualistic in their approach to work.

Appreciating Differences

These eight ways of working make a useful starting point for appreciating others. It's often tempting to see differences as a problem rather than appreciate their value. For example, those with a preference for Judging can easily see the value of organizing, structuring, and making decisions. They may find it more difficult to see the value of a Perceiving orientation and may conceptualize the preference in negative terms: unorganized, unstructured, indecisive. The important first step in developing understanding and appreciation is to see the positive aspects of all preferences and ways of working. Those with a Perceiving orientation then can be framed positively as flexible, adaptable, and open to new information.

Here are a few positive descriptors often associated with each element of the preference pairs. Keep these in mind and use them instead of negative descriptors, especially when working with others who have preferences that are different from yours.

EXTRAVERSION

- Quick to act
- Participative
- Possessing breadth of interest

INTROVERSION

- Careful
- Thorough
- Possessing depth of interest

SENSING

- Practical
- Realistic
- Observant

INTUITION

- Insightful
- Future-focused
- Able to integrate ideas

THINKING

- Logical
- Analytical
- Objective

FEELING

- Compassionate
- Considerate
- Appreciative

JUDGING

- Decisive
- Organized
- Productive

PERCEIVING

- Flexible
- Adaptable
- Open to new ideas

In a similar way, each of the eight ways of working has characteristic strengths. Here are a few for each.

RESPONDER

- Active
- Practical
- Adaptive
- Engaging
- Living for the moment

EXPEDITOR

- Decisive
- Active
- Responsible
- Structured
- Results-oriented

ASSIMILATOR

- Detailed
- Methodical
- Practical
- Task-focused
- Able to build from experience

ANALYZER

- Adaptable
- Flexible
- Analytical
- Self-reliant
- Independent

EXPLORER

- Enthusiastic
- Inspired
- Open to change
- Pursuing multiple interests
- Flexible

CONTRIBUTOR

- Collaborative
- Cooperative
- Organized
- Harmonious
- Expressive

VISIONARY

- Integrate information
- Broad perspective
- Future-focused
- Organized
- Follow-through

ENHANCER

- Authentic
- Appreciative
- Nurturing
- Flexible
- Harmonious

Adjust Interventions to Accommodate Different Preferences

As well as appreciating others, it is important to consider your personal strengths and biases as a helper. Everyone tends to approach situations in a way that feels natural. Sometimes this is not the best approach, especially when the person you are helping has very different preferences from yours. Sometimes it can even be a problem when you have the same preferences and thus the same blind spots as the person you are helping. To help you think about your biases, this section will show how personality type influences the way you tend to help others. One INTJ manager describes her ongoing focus on accommodating the preferences of others this way:

EXTRA EXTRAVERSION

For me, the issue is my "I" preference. I really don't like having to be around people all the time . . . but as a manager with a number of employees, superiors, and peers to interact with . . . I'm interacting with people for eight to twelve hours a day. I have to remind myself to reach out, check in with people, especially with phone calls or in-person visits (not just e-mail), because it's so tempting not to do so and I'm already emotionally tired just from mandatory and unavoidable interactions.

DETECT & DESCRIBE
Adjust Interventions to Accommodate Different Preferences

Don't see high performance

Evidence of not customizing interventions:

○ Ignoring individual differences among clients

○ Ignoring the effects of personal preferences in the helping process

○ Using the same strategies and processes for all clients

Do see high performance

Evidence of adjusting interventions to accommodate different preferences:

○ Acknowledging how others' preferences will affect potential interventions

○ Acknowledging personal biases in helping others

○ Comparing personal preferences with the client's and adjusting interventions appropriately

Ensure you are not expecting others to pursue their development using your personal work approach. Later in the process you can also work toward helping others see how their personality preferences create blind spots and problems for them. However, your initial task is to accommodate the client, rather than expecting or teaching the client to adapt to you and your approach.

A QUESTION OF BALANCE
Accommodating and Challenging

As a helper, you need to accommodate your clients' needs as well as challenge your clients to grow and develop. Consider when it is most helpful to engage in each part of this continuum.

While accommodating, you are considering how your clients prefer to do things. You work through their strengths. For example, with clients who prefer to learn in a practical manner, you will help them find ways to learn on the job rather than expecting them to attend training sessions.

However, sometimes your clients may need to take mandatory training. In this situation you will need to challenge them to find ways to cope with this nonpreferred activity. They may need your assistance to develop skills to maintain their interest and gain the maximum amount of learning from this activity even though they don't find it comfortable or natural.

The following sections describe the eight ways of working in terms of how each tends to prefer to help and be helped. You can use these descriptions to assess your own helping style. Understanding your unique approach and the way you add value to the helping process will be a good start.

But first, it is useful to look at some examples of how helpers are able to see and use their unique abilities. In each example, you can see how personality preferences affect the way they engage in helping. As you read these, consider what your greatest helping asset is.

TAILOR-MADE FOR THE WORK

- *My most valuable competency is helping others analyze the big-picture situations and see where they are falling short. (an INTJ)*

- *My most valuable competency is truly hearing what a person's weaknesses and strengths are and focusing in on those. (an INFJ)*

- *My most valuable competency is helping people make decisions and take action. (an ESFJ)*

- *My most valuable competency is helping others see possibilities they have not yet considered. (an ENFP)*

- *My most valuable competency is building credibility with my direct reports and others around me. (an INTP)*

- *My most valuable competency is supporting and bringing out the best in others. (an INFP)*

When you are working with clients, read their self-description to see where their style meshes and conflicts with yours. Incorporate examples, explain processes, and set up activities in a way that will suit their preferences.

RESPONDERS

Responders as helpers and clients tend to display the following qualities and preferences:

- Want to have fun and be playful
- Prefer real-life experiences and hands-on activities
- Are practical and use common sense
- Focus on interesting facts and events
- Like lots of action
- Demonstrate by doing
- Like to be the center of attention and enjoy group work
- Are entertaining and humorous
- Like lots of sensory stimulation
- Put play before work

- Are impatient with theory

- Adapt easily and improvise

- Like variety and change

- Are drawn to the most immediate task at hand

- Focus on the short term rather than the long term

When working with Responders to build workplace competencies, use a step-by-step approach. Show them how making concrete changes will achieve results. Provide them with real-life examples and opportunities for hands-on learning. Think of ways to make the development process flexible, interesting, fun, and interactive. Use practical language and focus on immediate benefits. Responders are grounded in the here and now. You may need to challenge them to focus on longer-term goals.

EXPLORERS

Explorers as helpers and clients tend to display the following qualities and preferences:

- Are enthusiastic, innovative, and adaptable

- Are generalists who integrate information from a variety of sources

- Multitask and like lots of stimulation

- Have a work style of inspiration rather than perspiration

- Like group work; need to talk and share ideas

- Read extensively and have wide interests

- Resist structure and rules; may challenge authority

- Improvise rather than prepare

- Like to initiate new ideas and seek change

- Are easily bored with details and may neglect routine tasks

- Test rules; may push the limits

- Like to start things more than follow through on them

- Need variety and change to keep their interest level high

- Are lively, spontaneous, and curious

When working with Explorers to build workplace competencies, use a big-picture framework. Show them far-reaching and broad effects and opportunities that can result from development. Do not expect Explorers to work steadily or follow step-by-step routines. Provide opportunities for them to jump in and try something new. Explorers like to interact with others to brainstorm and imagine possibilities. Encourage them to play with ideas, but also challenge them to focus on practical realities.

EXPEDITORS

Expeditors as helpers and clients tend to display the following qualities and preferences:

- Are decisive and like closure
- Analyze and evaluate what they see, read, and hear
- Like well-defined rules or principles
- Work well in a structured environment when they have some control
- Organize people and things
- Like to manage time and tasks
- Use a logical decision-making approach
- Enjoy competition and challenge
- Dislike disorder
- Set and achieve goals
- Want to organize the world around them
- Persevere and work hard and efficiently
- Have an open, direct communication style
- Are impatient with too much focus on the interpersonal
- Want to see clear and logical evidence

When working with Expeditors to build workplace competencies, use a logical, results-based process. Be sure to demonstrate your own competence before expecting them to listen to you. Provide opportunities to take action and complete tasks. Be direct in your communications. Allow them to question and critique both the information being gathered and the process being used. Let them take charge. Challenge them to see both the logical and personal side of situations.

CONTRIBUTORS

Contributors as helpers and clients tend to display the following qualities and preferences:

- Focus on communicating and cooperating with others
- Value appreciation, harmony, and a supportive atmosphere
- Take on many tasks; may overcommit themselves
- Focus on the needs of the group
- Coordinate people to complete projects
- Establish and maintain relationships
- Communicate by developing rapport and using empathy
- Give and like to receive positive feedback
- Are personable and supportive
- Link with a broad range of people
- Are collaborative leaders
- Have time management and follow-through as strengths
- Are devoted to human values and growth
- Make sure everyone is included and accepted
- Enjoy traditions and celebrations of people's success

When working with Contributors to build workplace competencies, create a supportive and collaborative setting. Provide opportunities to discuss personal feelings and values when defining tasks to work on. Create a structured plan with opportunities for cooperation, encouragement, and feedback. Use corrective feedback sparingly and gently. You may need to challenge Contributors to consider the logical as well as the personal side of situations.

ASSIMILATORS

Assimilators as helpers and clients tend to display the following qualities and preferences:

- Enjoy accuracy and precision and will master the facts
- Are task-oriented and inclined to work in a reliable, dependable way
- Take one thing at a time; systematic and careful

- Prefer quiet time to reflect on what they have learned and experienced

- Are independent and able to work effectively alone

- Are thorough perfectionists

- Are patient with detailed tasks

- Like to develop practical skills and learn practical information

- Focus on and tend to remember facts and details

- Need to relate what they are learning to their experiences

- Plan carefully before starting a task

- Like to learn about a topic of interest in detail

- Dislike metaphors and symbolism

- Prefer structure, routine, and predictability

- Work at a steady, careful pace

When working with Assimilators to build workplace competencies, use a practical, structured approach. Provide them with all the details, data, and resources necessary to complete the plan. Give them time to reflect and plan before expecting them to implement tasks. Create a plan that focuses on incremental growth using their current knowledge and expertise as a starting point. Link development to what they know to be true from their experience. You may need to challenge them to be open to unproven opportunities.

VISIONARIES

Visionaries as helpers and clients tend to display the following qualities and preferences:

- Take in ideas and make complex mental models

- Interpret and reflect on what they learn

- Prefer quiet environments; can work effectively alone

- Focus on theory and meaning underlying facts and experiences

- Are conscientious, determined, and strongly driven to meet goals

- Are questioning and seek new information

- Are systems thinkers and long-term planners

- Like to plan a project through completely before they take action
- Enjoy intellectual challenge and complex projects
- Need time to fit new information into a framework
- Like to implement their ideas through long-term projects
- Dislike routine or too much focus on facts and details
- See many different ways to look at information
- Are independent and self-motivated
- Enjoy metaphors, symbols, and other abstract figures of speech

When working with Visionaries to build workplace competencies, focus on long-term goals. Provide opportunities for them to create a vision and framework for their developmental process. Offer information and allow time to process theoretical explanations and the rationale for underlying behaviors rather than focusing only on changing the behaviors themselves. Integrate development with other aspects of their performance, goals, and plans. Visionaries are interested in broad, long-range change, and you may need to challenge them to focus on small, practical developmental tasks that have immediate results.

ANALYZERS

Analyzers as helpers and clients tend to display the following qualities and preferences:

- Examine and evaluate information analytically and internally
- Are independent and calm observers
- Need logical connections for new information
- Question decisions that seem subjective
- Want information presented in a clear and logical manner
- Prefer objective teachers and data
- Enjoy detailed, technical material
- Like to know why and how things work
- Struggle putting thoughts into action
- Like to solve problems; good at improvising
- Focus more on understanding situations than on taking action

- Independently evaluate their progress
- Question what they learn and seek competent teachers and leaders
- Detach if situations are too routine or predictable
- Need challenge and variety to keep their interest level high

When working with Analyzers to build workplace competencies, be as efficient as possible. Streamline the process so they can work independently whenever possible. Offer logical reasons to develop and be flexible about the way development is achieved. Allow Analyzers time to critique. You may need to challenge them to focus on the importance of connecting with others.

ENHANCERS

Enhancers as helpers and clients tend to display the following qualities and preferences:

- Focus on what is personally important
- Are comfortable staying in the background supporting others
- Are friendly, quiet, and easygoing
- Value harmony, collaboration, and a supportive environment
- Put great value on giving and receiving positive feedback
- Like to control their own pace and create their own structure
- Focus on how information aligns with their personal values
- Express themselves and their values in what they do
- Appreciate and work to improve the world around them
- Are open and adaptable unless something goes against their values
- Put others first and be focused on the needs of others
- Enjoy flexibility and variety
- Approach situations in a personal, individual way
- Avoid conflict and keep the peace
- Are sensitive and may take feedback personally

When working with Enhancers to build workplace competencies, take time to get to know and understand them. Seek to understand what is personally meaningful to them. Use corrective feedback carefully and gently. Provide a supportive, flexible, individualized process that allows them time to reflect. You may need to challenge them to focus on promoting themselves.

Putting It All Together

When working with individuals of each type, consider their preferences and adjust your interventions accordingly. Be especially aware of preferences that differ from your own. For example, if you are an Explorer, you will tend to focus on the future and link ideas in an open-ended way. When working with an Assimilator, you will find it important to focus on the present and start with what your client knows is true from personal experience. Then you can move step-by-step into making a practical, short-term development plan. This intervention will not represent your natural preferences, but it will be most useful for the Assimilator.

Refer to the Development Plan form in Chapter 2 (page 52). Fill in your client's personality type and have the client highlight some personal strengths. Think of specific things you will need to do to make the plan work most effectively for this client.

QUICK TIPS
Building Relationships

. . . .

Throughout the chapter you have seen the importance of building working relationships before you begin interventions to facilitate the development of others. Here is a quick overview of the main chapter points to help you review what you have learned.

- Focus on yourself first. Be sure you are modeling and developing workplace competencies yourself before expecting others to adopt them.

- Consider what components of the workplace competencies might affect your ability to help others. Are you self-responsible? Do you communicate effectively? Are you mindful, productive, and proactive?

- Maintain confidentiality.

- Be genuine.

- Work only within your scope of expertise.

- Be sensitive to personal factors that can influence others' performance.

- Acknowledge and appreciate personality differences.

- Be aware of how your personality preferences affect your interactions.

- Accommodate the personality preferences of others.

In the next chapter you will see how to create a development plan and learn practical interventions for facilitating development.

Chapter 2
Facilitating Development

Once you have established a working relationship based on trust and respect, you can start making a plan to facilitate development. An effective plan identifies specific outcomes, barriers, and strategies. This chapter uses a Gap Analysis along with a Development Plan form to help you identify what is needed to accomplish the plan and lay out the elements of what you and your client need to do. It also provides intervention tips to help implement the plan and evaluate its success. Note the list of the components of facilitating development in the order in which they will be covered in the chapter.

The following Gap Analysis addresses broad areas of behavior and will help you assess your development facilitating performance. Completing the analysis will help you identify specific components of the competency to focus on as you read the chapter. Before completing this tool you may find it helpful to scan the chapter content. This will privide a context for your assessment and will help you familiarize yourself with the specific behaviors considered within the five broad areas included in the Gap Analysis.

COMPONENTS OF FACILITATING DEVELOPMENT

Identify Outcomes, Roadblocks, and Strategies

- Assess needs and target specific behavioral outcomes
- Identify reasons for problems and roadblocks to improvement
- Create a structured development plan

Carry Out the Plan

- Coach the plan by supporting appropriate interventions
- Monitor effectiveness and results of the plan

GAP ANALYSIS
Facilitating Development

The pairs of statements that follow represent the endpoints of a continuum of possible performance in facilitating development. To assess your current level, place an X on each line at the location that best describes the approach you use now.

Identify Outcomes, Roadblocks, and Strategies

Leave outcomes unclear or unspecified	Assess needs and target specific behavioral outcomes
Work on problems without identifying underlying causes	Identify reasons for problems and road-blocks to improvement
Implement strategies in an ad hoc or unstructured manner	Create a structured development plan

Carry Out the Plan

Expect the client will implement a plan independently	Coach the plan by supporting appropriate interventions
Pay no attention to progress or to the effectiveness of the plan	Monitor effectiveness and results of the plan

Take time to reflect on facilitating development. Use the space below to write down any specific information or insights you have regarding your ability to apply this competency. You may want to ask leaders, colleagues, or clients to fill out the Gap Analysis to provide you with an external assessment to compare with your self-assessment. Before you leave the Gap Analysis with someone, take a few minutes to discuss the meaning of each element so they will understand the kind of behavior you want to review.

_____

_____

_____

INTRODUCING THE DEVELOPMENT PLAN

It is not realistic to expect competency improvement without a clear process and plan to facilitate development. A structured process can help you clarify expectations, set a measurable outcome, and evaluate your progress.

This chapter shows you how to apply a practical planning strategy for development. The planning process will also help you recognize and avoid potential roadblocks that can get in the way of your success as a practitioner. It is always a good idea to try any process first before expecting others to try it. Accordingly, you will want to complete a Development Plan for yourself before you use it with clients. As you work through the plan with your development in mind, you will grow familiar with the content and process involved. By clarifying all details in the plan, you are much likelier to achieve success. In Part Two, you will again use the Development Plan as you collaboratively create a plan with the person you are guiding.

REVIEW THE STEPS FOR
FACILITATING DEVELOPMENT

This planning process emulates the process you will use in helping your clients develop their competencies. First you will work with them to fill out a Gap Analysis for each of the five essential workplace competencies in Part Two. When you have identified performance gaps, you can move on to the Detect & Describe box of each competency chapter to choose specific positive outcomes to demonstrate. After you have worked through the materials for the workplace competencies, use the Development Plan as a guide to put the plan together collaboratively.

Once the plan is created, you can support and enhance the development process in a number of ways. Often you will need to challenge behaviors and beliefs. You will also need to, and find it valuable to, set safe conditions that allow your clients to try new behaviors with a minimal amount of discomfort. Strategies for making and evaluating the plan will help you keep on track.

Development Plan

Name: _____

Individual Considerations

What unique challenges do you have related to this specific situation that should be taken into account when making this plan? What strategies can be used to deal with these situational factors? Consider additional roles and responsibilities, any health or wellness concerns, and personal characteristics that are affecting your work success at this time.

Situational Factor	Strategy to Minimize Effects of This Factor

Personality Type

Strengths of my personality type are

_____

_____

_____

_____

The plan will accommodate my personality by

_____

_____

_____

Development Plan cont'd

Competency Components to Address

Look through your completed Gap Analysis and list up to five components you would like to demonstrate. These can be all from one competency or from different competencies. These will typically be components on which you have evaluated yourself furthest to the left. Then prioritize these from 1 to 5, with 1 being the most important component you want to address.

Priority	Component to Address

Write your number-one priority here. This is the positive outcome you will achieve.

_____

Refer to the Detect & Describe box in the appropriate chapter to identify up to three specific behaviors you will demonstrate to improve your performance on this component.

1. _____

_____

2. _____

_____

3. _____

_____

Development Plan cont'd

Intervention Strategies

If you are not already demonstrating these behaviors, identify the reasons. For each, describe what you need to do to remove or get around roadblocks.

Roadblock	Intervention Strategy	Resources Needed

Strengths

Refer back to the Detect & Describe box to identify and list up to three behaviors (strengths) you are currently demonstrating in this component. Next to each strength, show how you can use it to facilitate your development process.

Strength	Way to Use This Strength

Action Items

Write in specific action items and dates.

Action to Be Taken	Resources Needed	Completion Date	Initial

Development Plan cont'd

Execution

Who will be involved in evaluating the plan?

What data will you use for evaluating the plan? These should link directly to measuring the behaviors you have chosen to focus on.

How will you determine success using these data? That is, describe specific targets for improvement and specify what success looks like and how much and how well the behaviors will be demonstrated.

Who will collect the data?

What is the formative evaluation process and the date for its completion?

What is the date for the summative evaluation?

What will you do next if the plan is successful?

What are the consequences if the plan is not successful?

What are the rewards for success?

Your signature: _____   Completion date: _____

Signatures of others involved in the plan: _____

_____

Development plans are most effective if they are kept current. In collaboration with your clients, ensure the plan is implemented, evaluated, and adjusted. As a final step, you will be able to transfer the ownership of the development process to each of your clients. Ultimately you want them to be able to engage in self-development independently: The goal is for them to take control of their own learning and development when demonstrating the five workplace competencies.

IDENTIFY OUTCOMES, ROADBLOCKS, AND STRATEGIES

The first step in workplace development is to identify areas for improvement and then choose a positive outcome the client will work toward. The most powerful way to accomplish change is to focus on developing one positive, measurable outcome. Once someone has demonstrated an initial positive change, they can then choose a new behavior to focus on. This teaches them the continuous improvement process that high-performers naturally engage in.

Assess Needs and Target Specific Behavioral Outcomes

The Detect & Describe box helps identify negative behaviors that can be replaced with more positive alternatives.

Assessing Others

Assessment is a complex activity. Chapter 3 will examine tools and strategies to use to help a client carry out a self-assessment. This section considers the broader context of your assessment of the client's situation. Here is a list of questions meant to stimulate your thinking about what you need to consider and assess:

- What are the client's overall strengths?

- What are the client's weaknesses or areas for growth?

- Is the client suited to the work in question?

- Is the client satisfied in the work in question?

- Is the work a good match for the client's skills, interests, and personality?

DETECT & DESCRIBE
Assess Needs and Target Specific Behavioral Outcomes

Don't see high performance	Do see high performance
Evidence of working toward unclear or unspecified outcomes:	Evidence of assessing needs and targeting specific behavioral outcomes:
○ Taking a piecemeal rather than holistic approach	○ Carefully assessing an individual's overall strengths and areas for development
○ Focusing on the tasks at hand and not the characteristics of the person doing the task	○ Assessing and discussing an individual's suitability for the work in question
○ Describing areas for improvement in general or vague terms	○ Assessing measurable behaviors and identifying behavioral gaps
○ Using labels or overgeneralizations when describing behavior	○ Avoiding labels when describing behaviors
○ Neglecting to define specific outcomes for the development process	○ Specifically defining target behaviors for improvement
○ Seeking to stop or reduce negative behaviors without defining a positive option	○ Defining outcomes as demonstration of a positive behavior

- Are situational factors at work affecting the client's performance?
- Are systemic factors in the organization affecting the client's performance?
- Are situational factors outside the workplace affecting the client's performance?
- What is the client's relationship with people in the immediate work team?
- How do people describe the client?
- Is the work team supportive of the client's performance?
- What is the client's relationship to the immediate leader?
- Is the leader supportive of the client's performance?
- Is the leader a good match for the client?
- How well is the client performing the required work roles?
- Are there any complaints about the client's performance?

- Are the complaints from only certain sources or are they general among people who work with the client?

- Are the complaints about small, specific things or broader overall work performance?

- What type of evaluations has the client received in the past?

- Has the quantity or quality of work done changed recently?

- If so, why might that be?

- Is the client interested in self-development?

- What are the client's goals and expectations?

- Has the client assessed personal strengths and weaknesses?

- Does the client's self-perception match the perceptions of others?

- If not, what is different and why might it be different?

- What are the client's blind spots?

- Does the client tend to deny or ignore weaknesses or difficulties?

My suggestion that you consider the questions on this list does not mean you should create a comprehensive list of questions to read through when working with clients who are assessing their performance. These questions are simply the types of things you will be thinking about throughout the helping process as you define behaviors to work on, determine why behaviors are not being demonstrated, and create and follow a development plan.

One assessment task is to help your clients gather information and then interpret it accurately. To provide clarity and avoid widely differing interpretations of performance, the development process used here is focused on observable behaviors. Comparing self-assessment feedback and feedback from others is an excellent way to benchmark behavior. Usually, the more sources you draw on, the more helpful the information you gather will be. Feedback from different people may not always be consistent. In this case, you may need to help your clients interpret and understand why their performance is seen differently by different people.

At times, you will need to challenge a client's interpretation of information, especially if the client tends to disregard or distort information from others. We all have strengths and blind spots. However, some individuals seem to have a much more difficult time seeing these than others do. They may need to continue to refer to and gather additional feedback from others as they learn to develop an accurate self-portrait. It is useful for clients to self-assess very specific tasks or interactions and then immediately seek external feedback to see how well their perceptions match the perceptions of others. You may need to show clients how to read cues by showing them how others are reacting to their behaviors. Some people have difficulty interpreting these cues and miss feedback that is not direct.

Have clients list their skills and areas for development. Encourage them to find ways to use their strengths and compensate for or remediate their weaknesses. It is not always necessary to fix weaknesses. What is necessary is to make sure that the things clients don't do well are not getting in the way of their work performance. For example, someone who has trouble sequencing information can simply write down the few important sequences they need to remember. Many successful individuals use spell checkers rather than learn to spell. Finding ways of accommodating areas of difficulty can work very well. Encourage clients to think of simple types of accommodations whenever possible.

Clients need to recognize how they learn and use this knowledge to customize their learning activities to maximize effectiveness in developing any competency. Having a conversation about learning preferences can be a helpful way to start someone thinking about how they prefer to carry out learning and development.

With clients, decide what sources of information will help them in their assessment. Do they need to ask others for input? Review work that has been done in the past? Fill out inventories, checklists, or tests? Take time to reflect? Usually a combination of activities is best. When clients are seeking feedback from others, help them choose a process that will provide them with specific, useful data rather than broader, less usable opinions.

Research and apply resources that are already available to the client. Most organizations have feedback systems in place. Many also use competency models to clearly define relevant individual tasks, abilities, and gaps. Have your client access information from these sources to use in the assessment process. With self-employed clients, you may need to help them develop sources of feedback. They may benefit from the information gathered from interviewing customers, tracking sales and profits, or other measures to assess work effectiveness. Use the information gathered to clarify and specifiy performance gaps identified in the Gap Analyses throughout this book.

Encourage clients to listen carefully to the ideas of coworkers and customers. Help them look for links between the pieces of information. If they are having difficulties in learning or performance, help them determine and understand what is getting in their way, why it is a problem, and how they might be able to deal with it. Collecting and integrating information from a variety of sources can help clients define their current performance levels.

Many people who experience learning or performance difficulties try to avoid, ignore, or cover up problems. In the short term this strategy may work. However, in the long term it can create stress and performance difficulties that interfere with career advancement. Remember that people are often busy and will give the most useful feedback to your client if the needs for and purpose of the information are clear. Simply asking, "How am I doing?" is likely to result in vague generalities. Have clients use checklists, focused questions, or structured interviews to gather practical information. Some clients will already have good performance assessment information and may simply need your assistance to understand and integrate the information into a useful form. Here are some questions you can ask when helping a client complete a performance assessment.

- What resources does your organization have for assessing performance?

- How can you gather information?

- What information will be helpful?

- Whose perspectives will be valuable?

- Who can help you?

- What tools will you use?

- When can you do this?

More information on helping clients assess themselves is covered in the "Maximizes Effective Use of Personal Assets" section on pages 112–116.

Why Focus on Behavior?

Development is easiest to define and track when it focuses on demonstrating specific, observable, and measurable behaviors. Behavior is something the client and the coach can see and evaluate together. Focusing on behavior helps both parties separate the person from the feedback. You can point out certain behaviors that are appropriate and other behaviors that might be getting in the way of performance. A focus on behavior also helps you avoid labels and vague complaints about performance.

For example, it is not all that helpful to label someone as having a poor attitude. This statement is vague and negative and cannot easily be measured or corrected. What does a "poor attitude" look like? Is it blaming others when results are not achieved? Criticizing in a nonconstructive manner? "Blaming" and "criticizing" are behaviors and thus are much easier to see and measure than "poor attitude." It is possible to measure how often an individual acknowledges accountability for results rather than blaming others. You also can show someone how to provide timely and constructive feedback.

By focusing on measurable behaviors, the development process will also provide clear expectations. For example, your clients may not be aware that certain behaviors are unacceptable or may not understand or agree that certain behaviors are part of the roles required for the job. Once expectations are specified, you can clearly define what the desired behavior looks like in comparison to the behaviors that are currently being seen. You can identify specific gaps in performance and show a clear distinction between the areas for improvement and the desired behaviors.

Here is a powerful example of how one ENFJ trainer sets the stage for learning using a behavioral focus. Her approach to training reinforces the importance of building working relationships, as discussed in Chapter 1. Note how she describes her desired outcome—building a positive learning climate—with specific, concrete, behaviors. She is able to quickly evaluate how well she has accomplished her goals by checking to see if she has engaged in the required behaviors.

DEFINING SUCCESS

I think the most important competency for training professionals is the ability to build a positive climate right at the beginning of a group session. For me, this is critical and the interventions I use as a training professional have never let me down. Here are some of the interventions I use every time I do a training session or work with clients.

- *Arrive early and set up the training site for success. Have visual aids posted. Have name tags for students to write names on.*

- *Greet students or participants at the door, introduce myself, and welcome them to the room.*

- *Describe my role as facilitator (servant of the group) and talk about being neutral, nondefensive, and so on.*

- *Review the posted agenda and ask if everyone will agree to work on it with me. This ensures that everyone takes responsibility for the success of the event and is also a great intervention when dealing with difficult participants.*

- *Ensure that the participants introduce themselves and get to know each other through some kind of warm-up exercise, either social or topical. This is crucial when you want group participation in role plays of case studies later on.*

In this description it becomes clear what the trainer has decided to do to build a positive climate. Such well-described tasks and roles are easy to detect and define and thus teach and evaluate.

Why Focus on Positive Behavior?

Often when people are creating a development plan, they focus on solving a problem. It's usual to start by stating a behavior that needs to be changed. This is an essential part of the process, identifying what is not working. However, it doesn't do much good to focus only on eliminating what doesn't work. For example, say the client tends to give unsuitable types or amounts of feedback—a communication competency. In this case your goal would be to have the individual give both positive and corrective feedback. This reframing of the problem into a positive outcome allows you to focus on behaviors you want to see the individual demonstrate. If you don't do this, you put someone in a situation where their normal response is no longer appropriate, but they may be unsure of what an alternative response looks like. Your task is clear: You need to define and describe how someone can provide positive and corrective feedback and help find ways to demonstrate that behavior. You create a situation where the client is making an improvement rather than trying to simply extinguish something that isn't working.

The Gap Analysis at the beginning of each workplace chapter initiates this positive, outcome-based, focus by defining specific components that make up each of the workplace competencies. (The introduction to Part One outlines the function of the Gap Analyses and the Detect & Describe boxes.)

Why Focus on Only One Outcome?

Many individuals have several areas in which they could develop. It may seem overly restrictive to narrow the focus to one component of one competency. However, by working on one specific area at a time, you make it easier to make and evaluate a plan. Too often people try to fix too many things too fast and end up not accomplishing anything.

Pick the most important behavior to change and address it wholeheartedly. Once a change is seen in that behavior, you are ready to tackle another behavior. This step-by-step process will be the key to ongoing success. At times you may even find a natural transference of the change across the different components of competencies. Someone who is improving in one area will often discover how to achieve positive results in another component of the same competency or even in another competency area.

Who Should Identify the Outcome?

Ideally, individuals themselves should be able to assess, evaluate, and automatically adjust their behavior. However, it is unsafe to assume that everyone is able to carry out self-improvement activities efficiently and independently. This is especially true for people who are having difficulties with any of the five key performance competencies covered in this book. You may have to coach them through the development process. Once they have been guided through it enough to understand it, most people will be able to manage further development independently. As in any learning process, it is essential to start at each client's level of competence. You may need to provide significant teaching, coaching, and encouragement at first.

Without the competencies of self-responsibility and mindfulness, clients may have inaccurate self-evaluations. Most people are blind to at least some of their shortcomings and strengths. Your goal is to facilitate a process and provide tools to allow clients to assess and manage their development. However, at the same time, part of the learning process requires them to make an accurate self-assessment as well as to seek and use feedback from others. If they have difficulty in these areas, you may need to work on them first.

Even when these behaviors start to become established, it is always helpful for people to use multisource feedback to increase the accuracy of their self-assessment. This balance between self-feedback and accepting feedback from others is a fine line to coach and maintain. Your ultimate goal is to foster the development of individuals who are able to develop themselves. Then you can simply act as a resource to provide tools and fine-tuning tips. Some people are already self-managed in the areas of learning and development. Others may have a long way to go to reach that goal.

Identifying Desired Behaviors

Have clients complete the Gap Analysis at the beginning of Chapters 3 through 7. Have them place an X at the point on the continuum that best describes their current performance on each of the components within each competency. You will need to decide at this point if additional feedback is required. If clients are unfamiliar with the concepts addressed in the Gap Analysis, you may want to elaborate on the statements. This will help them make a more accurate self-assessment. Perhaps your client will need additional input from you, a supervisor, or a coworker or customer. This additional information may prove surprising and may be the first step to someone's understanding how others see their behaviors.

For many clients, this step of identifying a behavior to develop is a most difficult one. This is especially true when people do not seek or are not sensitive to the feedback and reactions of others. Honest feedback is of paramount importance to the ability to develop a self-image that agrees with others' perceptions. When someone denies or ignores problem behaviors, it is essential to put feedback processes in place so they can learn about and accept the impressions others have regarding their words and actions. Clients must see the need for, and the usefulness and importance of, desired behaviors. Otherwise they will have little motivation to make a change.

It is important to recognize that there may be more than one desired area for improvement and to prioritize when these will be developed. For some clients this process will need to be done in stages.

When reviewing a client's Gap Analysis, scan through the statements looking for those marked closest to the left side. As you look at each of these statements, ask your client whether it looks like a problem. Get a feel for how important it is for the client to change in each case. Add your perceptions as you work through the statements. Go through all five competency areas. When you are finished, identify up to five components the client would like to develop. There may be other areas that need to be developed, but stick to the most important five. List these on the Development Plan. Then prioritize the five components. At this point, choose the top-priority component to focus on developing first. This may be one the client has identified independently or one that is mandated because it poses a problem for coworkers, customers, or leaders.

Picking an Outcome

When choosing a specific component to focus on as an outcome, remember that behaviors work in tandem and problems in one area may result in a need for change elsewhere. For example, say someone makes a mistake and doesn't correct it. The real problem may be inability to communicate effectively or lack of the mindfulness required for solving problems. As you study the various components of the different competencies, remember these interactions and dynamics.

Once you have selected a priority to address, move on to the Detect & Describe for that component in the competency chapter to find a list of specific behaviors. Assess which of these component behaviors your client is and is not demonstrating. Identify and then write in the Development Plan up to three specific behaviors your client will begin to demonstrate or demonstrate more often to increase performance on this component. Write down the positive descriptors on the right, not the areas for development. This keeps the focus positive. There is a place to do this on the Development Plan on page 53.

It will be tempting to work on multiple outcomes, especially if the client has a number of areas for improvement. However, by choosing one component area as an outcome you can keep a specific, targeted focus on success. Under the positive outcome, indicate how you will measure success. This provides a clear target for the client to strive for.

You can revisit the plan and work toward another positive outcome later. Timelines should reflect a sequential rather than global approach. Address one area at a time in a step-by-step manner. If three outcomes are listed, focus on the top priority first and establish timelines for review and completion. You may choose to make timelines for additional behaviors at this initial stage, or you may prefer to implement the first part of the plan and create the additional timelines after the first behavior is demonstrated. No matter which way you approach the situation, if the client needs to demonstrate a number of new behaviors, make it clear that multiple changes are expected over time.

Identify Reasons for Problems and Roadblocks to Improvement

Once you have defined a positive outcome you need to understand why this behavior is not already being demonstrated. Be sure to engage the client to help you with this exploration, since self-understanding is an essential first step in the development process. Ask questions, make observations, and collect data until you have some insights into why the desired behavior is not occurring. Your plan can then reflect this and ensure that any potential barriers or roadblocks to change are avoided or overcome. As you are thinking about roadblocks, start to consider possible interventions to get around them.

DETECT & DESCRIBE
Identify Reasons for Problems and Roadblocks to Improvement

Don't see high performance	Do see high performance
Evidence of working on problems without identifying underlying causes:	Evidence of identifying reasons for problems and roadblocks to improvement:
○ Striving to eliminate behaviors before assessing reason	○ Taking time to analyze why a positive outcome is not being demonstrated
○ Neglecting to clarify expectations	○ Ensuring expectations are clear between the worker and others
○ Ignoring situations that reinforce undesired behaviors	○ Assessing and influencing current reinforcement systems
○ Neglecting to set up conditions to reward desired behaviors	○ Setting up conditions to reward desired behaviors
○ Ignoring systemic factors that contribute to individual performance	○ Considering how systemic factors contribute to individual performance
○ Failing to assess the effects of an individual's skills, knowledge, or abilities	○ Assessing the efffects of skills, knowledge, and abilities on performance
○ Ignoring health and wellness issues	○ Assessing health and wellness factors

Unclear Expectations

People are often unaware of all the expectations associated with their work roles. Sometimes subtle attitudinal and communication expectations are assumed but not written down. If the behavior is not being demonstrated simply because of unclear or unaligned expectations, it may be possible to correct the problem by clarifying, describing, and reinforcing the point that the desired outcomes are expected behaviors.

Tools such as work descriptions and feedback from others can provide clearer expectations for individuals. Often, however, a dialogue is necessary. You may need to intervene in this process by having the client discuss duties, responsibilities, and priorities with a supervisor, leader, or project manager. If the client and the leader disagree about what is relevant and important, performance is unlikely to be acceptable. Sometimes the dialogue itself is all that is necessary to correct problems based on unclear expectations. It may be appropriate to negotiate these expectations, especially if the client is able to demonstrate that the expectations of others are unrealistic. This may also be an opportunity to assess the resources in place and figure out if they are sufficient to allow the client to meet expectations.

In other cases, clients may need to reframe their roles to meet previously unclear expectations. This may require some coaching as they reorganize and reevaluate their workload and priorities. The following example from a human resources professional illustrates how important it is to clarify expectations.

GREAT EXPECTATIONS

An administrative assistant was scheduling candidates for recruitment testing. She would call the candidates, set an appointment, and then hang up. She did not realize it was her role to let them know how long they would be there, what they would be doing, and what they needed to prepare and bring to the appointment. When they came in, candidates were apprehensive and unsure. They were also unprepared for the activities they were undertaking. The recruiters discussed these problems with the assistant and she made a checklist of information to share with each candidate. As a result, candidates were better prepared and much less apprehensive about engaging in the recruitment process.

Positive Outcomes Are Not Reinforced

Learning theory can be a helpful tool when assessing reasons for the absence of desired behaviors. People rarely feel motivated to perform behaviors that are not reinforced and will have no motivation to stop using behaviors that have no negative consequences. Consequences are key when you are striving to adjust behavior. Assess how your clients are being motivated by external consequences. Are consequences in place to increase a desired behavior? It not, no one is likely to exert much energy in that area. In a case like this, positive reinforcement might be a useful tool to increase the likelihood of the behavior occurring.

Negative Behaviors Are Reinforced

On the flip side, also assess if undesirable behaviors are somehow encouraged or desirable behaviors are discouraged in the work setting. If this is the case, you may need to address what is acceptable to the whole work group, in addition to making an individual plan. Find out if some behaviors in the areas for development have been occurring over a period of time with no negative consequences. As with expectations, you may discover that certain problematic behaviors are ignored or, at worst, actually reinforced by peers. If this is the case, the problem lies both outside and inside the individual performer. Interventions need to be made to change the environment contributing to the client's difficulties. At the same time, it is important to remember that every worker is expected to take personal responsibility for behavior. Acknowledging that, at times, some people within the organization may reinforce unacceptable behaviors is not an excuse for those behaviors to continue. However, this needs to be considered and compensated for in the plan, since it is harder for anyone to demonstrate a desired behavior in a setting that does not reinforce it.

Systemic Problems

Sometimes it is difficult to demonstrate desired behaviors because people are working within inefficient systems. As with reinforcement, systemic problems should not be an excuse—but they do need to be addressed and compensated for in the plan. Many resources can help you discover and

A QUESTION OF BALANCE
Extrinsic and Intrinsic Rewards

. . . .

Individuals are motivated by both extrinsic and intrinsic rewards. *Extrinsic rewards* are external factors such as money and status that can be gained as a result of specific activities. *Intrinsic rewards* are internal factors, such as those generated when completing an activity, that are in themselves satisfying and rewarding. So someone who solves a problem only because it is a required work duty that results in pay is motivated by an extrinsic reward. Someone who solves the same problem because the process is interesting and challenging is motivated by an intrinsic reward. People can seek both extrinsic and intrinsic rewards in their work. When working with your clients, it can be illuminating to discuss these different types of rewards. Decide how clients prefer to be rewarded and incorporate a reward for a positive outcome in their development plan.

improve systemic factors that are detracting from organizational performance. Here are a few basic systemic factors to check for:

- Do the workers have clear procedures and processes to follow?

- Do the workers have the authority to make necessary decisions?

- Do the workers get sufficient feedback to adjust their performance?

- Is relevant, accurate, timely, and specific information available in an easily understandable form?

- Are expectations clear, realistic, and achievable?

- Is the flow of work well designed?

- Do the workers have sufficient resources to support performance (time, tools, people, and information)?

Be careful that systemic problems are not used as a scapegoat or an excuse for poor performance. People who blame the system for their poor performance are unlikely to implement any personal changes. Systems are indeed a factor, but people need to take accountability for their actions to succeed even within a poor system.

A QUESTION OF BALANCE
Systemic and Individual Interventions

As a development professional, you will find that your ability to obtain results is affected both by the system someone is working in and by the individual working in the system. To improve their performance, workers need to be actively engaged in a self-development process. However, systemic factors within an organization can have a tremendous influence on the workers' ability to do their tasks. There are many published resources that focus on how to make systematic changes to enhance performance across an organization.

Both individual and system problems are important and need to be addressed. Systemic change is just as important as individual development (and in some cases more so), but it is outside of the scope of this book to thoroughly address systemic change: so I focus on ways to help clients develop rather than on ways to change the systems they are working in. Nonetheless, each chapter includes questions designed to stimulate your thinking about the systems people are working within. In some cases, you are likely to see and need to address systematic changes. This is a challenge for development professionals, balancing an individual improvement plan with systemic barriers that may impair the client's ability to perform.

Lack of Skill or Knowledge

Clients may not have the necessary skill to demonstrate a behavior. It is unrealistic to expect behavior people do not understand or know how to do. They may not know how to develop rapport, summarize information, or identify trends in information. Knowledge gaps can often be addressed through training or through the use of instructional materials. Skill gaps are somewhat more difficult to correct than knowledge gaps, since it takes an application of knowledge and practice to consolidate them. Often skill development will need to be coached on the job rather than simply taught, seen, or read about. If skill or knowledge gaps are contributing to the situation, you may need to address them before you can expect a behavioral change.

Health and Wellness

Is the individual physically, mentally, and emotionally able to perform? People can be facing many work, family, and personal problems that impair their work. If work behaviors are reflecting a serious personal crisis or issue, it is likely that no development plan will succeed until these problems are resolved or managed. Stress, self-esteem, motivation, confidence, fitness, nutrition, substance abuse, illness, and financial difficulties may all reduce someone's ability to perform. As a trainer, leader, or coach, you are not expected to have the resources or the mandate to diagnose or address these issues. As discussed in Chapter 1, if you suspect a wellness or health problem, it is essential to recommend that the client see a professional.

Individual Capacity

As well as considering health and wellness issues, consider the client's ability to learn and retain information. Some people do well with routine and highly structured tasks but are not able to adjust to changing roles and responsibilities. A client may have specific difficulties such as a low reading level, a slow processing speed, or trouble comprehending verbal or visual information. In these cases, learning and performance may be slower than you would expect for the average person. These barriers must be identified and addressed if a plan is to be successful, although it may not always be realistic to attempt to accommodate them. In these cases, a specialized assessment may need to be carried out by a professional in the area of learning.

By taking time to explore factors that interfere with reaching the positive outcome, you will be in a better position to create a targeted development plan.

Create a Structured Development Plan

A development plan is most effective when it is specific and concise. A well-structured plan allows you to specify what needs to happen, when, and how. It includes a desired outcome and an intervention strategy, plus ways to measure success, action items, time frames, and consequences. Writing down and agreeing to outcomes defines and clarifies expectations for everyone involved.

DETECT & DESCRIBE
Create a Structured Development Plan

Don't see high performance

Evidence of implementing strategies in an ad hoc or unstructured manner:

○ Demonstrating no more than a vague idea of what results will be acceptable

○ Lacking a specific way to measure success

○ Neglecting to define or share consequences of success or failure

○ Lacking a clear intervention strategy

○ Leaving timelines and deadlines vague

Do see high performance

Evidence of creating a structured development plan:

○ Defining a clear, concrete outcome that will indicate when the plan is successful

○ Using specific behavioral measures to evaluate success

○ Defining specific consequences if the plan succeeds or fails

○ Using a targeted intervention strategy

○ Setting timelines and deadline

How Is Success Measured?

What will success look like? Clear, concrete targets and measures are essential to ensure you are able to measure progress against a development plan. For example, words such as *satisfactory, improved,* and *better* are subject to so much interpretation that they're useless as measures. Set your target behaviors in terms of observable, measurable behaviors. Here are some points to consider when setting up a way to evaluate the plan:

- How will success be measured?

- Are data already being collected that can be used to evaluate progress?

- What is needed to set up a way to measure progress?

- Who will be best to evaluate the client's progress?

- What information is needed to make an evaluation?

- Do feedback forms or other tools to facilitate evaluation need to be created?

- When should the evaluation take place?

- How will the information be shared with the client?

Discuss with the client ways to demonstrate achievement. Make these as simple and practical as possible. Use training, coaching, or evaluation sessions to share and appraise progress. You may need to establish a baseline to see how often a behavior is occurring now. Also be sure to write in a next step at this part of the planning. When the step is successful, what will happen next? What is the next behavior to address?

Defining Consequences

Provide specific information about what will happen if the development plan is completed successfully—and if it is not. This is not the time for ambiguity or vagueness. If you are working with someone who is already performing satisfactorily, of course, it may be unnecessary to worry about consequences. In an ideal world, this is how workplace development would work. High-performing individuals will always be fine-tuning nuances of behavior. However, at times, you will be dealing with people whose work is not acceptable. If you are working with someone who has been experiencing performance issues, a variety of consequences may be available, including lack of promotion, reassignment, retraining, demotion, suspension, and termination. In these cases it is important to provide every chance to succeed before you enforce negative consequences. If the client is successful, you may want to include a positive consequence. Be sure to document the plan, clarify your expectations, and inform the client of the consequences. Think carefully when setting these consequences and be sure you are willing to enforce them if results are or are not achieved. Discuss them openly to make sure your client knows exactly what is at stake.

Planning an Intervention Strategy

Now decide what interventions are necessary so the client will be able to demonstrate the behavior. Some of your choices include coaching, feedback, ergonomics, job aids, job and work design, learning, and training. Clarify what resources will need to be put in place as the intervention is being carried out. Once you choose a behavior to develop, it is important to return to your analysis of roadblocks before you choose an intervention. You will make a very different plan depending on the underlying reason for the gap.

Think again about someone who is making mistakes on the job. Here are some possible reasons for failing to correct mistakes, along with some samples of suggested interventions and the associated resources required.

Roadblock	Intervention Strategy	Resources Needed
Failure to recognize personal responsibility for correcting mistakes	Clarify expectations and define work roles Create a work description	Time for dialogue with leader Sample work description
Ignorance of ways to correct a mistake	Train on equipment or processes	Course materials Time for instruction or coaching
Lack of time to correct a mistake	Reorganize workload	Discussion of ways to adjust workloads Revised work descriptions
Failure to recognize a mistake when it occurs	Establish feedback processes and strategies for identifying mistakes	Coworker to initially provide feedback Coaching on strategies

As you can see, you will need to customize the plan by considering the roadblocks, situation, and needs of the individual client. For example, perhaps the lack of time to correct mistakes is related to a need to establish different priorities. People often need assistance in some of the productivity behaviors before they are able to find time to correct mistakes. (If so, you may choose to work on a productivity outcome first.) Or perhaps someone did not know they were making mistakes because they were operating under a lower set of standards than was expected. In that case, expectations will need to be clarified and agreed to. As you can see, it is crucial to link reasons behaviors are not being demonstrated to the appropriate interventions.

Here are a few general points to keep in mind.

- Roadblocks, interventions, and resources need to be clearly defined. The intervention and resources must clearly address the roadblock. In this example, if someone doesn't know they are making a mistake, making more time available will not contribute anything toward correcting the mistake.

- Be careful that roadblocks are not seen as excuses for avoiding the behavior. Some clients, especially those not yet demonstrating self-responsibility, will hold up roadblocks as reasons they will not be able to demonstrate the outcome. Deal with this directly and openly, being sure to clarify your expectations as well as the resources that will be available to support the change. Be sure to agree on what is needed and follow through on providing these resources.

- The resources must be in place to work the plan. If development time is not made available or support people are unwilling or unable to provide the assistance needed, then the plan is not likely to be successful.

Focus on general strategies as you fill out this section in the Development Plan (see page 54). Specific tasks and deadlines will come a little later in the process.

Don't Forget the Individual's Strengths

It is important to build on strengths as well as identify weaknesses. The Gap Analyses will clearly show what the individual does well. The Development Plan includes space for you to summarize strengths. Be sure to find ways to incorporate the individual's strengths as you create your plan.

CARRY OUT THE PLAN

Once the plan has been created, your role is to challenge and support the client's self-improvement efforts. A well-thought-out plan contains all the specific details about what, when, where, and how improvement will occur. Your task is to coach the implementation of the plan. Reinforce and encourage your client to accomplish the tasks that have been laid out, evaluate progress, and adjust the plan as necessary. Without this support and follow-through, many plans just gather dust in a drawer.

Coach the Plan by Supporting Appropriate Interventions

The general strategy embodied in the plan will allow you to begin to focus on specific action items, providing resources and coaching behavioral change. Many detailed strategies are available to you at this point in the process.

You may need to take on any of a number of roles at this stage of the process. Some clients may need assistance requesting, accessing, or negotiating for the resources they require to implement their plan. In this case you may need to take the role of advocate or coach. Others may need to learn specific information. You may then take the role of teacher or trainer as you transfer skills and knowledge. It is especially important to teach process as well as content. Often to accomplish this you will need to work through a real-life situation. For example, if someone has difficulties solving problems, you can explain a problem-solving process and then help them move step-by-step through the process while addressing a specific, real-life, work problem they need to solve. Sometimes the client is not confident or requires some support and positive feedback. In this case, your role switches to supporter. Other times, the client may be operating in blind spots or demonstrating inappropriate behaviors and you will need to challenge these behaviors or offer corrective feedback. The following sections outline some of the specific tasks and strategies to use when coaching a plan.

Identifying Specific Action Items

Translate the intervention strategy you have chosen into specific tasks. These might include attending meetings, completing training, engaging in a self-reflection exercise, making a list, buying some necessary resource, talking to someone, or practicing a behavior with a colleague. For each action item, set a specific date. Monitor the plan to make sure the actions are being carried out. Set a date for reviewing and completing the plan. Ensure that the action items include collecting the data to measure behavior change. Now you are set to take action.

Work with your client to make sure the necessary resources are available to implement each task. Allow clients to take as much responsibility

DETECT & DESCRIBE
Coach the Plan by Supporting Appropriate Interventions

Don't see high performance	Do see high performance
Evidence of expecting the client will implement the plan independently:	Evidence of coaching the plan by supporting appropriate interventions:
○ Failing to recognize or shift into various helping roles	○ Changing roles as necessary to lead, coach, teach, or evaluate performance
○ Being vague about plans to carry out assistance	○ Defining and carrying out specific tasks to implement a development plan
○ Neglecting to focus on the teaching process by asking questions	○ Using questions to help clients learn
○ Avoiding confrontation of unacceptable behaviors and beliefs	○ Challenging unacceptable behaviors and beliefs
○ Neglecting to reinforce progress	○ Reinforcing progress
○ Being unsupportive or discouraging	○ Providing support and encouragement
○ Expecting others to try new behaviors without support	○ Providing safe settings to take risks and try new behaviors

as possible for requesting, accessing, and negotiating the resources to carry out the plan. Help them develop their own lists of people to approach. If someone is uncomfortable requesting resources, consider rehearsing the process of making a request. If they are unsure of when to access resources, teach them how to find information about resources.

Questioning

Questioning is probably the most powerful tool those in helping professions can use. Questions can be used to challenge opinions, check for understanding, and promote self-reliance. Questions can also facilitate learning and development by encouraging thinking and triggering self-discovery.

If questioning is used incorrectly, however, it can become threatening or frustrating for the client. As with all communication, the content, tone, and context will have a significant influence on the way the question is received. Questioning is not helpful if you are trying to lay blame (Who did this?) or emphasizing a mistake caused by something a person should have known (Didn't you know you were supposed to—?). "Why?" questions can also be unhelpful and can create defensive reactions (Why did you do that?). Also, excessive questioning can seem to the client to be an interrogation.

If your client tends to respond to questions with "I don't know," it is tempting to simplify your questions in a desperate attempt to to get some kind of concrete input. However, oversimplifying questions can result in a condescending approach. Some people have not been exposed to this questioning technique and are self-protective. They may not want to give a wrong answer. Saying "I don't know" feels to them like a safer, more protective, response than hazarding a guess. You may need to encourage such clients by appreciating positive elements in their responses. Usually you can find some part of the response that can be directed in a positive way.

Questioning is not always appropriate. At times, the client simply does not have the necessary background or information to answer. Some clients, especially those with a preference for Introversion, may want time to think about a question before they answer and may find a questioning process overwhelming. With people of this type you may want to balance asking questions with providing information. And timing is important; clients who are in the middle of a busy day may not be interested in engaging in a learning process. Learning by questioning takes time and is not appropriate in all situations. Watch out for these contextual and individual factors when considering using questioning as a learning approach.

When choosing specific questions to ask, consider both the individual you are working with and the goal of the question. Use open-ended questions that require more than a yes-or-no answer. Frame your questions so they provide an opportunity for someone to reflect on what they know or are experiencing in a positive way.

Often you can reframe a client's question to create a teachable moment—that is, an occasion when a lesson can be taught as a natural result of the situation. For example, say someone with a list of tasks comes to you and asks, "What should I do first?" You could simply order the tasks yourself, but then the client would learn nothing about prioritizing. A more proactive approach would be to work through a process of prioritizing by asking a series of questions.

You could initially comment that the question is a good one to ask and reinforce that the client is showing thoughtfulness and planning. This is especially important if someone is hesitant to ask questions. Next you might focus on the process by asking about the criteria that would be good to use to prioritize these tasks. Then you could respond to the answer by asking how your client might be able to apply the criteria. For example, if someone says that it might be best to use the customer delivery date or some other external deadline, then your next question might be how to find out the deadlines. Even more productively, you could ask how it might be possible to include deadline information on the list of tasks to do. If someone is not identifying all the essential criteria, you could ask about what other factors might be important. This structured questioning helps the client think about the topic. Chapter 5, on mindfulness, presents numerous questions designed to help you demonstrate the importance of this aspect of thinking about actions and processes.

Well-developed questions encourage the listener to share information. Here are some characteristics shared by good questions on any topic:

- Thought out

- Specific and focused on a topic and purpose

- Brief

- Asked one at a time

- Neutral rather than leading, biased, or having one right answer

- Nonthreatening

- Open-ended

- Not too probing or personal unless rapport and confidentiality have been established

- Careful to avoid the word *why,* which can create a defensive response

- Interspersed with conversation so they don't come across as an interrogation

- Not demanding of an immediate answer—that is, allowing room for the person to think

Challenging Unproductive Behaviors and Beliefs

If someone is not highly motivated to change, it may be because unproductive behaviors or limiting beliefs actually make change seem undesirable or impossible. Such behaviors and beliefs can be especially challenging to work with because they are often well-established, habitual ways of thinking and acting. Some of the most critical problem behaviors and barriers to growth are linked to habits of mind and body. These habits can make it difficult for a client to treat others respectfully, persist on work tasks, take reasonable risks, and engage in many other essential workplace behaviors. Dealing with these ingrained patterns can be a daunting endeavor.

Often the process of exploring unproductive behaviors and beliefs is met with resistance, so overcoming resistance becomes the initial task to work on. First seek to understand the perspective of the client. Read Chapter 4, on the communication competency, to ensure you are demonstrating the ability to encourage others to express their perspective. Be especially careful not to judge, label, or engage in any other communication shutdowns. Seek to understand the perspective of the person you are working with. Remember that listening and understanding do not imply agreement with the perspective.

Once someone has explained a perspective, you can offer an alternative in a calm and objective way. It is not helpful to argue with or demean the perspective. Rather, use logic to introduce alternative ways of thinking. Remember that people are unlikely to remember and apply information that does not fit into their worldview. Continue to present information and find ways to explore and influence your clients' thinking over time. Changing attitudes and perspectives can be slow going.

What you can do immediately is clarify and set standards of behavior that is acceptable and unacceptable. For example, if a group of males have been harassing the first female to join their group, you are unlikely to be able to convince them to change their ingrained attitudes about the role of women in the workplace, or, at any rate, you won't be able to do so fast enough to make any difference to the current problem. However, you can and should immediately set and reinforce standards regarding the way that woman is treated. Identify specific unacceptable behaviors such as unfair assignment of tasks, sexual comments, teasing, and inappropriate practical jokes. Clearly define and reinforce consequences for engaging in these behaviors.

This strategy applies not only to attitudes about other people but to attitudes toward work itself. For example, if someone is not highly concerned or interested in completing precise work, you are not likely to quickly convert them into someone who is exacting. What you can do is set and enforce specific standards for precision. By focusing on the behavior, you can minimize the effect negative ingrained beliefs have on the work at hand.

Dealing with self-defeating behaviors and attitudes can be more difficult, since the person affected by them is the individual practicing them. However, you can still apply the same principles and focus on behaviors. You can encourage a person to replace self-deprecating comments such as "I can't do this" with more positive comments such as "I can do this if I work at it." The importance of self-confidence and positive self-talk is covered in more detail in Chapter 3, on self-responsibility.

Reinforcing Progress

The role of reinforcement is at times complex. Reinforcement is defined as anything that increases the probability of a behavior's occurring. However, what is reinforcing for one person may not be reinforcing for another. For example, if you decide to reward progress by taking a cake into a meeting, clients may react in several different ways. One may like that particular type of cake and be delighted; another may dislike it and unhappily pretend to be pleased. Still another may have an allergy to one of the ingredients and become deeply offended that you didn't remember this fact. Still another may be trying to lose weight and therefore may see the cake as an unwelcome temptation. Some clients thrive on public recognition and will be thrilled by the attention, while others will be made uncomfortable and embarrassed. Just as with the cake, any simple attempt at reinforcing progress can be more or less rewarding depending on the situation. Be sure to understand your clients and get to know the type and amount of feedback and encouragement each one prefers. This is true for verbal encouragement as well. Personality type can provide some clues in this regard. Chapter 4, on communication, explores personality preferences related to positive and constructive feedback.

Providing Safe Settings to Take Risks and Try New Behaviors

When people develop, they take on risks as they try out new behaviors. For many, this can be very uncomfortable. Here are a number of ways you can assist clients in this process:

- Behavioral rehearsal

- Successive approximation

- Role playing

- Guided practice

- Teaching process instead of content

Behavioral rehearsal is a powerful tool to use when someone is preparing to engage in an unfamiliar or uncomfortable task. Clients may want to use rehearsal to prepare for interpersonal situations such as interviews, making requests, speaking to a group, or preparing what to say when resolving a conflict. Chapter 4 includes a section on preparing for communication that helps clients plan specifically what they want to say. As you work through a communication plan, some clients will benefit greatly from an opportunity to rehearse. You can add to this process by helping clients anticipate and prepare for the types of questions and responses they may receive when they tackle the real situation.

In a similar way behavioral rehearsal can be used for a variety of tasks that are not related to interpersonal interactions. For example, someone may become very anxious at the thought of taking a test. You can create a mock testing environment to practice test writing. Set up an environment as similar as possible to the one the client will experience, including time frame, types of questions, and physical setting. Prepare for the mock test by sharing strategies for managing test anxiety. In this way, you can help someone rehearse any behavior they need to demonstrate.

Successive approximation, sometimes called *shaping,* uses a gradual improvement process to reach a goal. You will incorporate a shaping process to some extent with the other strategies such as behavioral rehearsal and role playing. However, it is worth discussing as a strategy in itself. The gap between existing performance and the target behavior you are expecting your client to exhibit can often be quite large. It may be unrealistic as well as frustrating for your client for you to expect the target behavior to emerge in its ideal form immediately. Consider the size of the gap and then define smaller, more realistic, gains that will gradually shape the behavior. These successive approximations toward the goal can be coached and then rewarded. By rewarding this incremental progress, you can close large gaps successfully.

Role playing is a tool similar to rehearsal that takes the process a step further. In this case, you help your clients prepare for interpersonal inter-actions by actually taking on the role or roles of others who will be involved (or having an associate do so). For example, you can role-play an interview by acting as the interviewer would. This tool is especially helpful when a client needs to prepare to respond to someone else. It can be a powerful way to work on the communication competency in areas such as listening, sharing information, and conflict resolution. Role playing is especially helpful when you build into the process a way to obtain feed-back. The people involved can simply review the experience, but because they were engaged in it, they can miss some potential learning if they rely on just their feedback. Videotaping the role play or having someone else assigned to an observer role to report back can be more informative. Make sure your observers are skilled at providing feedback. If you are using a role-play situation with an observer, you may want to create a checklist or observation sheet for the person giving feedback.

Guided practice is a familiar technique used when an individual tries a new behavior with someone watching and coaching. When using guided practice, your challenge is to encourage the client to work as indepen-dently as possible, while at the same time using "teachable moments" to fine-tune performance. You may want to use an incremental approach to this process by completing the task first yourself with the learner as an observer and then gradually letting the learner take on more and more of the task. You will find that some learners will be more or less motivated to learn by doing and will have more or less patience for learning by watch-ing. This is an especially helpful tool for learning motor skills, but it can be used in a variety of situations. For example, guided practice can be used to coach a process such as problem solving or decision making.

Teaching process instead of content makes people much likelier to try new behaviors because it helps them understand the process and gives them a planned strategy to follow. For example, say you are working with someone who is experiencing a conflict with a coworker. If they under-stand the steps in the conflict resolution process and have developed a communication plan, they will be more comfortable and likelier to be more successful in their efforts to address the conflict. They have a good idea of what to do and how to do it. Without this understanding of steps and strategies, the client will be more hesitant and uncomfortable facing a new situation. Be sure to share the appropriate processes and strategies before expecting anyone to demonstrate a new behavior. Use this in conjunction with role play, guided practice, successive approximation, or behavioral rehearsal to reinforce learning.

One helper demonstrates how she used a combination of techniques to coach an employee into a leadership role. Note how she is addressing the employee's mindfulness and well as her supervisory ability.

EFFECTIVE INTERVENTIONS

I mentored an employee who joined us in an entry-level position and helped her progress all the way up to a senior vice presidency. The most important competency was managing others for results. I met weekly with the employee and had her share her challenges and how she planned to solve and address them. We role-played her planned actions as well. I gave her feedback on how well she had thought through the problem and provided constructive suggestions periodically. She started with one person reporting to her, and now she has dozens.

Monitor Effectiveness and Results of the Plan

Be sure to follow through and evaluate the success of the plan. If it is not successful, you may need to revisit the roadblocks and adjust your strategies. If there are consequences or rewards, be sure to enforce them. If your plan is successful, your client can choose another behavior to address. Once you have coached someone through the process, they will be able to complete it more independently in the future. Your role in this essential follow-up stage is to ensure the client is making an accurate self-assessment and is able to evaluate performance. People may need coaching in either or both of these aspects of the development process.

An effective plan always includes careful definitions of what success will look like and how and when the plan will be evaluated. It also specifies consequences for accomplishing or failing to accomplish each projected step. When you have defined the evaluation process clearly in this manner, it is relatively easy to follow through.

It is a good idea to have checkpoints for evaluating the progress of the plan well before the date when consequences are to be applied. This provides the opportunity to give formative rather than evaluative feedback. *Formative feedback* is given during a process. Its purpose is to show some-

DETECT & DESCRIBE
Monitor Effectiveness and Results of the Plan

· ·

Don't see high performance	**Do see high performance**
Evidence of unconcern about the progress or effectiveness of the plan:	Evidence of monitoring effectiveness and results of the plan:
◯ Failing to set regular times to track progress	◯ Checking client progress regularly
◯ Ignoring roadblocks the client is experiencing	◯ Working with client to move or get around roadblocks
◯ Providing unclear or vague feedback	◯ Evaluating progress and providing clear feedback
◯ Providing only summative feedback	◯ Providing both formative and summative feedback
◯ Sticking to a plan even when evidence indicates it is not working	◯ Adjusting the plan as necessary
◯ Failing to apply consequences	◯ Applying consequences

one how they are doing so far. If the plan is not on track, there is still time to adjust. This type of feedback is proactive and supportive. You may want to set regular checkpoints and meetings with the client to discuss progress and provide formative feedback, see what is working and what is not working, and adjust the plan accordingly. Be careful that clients do not simply blame external factors or extend deadlines because of procrastination. In these cases, you may need to challenge a lack of results and coach self-responsibility and productivity.

As you are helping with the implementation phase of the plan, work with clients to evaluate the progress being made toward their goals. Measure behavioral changes and encourage reflection on experiences, struggles, and successes. Help clients identify and deal with roadblocks that are getting in the way of the plan. Listen to fears and consider ways you can support and guide progress.

Allow clients to take as much control as possible in evaluating personal development. Your ultimate goal is to foster the development of people capable of accurate self-assessment. When you suspect a client is seeing progress inaccurately, seek alternative opinions. Some clients will

A QUESTION OF BALANCE
Action and Reflection

. . . .

Development requires a combination of action and reflection. Individual clients will vary in the amount of time they spend in each part of this cycle. Assess your client's tendency to balance these two sides of learning to maximize personal growth. Some clients will want to approach a particular activity by acting first and reflecting later. Others will want reflection time before they take action. Accommodate these needs as you encourage clients to take advantage of both the action and reflection processes.

Action provides an opportunity for clients to try out behaviors. It is outwardly directed. Clients are able to directly experience what they are working toward and can get immediate feedback from their environment as to how they are doing. This is often desirable, but too much action without reflection can create a situation where mistakes are repeated.

Reflection provides an opportunity for clients to think about what they have done or plan what they will do. It is inwardly directed. When people reflect, they are able to think about how successful their previous actions were. They can analyze what worked well and what could be improved. Reflection provides an opportunity to think how the action might be improved next time. However, too much reflection without action does not allow skills to be applied.

tend to under- or overestimate their development. Work with them to complete an accurate and realistic evaluation of their progress.

As well as evaluating individual progress, you will also want to work with each client to evaluate the plan. This level of evaluation will help people adjust the development process itself to better suit their learning style and needs. For example, someone may discover that it would have been preferable to rehearse behaviors more before trying them out or that it would have been more helpful to read about a topic before discussing it. By reflecting on the process of development, your clients will be able to make a better development plan next time.

Barring serious life situations such as death of a family member or a medical emergency, do be sure to implement the consequences that were set when the plan was created. If consequences are not enforced or are enforced in a casual way, the development process will be seen as unimportant or even irrelevant.

As you can see from these first two chapters, the professional developer's roles include role modeling, advocating, teaching, coaching, challenging, and supporting. Your challenge is to use these roles in a timely and appropriate manner for each of the clients you are helping.

In the next section of the book I describe ways to apply these two chapters when helping clients prioritize and develop the five basic workplace competencies.

QUICK TIPS
Facilitating Development

Throughout the chapter, I have emphasized the importance of using a structured plan and providing support to facilitate development. Here is a quick overview of the main chapter points to help you review what you have learned.

- Enlist your clients in the process. Have them take as much ownership as possible in assessing, planning, and evaluating their own performance.

- Complete a thorough assessment of how your clients' needs, barriers, and characteristics may be affecting their performance.

- Look carefully at any systemic or other external factors that may be affecting performance.

- Assess your clients' performance using specific, measurable, behaviors.

- Avoid vague evaluations, labels, and generalizations.

- Define a positive behavior as an outcome for the client to demonstrate.

- Assess the underlying reasons why the outcome is not being demonstrated.

- Create a development strategy that will take into account the reasons the outcome is not being demonstrated.

- Define specific ways to measure success.

- Define timelines, deadlines, and consequences.

- Help clients implement their plans using a number of strategies and helping interventions.

- Monitor the effectiveness and results of the plans.

- Enforce consequences.

PART 2

Workplace Competencies

Part Two explores five workplace competencies that enhance everyone's ability to be effective in the workplace: self-responsibility, communication, mindfulness, productivity, and proactivity. Besides providing practical tips and strategies to help people develop these critical workplace competencies, each chapter includes a Gap Analysis to help identify specific strengths and areas for improvement you can focus on with each client.

Before you work through the next five chapters with a client, you will find it helpful to overview the chapters and complete all the Gap Analyses for yourself. Familiarizing yourself with the content of the chapters and completing a personal assessment will provide a useful background for working with a client on the same material.

When you are working with someone else, it is often most useful to fill out the Gap Analysis together to ensure you are both seeing the client's strengths and weaknesses in the same way. This collaborative process also allows you to elaborate on and explain the statements in the Gap Analysis. If you are not familiar with your client's performance, your client will need to fill out the Gap Analysis alone or obtain additional feedback.

Have a discussion with your client to identify people who would be able to provide helpful feedback. Clients may want to ask leaders, colleagues, or customers to fill out the Gap Analysis to provide additional information to compare with your assessment and your client's self-assessment. These multiple sources of feedback will give a more global perspective.

Provide additional feedback on the bottom of each page by adding specific information or clarifying your rationale for the choices on the Gap Analysis. You can make the Gap Analysis more complete by writing in specific behaviors you have observed. As with any feedback tool, specific examples will help clarify problems and areas for growth. Be sure to focus on specific behaviors and not labels or generalizations.

As in Part One, each chapter covers ways to develop the components that make up each specific competency. The Detect & Describe boxes will help people become aware of their strengths and weaknesses and will help you measure change in those particular areas. Don't forget to use the Development Plan worksheet in Chapter 2 as a guide in creating a plan—for yourself, then with your clients—as you progress from chapter to chapter.

Chapter 3
Self-Responsibility

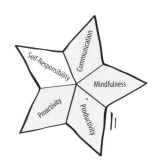

Self-responsible people—those who take a positive approach toward and active ownership of their work—are the likeliest ones to improve in any of the competency areas. Self-responsibility consists of showing up ready and willing to work and taking ownership of successes and mistakes. People who do not demonstrate self-responsibility will appear unmotivated, passive, complaining, dependent, helpless, or pessimistic. They will tend to blame others and will ignore, avoid, or deny their part in failures and even in successes.

Self-responsibility is a powerful competency. It enables people to take control and make choices to accept or improve their situation. Self-responsible people have a good work ethic and a positive attitude, and they appear committed, determined, dependable, reliable, and dedicated—all qualities much needed in the workforce.

The self-responsibility competency consists of two distinct components of behavior. I summarize the first group of behaviors as "Shows Up Ready and Willing to Work"; it includes the things people need to do to take on their work duties in a positive and determined way. The second group—"Takes Ownership"—reflects the willingness to be accountable for performance and to work at improving it. Note the list of the components of self-responsibility in the order in which they will be covered in the chapter.

> ### COMPONENTS OF SELF-RESPONSIBILITY
>
> **Shows Up Ready and Willing to Work**
> - Has a realistically optimistic outlook
> - Maintains energy and alertness
> - Independently works toward goals
>
> **Takes Ownership**
> - Demonstrates personal accountability
> - Maximizes effective use of personal assets

GAP ANALYSIS
Self-Responsibility

The pairs of statements that follow represent the endpoints of a continuum of possible performance in self-responsibility. Place an X on each line at the location that best describes the current level of performance.

Shows Up Ready and Willing to Work

Pessimistic or overly idealistic	Has a realistically optimistic outlook
Tired or distracted	Maintains energy and alertness
Overly dependent or too independent	Independently works toward goals

Takes Ownership

Does not accept accountability	Demonstrates personal accountability
Over- or underutilizes personal assets	Maximizes effective use of personal assets

Take time to reflect on self-responsibility. Use the space below to write down any specific information or insights you, your client, or others may have regarding your client's ability to exercise self-responsibility in the course of daily work activities.

_____

_____

_____

SHOWS UP READY AND WILLING TO WORK

People who are ready and willing to work are energetic and alert and have a positive outlook. They see possibilities and challenges in problems, and they persist on a task even when it is mundane or highly challenging. When the strategies they are using don't work to accomplish their goals, they look for and find alternative ways of approaching the situation. They cooperate with others and are also able to work on their own.

Has a Realistically Optimistic Outlook

People's basic belief system and outlook toward work and life have a huge effect on their performance on the job. Employers know they are looking for people with the "right attitude" or a "positive outlook." However, the terms *attitude, outlook,* and *perspective* tend to be somewhat abstract; the qualities they describe are difficult to measure. To work with them, it is essential to translate these abstract concepts and words into concrete behaviors, defining and measuring specific behavioral expressions. The Detect & Describe box on page 94 has a checklist of specific behaviors people engage in when demonstrating a realistically optimistic attitude. Focus in on and use these when you are seeking and measuring behavioral change for clients who are working on this area.

When working with clients, be sure to bring their attention to their use of statements, body language, and other behaviors that come across as negative or overly idealistic. For each negative behavior you identify, have your client replace the behavior with a more positive alternative. Sometimes people develop a negative set of behaviors that, over time, have become unconscious and automatic. They may not even be aware of how much their negative outlook comes across to others. Identifying negative comments and actions will help them focus on how they are seen. These behaviors can then be minimized and replaced with more positive options.

People tend to develop characteristic ways of responding to situations and others. Because these attitudes are demonstrated as ingrained, habitual, orientations toward work and life, it can seem an overwhelming task to change them. However, it is appropriate to set specific behavioral expectations as to how clients express themselves in the workplace. It is reasonable to assume they have a responsibility not only to show up at work but also to present a positive demeanor. It is realistic to expect them to express behaviors that show they are cheerful, positive, and hopeful.

DETECT & DESCRIBE
Has a Realistically Optimistic Outlook

Don't see high performance

Evidence of an overly pessimistic or idealistic attitude:

○ Showing dissatisfaction through body language such as frowning and slouching

○ Ignoring or avoiding others

○ Showing no interest in others

○ Saying mostly negative things about others

○ Saying mostly negative things about personal behavior and attributes

○ Commenting mostly on negative aspects of situations

○ Predicting negative outcomes to situations

○ Complaining frequently

○ Expressing negative emotions such as anger and frustration

○ Arriving late for meetings and not ready for commitments

○ Dressing inappropriately or having poor hygiene

○ Ignoring or avoiding unpleasant realities

○ Being overly enthusiastic, even in situations where enthusiasm is inappropriate

○ Focusing on goals without considering facts, details, and status quo

○ Setting unrealistic expectations both personally and for others

○ Glossing over rather than dealing with barriers and constraints

Do see high performance

Evidence of a realistically optimistic attitude:

○ Showing energy and engagement through body language

○ Greeting and acknowledging others

○ Being friendly and interested in others

○ Saying mostly positive things about others

○ Saying mostly positive things about personal behavior and attributes

○ Commenting mostly on positive aspects of situations

○ Predicting realistic positive outcomes to situations

○ Complaining rarely

○ Exerting control over negative emotions such as anger and frustration

○ Arriving on time and ready for commitments

○ Being neat, clean, and appropriately dressed

○ Dealing gracefully with unpleasant realities

○ Refraining from excessive enthusiasm in situations where others are more sedate or cautious

○ Aligning realistic goals with current realities

○ Setting realistic expectations for self and others

○ Finding solutions to barriers and constraints

A QUESTION OF BALANCE
Optimism and Pessimism

Personal outlook can best be thought of as falling on a continuum from highly optimistic to very pessimistic. Optimists tend to expect and hope for the best, whereas pessimists expect the worst. Positive beliefs about oneself and one's ability to meet challenges and accomplish goals are certainly valuable assets for any individual. People need to be able to dream and have lofty goals and visions—that's what allows them to attempt and accomplish things others believe are impossible. The drive and initiative to strive toward a goal requires optimistic thinking and persistence.

However, being overly optimistic can translate into having overly ide-alistic expectations. People who do not consider the practical realities of situations are apt to do themselves a disservice. They will expect tasks will be done sooner than possible and will not anticipate problems that might occur.

Successful workers draw from both optimism and pessimism. Pes-simism and realism allow people to think about and predict potential roadblocks and challenges. However, once roadblocks and challenges are identified, optimism is what allows people to work toward overcoming them and achieving the results they want. Because of the nature of this continuum, be careful not to coach clients to simply replace pessimism with optimism. Instead, teach them to project realistically optimistic out-comes. At the same time, watch out for the tendency of people to limit themselves by grounding their dreams too soon. Walk the fine line be-tween helping clients envision themselves as being the best they can be and making sure they are able to actualize that vision.

PERFORMANCE PREFERENCES
Optimism and Pessimism: Sensing and Intuition

Sensing (S) types tend to be practical and realistic in their approach and may seem less optimistic than Intuitive types because they are usually more focused on and aware of the specific situational factors that will affect their efforts. Intuitive (N) types tend to focus on possibilities and the world of ideas. Because of this they can come across as overly idealistic and unrealistic, especially to Sensing types.

When working with Sensing types, be sure to start with the realities and accept and assess the barriers they face. Once this is completed, you can then help the Sensing types move past the barriers to increase their optimism. When working with Intuitive types, you will need to ground their optimism with a reality check by helping them see the facts and details of the situation.

Sometimes people are not aware of the cues they are sending, especially in the nonverbal areas of communication. When helping clients display a more positive outlook you may find it helpful to show them what their behaviors look like to others. Here is an example of someone who was not aware of the message she was sending.

ABOUT FACE

One ESTP woman, when attending meetings, would become frustrated when her points were not well received by the group. She would then slouch and frown for the rest of the meeting. Her facial expressions clearly conveyed her disapproval. When frustrated, she would also stop contributing to the meeting. When her supervisor discussed these behaviors, the woman admitted she was aware that she tended to shut down when frustrated. She knew she needed to improve by making an effort to stay engaged, but she had no idea her facial expressions were bothering people. Her supervisor suggested that she look into a mirror and then re-create her mind-set in situations where she became frustrated. She was shocked to see how overtly her emotion was reflected in her expression. She was then

PERFORMANCE PREFERENCES
Optimism and Pessimism: Thinking and Feeling

Individuals with a preference for Thinking (T) tend to analyze situations and spot flaws. When working with Thinking types, be sure to recognize the usefulness of this approach as well as show them how an approach that is overly focused on critiquing can be demoralizing to others. This is especially true when they are working with people who have a preference for Feeling (F). The Feeling types will want to focus on appreciating and validating what is working before looking at problems and flaws. You will need to take this into account when working with Feeling types.

Thinking types may not react well to being asked to create overtly optimistic projections and outlooks, which seem to them illogical, unrealistic, and idealistic. In fact, individuals who seem bubbly, positive, and enthusiastic can irritate Thinking types. Thinking types can also be skeptical about information that is being shared in such an enthusiastic way. Everyone, regardless of preferences in this area, will benefit from understanding this difference in approach. Feeling types, especially those who also have a preference for Extraversion (E), can learn to tone down their passion and enthusiasm. Thinking types can learn to interpret the enthusiasm as an expression of a valid personal approach to the world.

When helping clients develop a positive orientation, you need to think about where they are starting from and coach accordingly.

able to begin to make a much greater effort to control the way she was coming across to others.

Some workers may object that the way they choose to interact and come across to others isn't related to their ability to complete tasks and perform well. Those who believe this are not likely to adjust their behaviors in this area. If this is the case with any of your clients, you may need to show them the value of projecting themselves in a positive way. They may need concrete examples of how a negative demeanor affects organizational morale and customer service. They need to understand that even when they are not in a direct service role, people outside the organization will judge the organization on the basis of their demeanor.

PERFORMANCE PREFERENCES
Expressing a Positive Outlook: Extraversion and Introversion

People with a preference for Extraversion (E) may be likelier to greet others and be enthusiastic in their approach to them, but they may also be more vocal in their complaints and in their expression of both negative and positive emotions. Use their outward focus to build on the positive comments and behaviors they demonstrate. They may need coaching to think before they speak, especially if their comments might be damaging to customer relations or organizational morale. As well, they may need to learn to be careful about expressing their body language, especially when it is negative.

Individuals with a preference for Introversion (I) may not always be oriented toward overtly demonstrating a positive outlook. They may be less likely to share their feelings and thoughts, especially to casual contacts. Build on their thoughtful approach. They are less likely to say things they will regret later. They may, however, need coaching to be a bit more outwardly positive and to show their enthusiasm to others. Individuals who prefer Introversion may also need to learn to express more interest outwardly through their body language.

Speakers look for cues from listeners to help them gauge reactions. The following example illustrates difficulties that can arise if a speaker is not receiving cues.

WHAT ARE YOU THINKING?

An INFP man proved almost impossible for colleagues to read. He would not say anything in response to attempts to share information and would sit there with a blank face and without nodding or using any other active listening cues. When challenged on this behavior, he replied that he had been actively listening to and thinking about the information but had not been putting any energy into acknowledging the input. His working relationships improved when he began to focus outwardly when hearing information to demonstrate interest and enthusiasm about what was being said.

Situational Factors

Personal outlook can be strongly influenced by situational factors. Almost everyone has felt dispirited or not overly friendly or optimistic at times. If someone's outlook has changed dramatically and relatively suddenly, then mental health or personal or interpersonal difficulties may be the cause, and a referral to counseling services may be in order. Someone whose personal problems are making it difficult to take a positive approach or whose situation is overly stressful may need to consider taking a leave from the workplace. And those who are unhappy with their work may realize on consideration that they are simply working in the wrong place.

Before addressing a client's outlook, be sure to assess overall organizational morale. It can be an organizational norm to complain about the workplace and its leaders, decisions, and processes. At times negativity increases when no one seems to listen to or act on concerns. Sometimes changes in individual demeanor are a symptom of this decrease in morale across the organization. Times of change and uncertainty can produce fear of job loss or of increased workload. People who lack information about change tend to fill the gap with rumors and speculation, creating fear. If morale is especially low in your organization, you may need to make changes in your systems and processes to reward and recognize people and their efforts. In these situations, simply encouraging others to show a more positive face to the world is rarely a successful strategy. You may need to take a more systematic approach and address morale at the organizational level rather than working with individuals.

Be careful to recognize that people do need to process negative thoughts and feelings. Your goal is not to have them mask their true opinions with a falsely positive face. Acknowledge concerns and encourage others to see the positive side of things. Concerns aren't as likely to grow if people have opportunities to share and deal with them. Most organizations have problems and issues that need to be faced. If the organization listens to its people and addresses issues directly and promptly, complaining and commiserating will decrease.

Self-Confidence

Lack of self-confidence may underlie negativity. When people are unsure of their abilities and perceive themselves as lacking, they often relate to others in a defensive or pessimistic manner and tend to give up more easily and take fewer risks. Those with low confidence can come across as either unsure of themselves or overconfident. Both demeanors tend to be unsuccessful when dealing with others.

Here are some ideas you can use to boost a client's confidence:

- Discuss the topic of confidence.

- Decide, with the client, if self-confidence needs building.

- Point out and emphasize the client's strengths.

- Offer positive feedback.

- Help the client make and meet small, realistic goals.

- Acknowledge success and growth.

- Reframe negative and limiting thoughts through self-talk.

Positive Self-Talk

What people say to themselves, their *self-talk,* can have a powerful effect on their behavior. One confidence-building tool requires reframing negative and limiting beliefs and self-images. That is, people must first become aware of the issue by listening to their self-talk, since negative expectations limit the ability to take on responsibility, face challenges, and learn new things.

Have clients create a list of negative or limiting statements they hear themselves saying or thinking. This step is important, because much self-talk is internal. Here are some common examples:

- I can't do this.

- This is really hard for me.

- I'm not good at . . .

- I'll never be any good at . . .

Work with your clients to reframe their limiting statements into more positive ones, but be sure the new messages are realistic and believable. If someone complains about being inept at managing time, don't try to reframe the statement as "I am wonderful at managing time." Try a more realistic replacement such as "I can focus on managing my time more effectively by using my planner." Don't ignore or minimize areas of difficulty. Your goal is to ensure that clients are able to see themselves in a positive way.

Maintains Energy and Alertness

People require energy and alertness to tackle daily tasks. When sufficiently rested and alert, they can focus effectively; when tired or distracted, they may make mistakes and engage in unsafe work practices. Self-responsible people don't use lack of energy as an excuse; instead, they make an effort to live a healthy lifestyle and maintain a balance between work, other responsibilities, and recreational time. To maintain their health, they get regular sleep, eat well, and exercise.

Although you may not be able to directly observe health and lifestyle practices, the consequences of unhealthy behaviors show up as a lack of energy and decreased alertness. It may not be reasonable to expect clients to change their personal habits, but if these habits affect performance, it is reasonable to expect behavioral change at work.

Your company is entitled to expect top performance from its workforce. People have the responsibility to attend work regularly, to maintain their energy and alertness, and to address any conditions that may endanger themselves or others in the workplace. That being said, at times people may not be aware of how their health and wellness issues are affecting their performance. When health issues affect clients' ability to be ready and willing to do their work, you need to address these issues.

Physical health problems and medical conditions can affect physical energy levels and mental abilities. If you suspect a health problem you may want to share your observations with your client and encourage a visit to a physician.

DETECT & DESCRIBE
Maintains Energy and Alertness

Don't see high performance	Do see high performance
Evidence of a lack of energy and alertness:	Evidence of energy and alertness:
○ Slouching, yawning, walking slowly	○ Walking vigorously and looking wide awake
○ Being slow to move or get up to do things	○ Readily moving around to get things or perform tasks
○ Being unresponsive to cues or events	○ Responding quickly to cues and events

Stress can also contribute to and even create inability to perform adequately on the job. People can be facing many work, family, and personal problems, or any of a number of other emotional, physical, and situational factors that can contribute to performance problems. Often when people are experiencing stressful situations their sleeping patterns are affected, which further diminishes their energy and alertness.

Here are some cues that might lead you to suspect work performance issues are related to personal issues:

- Increased work absences

- Changes in typical behavior patterns

- Reduced productivity or quality of work

- Variable work pace

- Missed deadlines

- Mood swings

- Emotional outbursts

Generally, when personal and health issues affect performance, you tend to see a noticeable change in behavior. However, if you think a performance concern is related to one or more personal issues, it is not your job to diagnose the exact cause. What you can do is show concern—but don't pry. Don't try to identify or solve the problem yourself. Refer the client to any support services that may be appropriate and available. See Chapter 1 for more information about dealing with people's personal situations.

Eating well and exercising boosts energy levels. Assess how well your company promotes good habits. What types of foods does your company provide for individuals to purchase? Too many organizations fill their vending machines with junk food rather than healthy choices. Too few encourage individuals to bring healthy food to work by providing a refrigerator and a way to heat food. Are breaks adequate to eat well rather than grabbing something and eating on the go? Are there any drinks other than coffee and soda? Is there a good source of drinking water? Are a time and a place for exercise provided for people to use during breaks? Does the company have information and referral services to help individuals make healthy lifestyle choices? It may not be practical to have all these elements in play in any specific work site. However, if you are encouraging individuals to be healthy, you must model and provide ways for them to accomplish good health.

No matter how many systems the company puts in place to encourage healthy choices, however, the choice is still up to the individual. Once medical conditions are explored and information and tools are provided, it will be essential to clearly define what the workplace expectations are for energy and alertness. At this point, it may be reasonable to put negative consequences in place for a lack of performance. This is especially critical if the safety of the individual or others might be at risk as a result of a mistake.

Independently Works Toward Goals

When starting to work with someone on this component, be sure to call any negative behaviors to their attention and start to minimize their use of such behaviors. For each negative behavior you identify, have the client replace the behavior with a more positive alternative.

As with all behaviors, consider the personality preferences of clients when coaching them to work independently.

The general expectation on the job is that people who understand the task at hand and have the skills and knowledge to do the work will be able to carry out their duties independently. Workers may need to check in

DETECT & DESCRIBE
Independently Works Toward Goals

Don't see high performance	Do see high performance
Evidence of a lack of independence:	Evidence of independence:
○ Requiring frequent supervision	○ Deciding what needs to get done next
○ Depending on others for direction	○ Taking control of situations by taking action
○ Avoiding action to improve situations to achieve success	○ Improving situations to achieve success
○ Expecting big results from a small amount of effort	○ Putting in the effort required to achieve the results desired
○ Being helpless and passive	○ Being active and resourceful

PERSONALITY PREFERENCES
How Different Types Work Independently: Thinking and Feeling

Individuals with a preference for Thinking (T) as a decision-making style may be more self-evaluative than those who have a preference for Feeling (F). If they also have a preference for Introversion (I), they may prefer to work mostly independently and may not seek feedback on progress. People with these preferences (IT) may be seen as overly independent. When working with them, you will need to establish yourself as a credible source of feedback before they will accept your input.

Feeling types tend to thrive on positive feedback and like to hear support and encouragement as they work. This is especially true if they also have a preference for Extraversion (E). Individuals with these preferences (EF) may ask for direction as a way of connecting and interacting and thus may come across as dependent. When working with them, it will be important to separate their ability to work independently from their need to interact with others.

In both cases, helping individuals understand their preferences and the preferences of others will help them see the differing needs in the areas of interaction and independence.

A QUESTION OF BALANCE
Independence and Involvement

People need to exercise the level of independence expected on the job—but no more. Those who go off on their own may make decisions that take others by surprise, interfering with the overall effort. They may change procedures without consulting people whose work needs to mesh with theirs. They may complete work others don't see as a priority or as even necessary. Others may duplicate their efforts without realizing tasks have already been done. Resources may be used on one project that others wanted to apply elsewhere. For these reasons, it is important to put checks and balances on the amount of independence you encourage. Your clients do need to link their efforts with the efforts of others. Ask yourself, "Where on the independence-involvement continuum do I want clients to be and how can I get them there?"

with a supervisor, peer, or leader in unusual circumstances or when faced with complicated problems or demands. Usually the employer does not see this as a problem. When someone frequently asks for instruction and seeks direction well after the tasks have been learned, however, then the behavior can be a problem and a draw on resources. At the same time, someone who works too independently can also be seen as a problem.

Individuals may have many reasons for not acting independently. Be sure to assess why a client is not showing independence before you try to implement a plan. The strategies you use must match the reasons for the behaviors or your efforts are not likely to be effective.

Learned Helplessness

Some people have learned to take a passive approach. Situations have trained them to think their actions will not be effective in achieving results, so they do not take any action. Also, they find it easier to ask and be directed than to figure things out for themselves. This approach allows them to avoid any sense of personal responsibility, thinking, "I was only doing what they told me to do."

If you sense that your client is able to act independently but is more comfortable being told what to do, you can intervene through a process of questions and discussion. When such individuals seek direction about how to do something, ask them how they think it could be done. If they are unsure of which task to complete, encourage them to discuss what they think they should do next. You can also have clients tell you what they plan to do or encourage them to make and share a list of their duties. Find opportunities to discuss priorities and responsibilities. Avoid simply telling clients what to do in these situations, since this will encourage their passivity.

Organizations often reinforce learned helplessness by neglecting to give their people any authority to work independently within their scope. When an action is to be taken or a decision is to be made, are people in your organization expected to check with the supervisor? Or do they have the authority to make a decision? If they are expected to take action or make decisions, do they have the tools, guidelines, processes, criteria, or procedures in place to allow them to act independently? Sometimes the system itself creates a need for extensive supervision and direction, and then management is disappointed when workers don't act more independently. This systemic problem must be addressed before you can expect people to change their behavior.

PERSONALITY PREFERENCES
How Different Types Work Independently: Sensing and Intuition

People with a preference for Sensing (S) and those who combine Sensing and Judging (SJ) may hesitate to act independently when they are unsure of expectations or lack a clear understanding of the situation at hand. Clear, specific, and well-defined processes, procedures, and criteria for decisions will help people with these preferences maintain their independence at work.

Intuitive (N) types will be best able to work independently when they see how the tasks at hand are related to and contribute to larger goals or visions. Before acting independently, they will want to see the implications and future results of their actions.

Uncertainty About What to Do

People can be especially hesitant to take risks and work independently when moving into new roles and duties. Someone who is totally unfamiliar with a task may need information, training, supervision, reminders, evaluation, and positive feedback before they will be able to work on it independently. This tends to be a gradual process. Workers become more independent in performing tasks when they develop confidence and competence. Be sure your clients know specifically what the scope of their work is and the expected standards. This will allow them to feel comfortable with their duties and establish competence in them.

Be careful to be encouraging and not judgmental when people are confirming or clarifying what they are supposed to do. You do not want to create an artificially positive situation where someone stops asking for direction but is then unsure of how to do the work. Your goal is to increase clients' ability to work independently, not to simply discourage asking for direction. If someone is unsure, it may be because they were not oriented to the role adequately or not given clear expectations.

Leadership Practices That Encourage Dependence

Leadership style and practices can also greatly influence the amount of independence people demonstrate at work. Some supervisors and leaders

PERSONALITY PREFERENCES
How Different Types Work Independently: Extraversion and Introversion

Extraverted (E) types may seek input as a way of thinking about and understanding a task. They are not necessarily seeking direction; rather, they are simply thinking out loud. However, this behavior can come across to others as somewhat needy or dependent. It will be useful to share with Extraverted individuals how others might interpret their thinking out loud.

Introverted (I) types may be likelier to reflect on situations and work the options through before seeking input. They may come across as more independent. It is possible for people with Introverted preferences to stop working on a task because they are unsure of how to proceed. They may hesitate to ask for direction. Be sure to check in with Introverted clients to assess if any barriers are getting in the way of their taking independent action.

are very directive in their leadership approach and can discourage workers from acting autonomously. If leaders are interested in maintaining control and want workers to act in specific ways, the workers are unlikely to respond autonomously to situations for fear of reprisal. When leadership changes, often workers are unsure what level of autonomy is expected of them. If the new leader has different expectations than the previous one did, the workers' behaviors will probably not match up. Be clear how much autonomy you expect from your clients, and follow through by allowing them to take action and make decisions within their scope.

TAKES OWNERSHIP

When people take ownership, they acknowledge their role in events and situations. They demonstrate personal accountability by holding themselves responsible for the results of their actions. They are aware of and maximize their personal assets to be as effective as possible.

Demonstrates Personal Accountability

Blame is a huge waste of resources in organizations today. Although it is important to analyze errors and correct mistakes, many people spend a lot more time and energy trying to find ways to absolve themselves of responsibility than acknowledging accountability and then moving forward to correct or compensate for errors and flaws.

People who place blame elsewhere when results are not achieved are unlikely to improve their own performance. They can become immersed in blaming, passing off responsibility, and making excuses. These types of behaviors will decrease productivity and create situations where mistakes and problems are covered up rather than dealt with.

You can measure people's investment in personal accountability by what they say and do. Look for statements and actions that show the client is acknowledging responsibility and not blaming others. The Detect & Describe box lists behaviors that demonstrate the level of acknowledgment of personal accountability. Focus on and work toward replacing negative behaviors with positive ones when you are measuring change in this area.

When people don't take personal accountability, their failures and successes are outside their control. They attribute their failure or success to luck, chance, or the actions of others. It is difficult to encourage people to improve when they don't see themselves as responsible.

Several strategies will prove useful when you help clients take personal accountability. Remember that you can't give responsibility to clients, you can only encourage them to take it. Ultimately progress on this behavior must result from the decision to own their behaviors and the subsequent consequences.

Blame and Responsibility

It can be helpful to discuss the ideas of blame and responsibility with your client. You may want to challenge words and behaviors that demonstrate a lack of control over actions or consequences. Treat these types of statements the same way you treat negative self-talk and find positive replacements for them. Listen for and challenge phrases such as "It doesn't matter what I do" or "It's not my fault." These reveal a sense of powerlessness or a detachment from personal accountability. It is virtually impossible to help anyone improve their performance if they believe factors outside their efforts are responsible for their success or failure.

DETECT & DESCRIBE
Demonstrating Personal Accountability

. . . .

Don't see high performance	Do see high performance
Evidence of not accepting accountability:	Evidence of demonstrating personal accountability:
○ Blaming others for problems and situations	○ Acknowledging a personal contribution to problems and situations
○ Blaming others for lack of results	○ Taking responsibility when results are not achieved
○ Making excuses for lack of results	○ Making no excuses for lack of results
○ Asserting inability to do something	○ Expressing belief in personal ability to accomplish goals
○ Not attempting tasks	○ Attempting tasks, even when unsure of the outcome
○ Denying, ignoring, or detaching from faults	○ Admitting to faults
○ Trusting luck or fate for success or failure	○ Linking effort to success
○ Not focusing on areas for professional development	○ Focusing on areas for professional development

Benefits of Accepting Accountability

When encouraging clients to accept personal accountability, it is essential to make sure they can see the benefits and disadvantages of being accountable. Discuss how it often may appear easier to not take responsibility in the short term, but the long-term consequences are apt to be less favorable. In your discussion you can offer choices and options and have your client explore the consequences of different types of approaches. Especially consider situations where errors have been made.

It can also be helpful to share your perspective or the perspectives of others regarding specific work areas where the client has displayed a lack of accountability. Discuss how and why these actions could create further problems and why accountability is necessary. This might require focusing on a bigger picture and on the effect of the behavior on the client and on others in the longer term. However you approach your explanation and discussion, your goal is to help clients see the links between their decisions, actions, and results.

Individual Understanding and Motivation

Sometimes someone who is not taking responsibility may simply not understand the task or may not be motivated to complete it. Explore these possibilities to understand what is driving the unsatisfactory performance. Set clear expectations with your clients and provide opportunities for their actions to be linked to specific consequences—both good and bad. Sometimes people need to see immediate negative consequences before they will be motivated to change their behavior.

Organizational Culture

Blaming may be a part of your organizational culture. What are the consequences of making mistakes? When mistakes are made, how do people characteristically respond? Do leaders tend to hold themselves accountable or is blame passed on to others? As with other behaviors, you are not likely to change the actions of your clients unless the culture supports the behaviors you recommend.

The Positive Side of Making Mistakes

Making mistakes is an essential part of learning. If someone is making a number of mistakes, look at the types and patterns of mistakes being made. This will help you focus on ways to learn from them and do the work with fewer errors. The key to this is analyzing what happened.

If individuals are making calculator errors, for example, teach calculator use. If errors are being made in transferring data, have people check for accuracy. Some mistakes are simply the result of carelessness. Coach people to check their work to reduce the frequency of this type of mistake. In a similar way, many mistakes are made when people are distracted. You may need to reduce or remove distractions in the workspace. If some mistakes are easy to make in a specific setting, come up with a long-term solution. If something is being spilled, put it in a different place or in a different container. If something is being misplaced, create a specific process to handle it. Whenever possible, engage the people who are making the errors in creating long-term solutions.

Don't get caught up in a discussion about blame and fault when mistakes are made. Analyze what happened and fix it. Some of the more complex errors will take a bit of time to analyze and understand. Lack of feedback may mean that people simply do not understand that they have made mistakes. Be sure to keep the feedback lines open so mistakes are brought to the attention of people who make them. Not only should people become aware of errors, they should be encouraged to process them and learn from them.

Be careful not to discourage taking risks and making mistakes. It is a necessary part of learning and development to try things and make mistakes. Mistakes usually become a problem only when individuals make the same mistakes several times without correcting them. However, there are some areas in which it is not safe or prudent to take risks. People need to be aware of these limits and choose carefully when they are trying on new behaviors and finding different solutions.

Control and Accountability

Part of being accountable is separating what an individual can and cannot control. Help your clients focus on being personally accountable for what they can control. Teach them to be accountable for their reaction to what they can't control: Everyone can control the way they react to a situation. Also be sure to encourage people not to hold themselves responsible for things that are out of their control, as those who do so are likely to create high levels of stress for themselves.

People can identify what is within their control. They can plan and act to deal with things within their control. When required to deal with situations that have factors outside their control, they can learn to evaluate, adjust, and compensate.

Be sure to acknowledge that there are times when others have an influence on the client's success and failure. However, make it clear that this should not be used as an excuse. People need to recognize their patterns of blaming, trusting luck, or denying their part in a situation. We are responsible for how we react when others are impeding our ability to achieve results. You may need to coach clients on ways to access what they need or negotiate timelines when others are not delivering necessary resources.

One Step at a Time

Accepting personal accountability may need to be encouraged through gradual changes. Set clear goals that can be accomplished and ensure follow-through. Have the client accept accountability for one specific thing and be sure to track the results.

A QUESTION OF BALANCE
Accountability and Privilege

Sometimes people forget to make a link between the privileges and benefits they have and the responsibilities those privileges and benefits entail. For example, it may be considered a benefit to telecommute; however, there is an implied responsibility for accomplishing the same amount of work that would be done if the individual were working on-site. Perhaps when individuals complain about responsibilities or look for additional benefits you will be able to show them the logical links between accountability and privilege. Here are a couple of examples to get them thinking:

Want a raise? Demonstrate how you are adding value to the company.

Want to attend a professional development opportunity? Show how the course will help you perform your work more effectively.

Maximizes Effective Use of Personal Assets

People who demonstrate self-responsibility make the most of their personal assets. They accomplish this by being aware of their unique strengths and weaknesses. They capitalize on strengths without overusing them and find ways to accommodate and remediate their areas of weakness. Their ability to do this evolves out of a thorough and accurate self-assessment.

To maximize personal assets, someone must first be motivated to and able to complete an accurate self-assessment. Most people have some blind spots and many need assistance in carrying out this process. They need to assess what they can do well and what they find difficult. This process will be most effective if people also take time to assess their preferences. Considering their personality, interests, values, lifestyle choices, and personal constraints will ensure they are engaged in suitable work. Looking at what they prefer to do will help them focus and direct their career path. (See Chapter 7 for more on this type of proactivity.)

DETECT & DESCRIBE
Maximizes Effective Use of Personal Assets

. . . .

Don't see high performance	**Do see high performance**
Evidence of over- or underutilizing personal assets:	Evidence of maximizing personal assets:
○ Being unable to describe personal strengths	○ Listing and describing areas of personal strength
○ Doing congenial parts of a job and ignoring the rest	○ Completing all work functions, even those that are unappealing
○ Being unaware of or ignoring areas for personal development	○ Compensating for or remediating areas of weakness
○ Neglecting to focus on developing skills	○ Improving skills systematically
○ Under- or overrepresenting abilities	○ Representing skills and abilities appropriately
○ Overusing personal strengths	○ Refraining from overrelying on strengths to the point where they become a liability

Assessment Tools

The first step toward enhancing clients' ability to make an accurate self-assessment is to ensure they have the proper assessment tools. Your organization probably has some tools already in use to help individuals pinpoint skills and areas for improvement. Sometimes these tools are linked to different human resources and leadership processes and are not readily available or offered to all individuals. For example, job descriptions are sometimes used only when recruiting for positions or addressing performance concerns. Individuals may not regularly use job descriptions to review, discuss, or modify their performance. Performance appraisals are sometimes used as checkpoints linked to compensation rather than as tools to define learning and development opportunities. Once the performance assessment is over, the information may simply be filed and forgotten. Multi-source feedback, inventories, career dialogues, learning plans, and career plans are often used ad hoc as separate development tools in workshops and other types of development sessions. Some people have used the same tool more than once and others have never used it. This hodgepodge of assessment processes can be confusing and ineffective.

Many organizations are working toward integrating their human resources tools. When you are working in an individual development role, your task is to ensure that clients have access to tools to help them assess both their preferences and their performance. Inventory the tools you have on hand to see if they are adequate. Consider when each tool is used and which groups of individuals have access to it. This is especially important if self-assessment information is being offered to workers in small, unrelated pieces. Once you inventory the tools on hand, check to ensure the resources are integrated for the workers to use easily.

Also be careful to use more than one source of information. Each tool and source of feedback will provide a slightly different perspective, and interpreting and integrating these perspectives will be the most complete way to assess individual strengths and areas for development.

Interpretation and Feedback

Tools are a good start for self-assessment. However, just having the tools is not enough. Even the best of tools, if used improperly, can be misleading and limiting, and many clients lack the time, integrative skills, or inclination to interpret and apply the information they provide. Many tools are presented and used in a short time and limited context, without proper explanation of limitations and appropriate applications. Often there is too much information and too little interpretation or application. Self-assessment is a process that must be coached and encouraged to be of benefit.

Be sure to check the accuracy of clients' self-perceptions while you help them with the interpretation of self-assessment information. If these perceptions are too different from the data revealed in the assessment, the phenomenon known in psychology as *cognitive dissonance* may come into play. That is, people are likelier to accept and believe information that fits with (is consonant with) what they already believe and to discredit information that does not fit (is dissonant with) their belief system. They tend to have a set of firmly held beliefs about how well they are doing their job and how well they interact with others. These beliefs may or may not be accurate. At times, your task will be to convince clients that they are not performing as well, or as poorly, as they think they are. To do this, you may need to use considerable persuasion and present a number of different forms of evidence. Once you help clients access, utilize, and interpret tools, they will be able to summarize who they are and how well they are performing.

Personality Differences

Compounding the difficulty of accurate self-assessment, personality differences also greatly affect how workers are evaluated. It is not uncommon for someone to receive a positive evaluation from one coworker or supervisor and then to receive a much different, negative, evaluation from another. This can be especially pronounced in an open-ended evaluation process. In these situations, clients may tend to focus on only the positive evaluation and may feel justified in ignoring or discrediting the negative evaluation. You will need to help them see themselves through the eyes of others and explore how they come across to others. Stress that differences are not matters of right and wrong; they are an expression of different preferences. Help people understand how to accept and accommodate the preferences of others, since differing perspectives can create potential conflicts. The following example shows how different personality types interpret the same behavior differently.

A POSITIVELY CHARGED SITUATION

An ISTJ individual commented that one especially bubbly ENFP coworker was too "perky" in the mornings. The ENFP would come to work full of energy and wanting to talk about upcoming events and what the day might bring. The ISTJ wanted to focus on the work at hand and was not interested in socializing. The ENFP found this behavior unfriendly and the sign of a negative attitude. Each woman was convinced that she was demonstrating the more appropriate behavior.

Overuse of Strengths

Someone's greatest strength can become their greatest weakness when overused. For example, the highly organized, efficient leader may be so concerned with results that others are excluded from the decision-making process in an effort to save time. Excellent results are achieved time and time again, but colleagues become increasingly frustrated and alienated. Or the highly creative idea person has many brilliant ideas and sees countless possibilities in situations, yet fails to follow through with the small details whose lack makes it impossible to bring the ideas into reality.

You can probably think of many other examples when strengths become a disadvantage. When working with clients, assess whether they

QUICK TIPS
Developing Self-Responsibility

Throughout the chapter you have seen many aspects of self-responsibility and factors that can influence whether someone will demonstrate self-responsibility. Here is a quick overview of the main chapter points to help you assess what areas of intervention will be most applicable in your situation:

- Explore clients' belief systems around their work attitude and demeanor.
- Describe behaviors you expect clients to use to demonstrate a positive demeanor.
- Take a look at organizational morale before focusing on an individual client.
- Consider whether personal circumstances are affecting your client's ability to perform.
- Show clients how to develop positive self-talk.
- Find ways to enhance each client's self-confidence.
- Ensure clients are suited to their work roles.
- Provide clients with the tools they require to work independently.
- Advocate healthy lifestyle habits.
- Discourage blaming and making excuses.
- Allow clients to take reasonable risks and try out new behaviors.
- Encourage accepting personal accountability.
- Inventory, align, and integrate the self-assessment tools used in the organization.
- Facilitate the self-assessment process.

are using their strengths wisely. Do this by identifying their greatest strengths and then exploring the possible problems that can occur when the strength is not harnessed well. Come up with ways to temper the strength to ensure it is used effectively with a minimum of negative side effects.

TLC FOR ALL TYPES: SELF-RESPONSIBILITY

All personality types can demonstrate self-responsibility. Here are some of the special challenges of developing this competency that relate to personality preferences. As you choose an intervention, be sure to take the personality type of your client into consideration.

RESPONDERS (ESTP AND ESFP)

Responders tend to take an active and immediate approach. They usually demonstrate a practical and realistic outlook. Wanting to be active (and wanting to avoid sitting in boring meetings), Responders may appear overly independent to others.

Responders are not highly motivated to complete self-assessments, especially if they require filling out paperwork and sitting down to complete a long-term plan. They will not naturally look for conceptual themes or underlying motivations for behaviors.

Responders are focused on the here and now and are most comfortable considering current problems and situations. When working with them in the area of self-responsibility, be sure to give them practical information they can use immediately. Use real-life examples and then model and have them try new behaviors. Minimize the amount of paperwork and analysis in the process and focus on making practical changes.

Logical Responders (ESTP) are attracted to analyzing situations. They may appear skeptical and may demonstrate a cynical sense of humor. Compassionate Responders (ESFP) approach situations focused on helping others in a practical way and may react or show their displeasure openly when frustrated or undervalued. Responders will benefit from understanding how others may interpret these behaviors.

EXPLORERS (ENTP AND ENFP)

Explorers tend to be more optimistic and long-term focused than realistic and practical in their approach. Because of this, they may think they can get more done than they really can in a given time frame. Others can then see them as overly enthusiastic, idealistic, or unrealistic. Explorers find it easy to see possibilities but may need assistance focusing on the practical details and path forward. They may need to be careful not to come across as overly optimistic and unrealistic about what they are able to accomplish.

When completing a self-assessment, Explorers are likely to be able to see themes and integrate information easily. They will enjoy completing inventories and will want to collect and compare information from a variety of sources. Explorers like to have input when working, especially when creating ideas. They want to brainstorm and discuss possibilities. Those more oriented toward completing tasks may interpret this tendency as procrastination or dependence.

Logical Explorers (ENTP) approach situations in an analytical way. They may be direct when discussing problems and possible causes. Although they are simply critiquing the problem, others may interpret these behaviors as cynical and blaming. Compassionate Explorers (ENFP) do not want to limit possibilities, especially for people. They want to explore how the work they are doing is personally meaningful as well as helpful to others.

EXPEDITORS (ESTJ AND ENTJ)

Expeditors may not see the value of being highly expressive about positive aspects of situations and tend to critique and spot flaws rather than share positive comments. They are comfortable working independently and often are self-reliant and comfortable taking charge and making decisions. They expect others to be independent as well and may engage in blaming and judging when results are not being accomplished.

Expeditors may need to have logical reasons for completing self-assessment tools. They want to take the information and apply it quickly. Expeditors need to know that the person assessing them is competent and knowledgeable. Otherwise they will likely dismiss the assessment.

Practical Expeditors (ESTJ) are realistic and take initiative to complete tasks at hand. They may find it more difficult to accept accountability when they are working toward vague goals. Practical Expeditors are most effective with self-responsibility when expectations are clearly defined and the situation is structured. Insightful Expeditors (ENTJ) are more interested in completing long-term goals and are less focused on the details and realities of a current situation. They may become impatient with immediate tasks. Others may perceive this as detachment or arrogance, and the Insightful Expeditor may be labeled as overly idealistic or demanding.

CONTRIBUTORS (ESFJ AND ENFJ)

Contributors are generally highly positive and supportive in outlook. However, if their morale or organizational morale is low, they can become very focused on the negative aspects of situations. They often act as an organizational barometer, so you will hear the Contributor raising and focusing on the concerns of all individuals. A dissatisfied Contributor will tend to find it difficult to present a positive outlook until the needs of others have been dealt with in a positive manner.

Contributors enjoy the process of self-assessment and will focus on how they can collaborate and cooperate with others to make a contribution to the goals of the organization. They are interested in self-improvement and will strive to improve. However, many Contributors find it difficult to accept negative feedback and may benefit from coaching to help them in this area.

Practical Contributors (ESFJ) organize the details of situations and are practical and realistic in their approach. Insightful Contributors (ENFJ) focus on supporting the development of others and may be seen as overly idealistic.

ASSIMILATORS (ISTJ AND ISFJ)

Assimilators tend to be quietly focused on using past experiences to help them complete current tasks. They are generally practical and independent when they know what is expected. Assimilators may be less independent when they are unsure of what, specifically, they are supposed to do. They do not usually show high levels of enthusiasm except when they are discussing familiar and well-researched topics. They also tend to be more outwardly enthusiastic with people they know and trust.

When assessing themselves, Assimilators focus on specific examples and situations. They want to focus on facts they know to be true from their experiences. They may need assistance to see themes or set more abstract long-term goals. Assimilators like to develop specialized, in-depth, information and experiences related to a few selected topics. When working with Assimilators to identify their strengths, strive to find these areas of expertise.

Logical Assimilators (ISTJ) tend to analyze situations impersonally and may appear skeptical and critical. They may need to work toward showing more optimistic responses. Compassionate Assimilators (ISFJ) tend to be quietly and realistically optimistic and supportive of others. Both types of Assimilators may react negatively in situations of unexpected change.

VISIONARIES (INTJ AND INFJ)

Visionaries tend to be quietly focused on building complex mental models to help them form and implement long-term plans. They are typically more optimistic and idealistic than realistic in their perspectives and may need coaching to see the practical side of situations. Visionaries may be seen as overly independent, especially at the early stages of a project when they seek time alone to conceptualize and structure the work to be done.

They will want to complete a comprehensive self-assessment integrating information from a variety of sources. Visionaries will see themes and will be motivated to synthesize multisource data. They want to see an overall framework and purpose for assessing their assets.

Logical Visionaries (INTJ) are inwardly focused, analyzing situations and integrating ideas. People may see them as detached or uninterested in others. Compassionate Visionaries (INFJ) tend to be quietly focused on seeing possibilities and supporting the development of others. They may be seen as overly idealistic.

ANALYZERS (ISTP AND INTP)

Analyzers tend to be more doubtful and analytical than optimistic in outlook. They need to see logical reasons for presenting a favorable outlook because this will not be necessary or appealing to them. Analyzers do not want to state the obvious and will resist attempts to encourage them to be optimistic or idealistic.

Analyzers are independent and self-reliant in their work and self-assessment process. They may tend to dismiss feedback that doesn't fit with their own judgment. This tendency can make them appear even more independent and even somewhat aloof. They may need coaching to listen to and accept information outside their perspective.

Practical Analyzers (ISTP) are realistic. Preferring to operate in the here and now, they are not highly motivated to make or independently follow through with long-term goals. Insightful Analyzers (INTP) are more interested in long-term possibilities to improve systems and may lack independent follow-through on immediate tasks, especially if those tasks are routine and not challenging.

ENHANCERS (ISFP AND INFP)

Enhancers tend to be encouraging and quietly supportive of others. They tend to be positive unless they are in a situation that is creating an internal conflict with their personal values. In this case an Enhancer can become negative. Although Enhancers are normally flexible and accommodating, they may appear stubborn and resistant when their values are being challenged.

Enhancers are interested in the self-assessment process. It may take some encouragement to turn the focus to an Enhancer's personal assets, since often the Enhancer's greatest asset is the ability to help others maximize their assets. Enhancers tend to minimize their contributions and turn the focus to the accomplishments of others around them. They may need encouragement to highlight their own contributions, abilities, and accomplishments.

Practical Enhancers (ISFP) are likeliest to show independence when they are engaged in realistic, practical tasks. They may not be as self-responsible or positive in outlook when focusing on or working toward long-term goals. Insightful Enhancers (INFP) are likely to demonstrate self-responsibility when focused on long-term possibilities and may be less positive in outlook when working on routine or highly detailed tasks.

Chapter 4
Communication

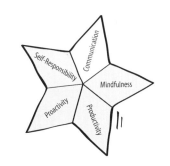

No matter what type of work someone is doing, communicating with others is an essential part of it. Effective communication is a key competency for learning, obtaining feedback, understanding the needs of others, and sharing information. People who communicate effectively express themselves well, give and receive feedback, make connections with others, and are seen as amicable and cooperative. They come across as clear, articulate, pleasant, straightforward, diplomatic, empathic, understanding, tactful, nonjudgmental, open-minded, and considerate.

Without a well-developed communication competency, almost anyone will have difficulty in almost any type of role. When people are not demonstrating the communication competency, others find it frustrating and unrewarding to interact with them. Poor communicators do not respond well to feedback and may have many conflicts and unresolved issues with others. They tend to appear obtuse, unclear, confusing, defensive, judgmental, argumentative, passive, indirect, pretentious, domineering, and aggressive.

The communication competency consists of two distinct groups of behaviors. I call the first group "Listens Carefully," because it includes behaviors necessary to encourage, clarify, and appreciate the communications of others. The second group, "Shares Information Effectively," explores an individual's interactions with others and capacity for clear self-expression. Note the list of the components of communication in the order in which they will be covered in the chapter.

COMPONENTS OF COMMUNICATION

Listens Carefully

- Encourages others to express differing opinions
- Clarifies and acts on communications
- Incorporates corrective feedback

Shares Information Effectively

- Customizes messages to show purpose, planning, and precision
- Gives positive and corrective feedback
- Resolves issues

GAP ANALYSIS
Communication

The pairs of statements that follow represent the endpoints of a continuum of possible performance in communication. Place an X on each line at the location that best describes the current level of performance.

Listens Carefully

Is unreceptive to or intolerant of alternative views	Encourages others to express differing opinions
Misinterprets communications	Clarifies and acts on communications
Rejects or ignores feedback	Incorporates corrective feedback

Shares Information Effectively

Messages are impulsive, unfocused, or lacking in clarity	Customizes messages to show purpose, planning, and precision
Gives unsuitable types or amounts of feedback	Gives both positive and corrective feedback
Avoids or ignores issues	Resolves issues

Take time to reflect on communication. Use the space below to write down any specific information or insights you, your client, or others may have regarding your client's ability to communicate in the course of daily work activities.

_____

_____

_____

LISTENS CAREFULLY

Listening is the most important and often the least developed aspect of communication. Good listeners suspend their beliefs and curb their responses as they strive to understand the perspectives of others. They are nonjudgmental and considerate when listening. When given information, including feedback, they clarify and act on it.

Encourages Others to Express Differing Opinions

To listen effectively you must first encourage others to share information with you. No one is eager to interact with someone who appears uninterested. Most people will watch for active-listening behavioral cues to guide them in deciding whether communication efforts are worthwhile. Review these cues with your clients to assess whether they regularly encourage others to communicate.

DETECT & DESCRIBE
Encourages Others to Express Differing Opinions

Don't see high performance

Evidence of not listening or being unreceptive to alternative views during a conversation:

- ○ Answering the phone or trying to accomplish something else
- ○ Fidgeting or fiddling with objects
- ○ Rushing in with comments whenever there is silence
- ○ Interrupting
- ○ Clock watching
- ○ Using physical space as a barrier to the speaker
- ○ Sitting with arms or legs crossed

Do see high performance

Evidence of encouraging others to express differing opinions:

- ○ Turning off or leaving off distracters such as the computer or telephone
- ○ Leaning forward attentively
- ○ Minimizing talking
- ○ Nodding or tilting the head to one side
- ○ Using eye contact without staring or intimidation
- ○ Judging what is a comfortable personal space
- ○ Keeping a neutral or positive expression and stance

Someone who engages in active-listening behaviors is setting the stage for others to begin to communicate. Encourage these behaviors. If someone demonstrates a lack of active-listening behaviors, have them focus on one or two behaviors to improve their receptivity. Once clients are aware of a specific behavior they need to adapt, the behavior is usually quite easy to demonstrate.

Communication Shutdowns

It is possible to use positive behavioral listening cues and then respond to what is being said in ways that discourage others from communicating. There are a number of communication shutdowns to watch out for. Some of these ways of responding are appropriate in certain situations or may be acceptable in certain groups of individuals and types of communications, so be careful to assess the situation and tailor your recommendations. However, in general, communication shutdowns do not encourage others to continue to express and elaborate their views.

Go through the list that follows with your clients to see if any of these common communication stoppers are getting in the way of their ability to be good listeners. Once clients check behaviors they tend to overutilize, you will want to select alternative responses such as the ones described in the next sections.

- Judging
- Diagnosing
- Labeling
- Blaming
- Being sarcastic
- Criticizing flaws
- Preaching
- Saying "I told you so"
- Evaluating
- Threatening
- Advising
- Offering solutions

- Moralizing
- Arguing with the speaker's logic
- Debating the speaker's feelings
- Ignoring feelings
- Avoiding or ignoring concerns
- Showing a lack of response to what is said
- Being overly reassuring or sympathetic
- Being condescending or patronizing
- Pretending to understand
- Asking a lot of "Why?" questions
- Defending personal views or actions
- Breaking confidentiality

Everyone uses some of these communication shutdowns. At times, it might be helpful to diagnose a problem or offer a solution. However, when the intent is to listen, any of these types of responses can make the speaker sense that it is not safe to continue. This is especially true when the listener is in a position of authority over the speaker or the speaker lacks confidence. The following example given by an INTP leader illustrates how one employee struggled with teamwork because he was using communication shutdowns.

I'M RIGHT, YOU'RE WRONG

I had an INTJ employee who was finding it difficult to become a team player because he couldn't accept illogical or nonoptimal decisions. It didn't help that his ideas and solutions were, in 80 percent of the cases, clearly better than the team decisions. He was unable to communicate with or persuade his team members because he wasn't interested in seeing their perspectives or helping them. He was only interested in showing them they were wrong. I had to help him become more accepting, flexible, and practical so he could change the effect his behavior was having on people.

Personality type has an effect on what behaviors may be perceived as communication shutdowns. One manager describes the Thinking–Feeling communication difference with the following example.

WHO'S A JERK?

Our work group is mostly composed of individuals with a preference for Thinking who have to carefully monitor their interactions with a particular INFP supervisor and a few other staff with a preference for Feeling. Their Thinking communication style is to be objective, and even blunt, about problems, including their perceptions of the people who contributed to those problems. This can come across as criticism to people involved who have a Feeling preference. These people then react negatively and phone me to report that the person analyzing the problem is being a jerk. Doing the MBTI personality inventory and discussing types with my employees helped them better understand and moderate their communications.

PERFORMANCE PREFERENCES
Communication Shutdowns: Thinking and Feeling

· ·

When helping Thinking (T) types, you may need to take extra time to explore various communication shutdowns carefully. Individuals with a Thinking preference tend to prefer to critique situations. Because of this preference, Thinking types can be prone to interacting with others by spotting flaws, advising, offering solutions, debating, and arguing. These types of communication activities are comfortable and stimulating for the Thinking types, who can be surprised to find out that others simply want to be heard and understood. Open-ended listening and validation is not their natural style of interaction.

Feeling (F) types tend to find validating what others are saying a more natural approach. However, Feeling types are prone to focus on the personal side of communications and can be overly sensitive to what they hear. You may need to help them learn to listen more objectively and not react personally to what others are saying.

Communication Encouragers

Once clients are aware that their response style may discourage others from talking, they will need some positive replacement behaviors to use. Show them how to use verbal encouragers such as short comments or questions to show interest. Here are a few examples:

- What happened then?

- Wow!

- Oh!

- What did you do then?

- How did that turn out?

- Tell me more.

- Oh no!

People who are unfamiliar with using listening encouragers tend to find these comments difficult to use at first. They feel artificial and contrived. It takes practice and feedback to be able to encourage others to communicate. These are good behaviors to model and role-play.

Once people know how to encourage listening, they can begin to use techniques to show they understand what the speaker is saying. One simple technique you can teach clients is to summarize, in their own words, what they have heard. They will need to focus on the feeling underlying the words as well as the content. Here are a few examples of how listeners can summarize part of a conversation to show they understand and are engaged in listening:

- That guy wouldn't give up, would he?

- Sounds like you're swamped with work.

- Every time you turned around you ran into another problem.

Of course, these summaries must be specifically related to what the speaker is saying. It's easy for the listener to tell when summaries are correct because the speaker will say something like "Exactly" or "That's for sure." When the summaries are wrong, the speaker will let the listener know right away. As with encouragers, these summaries can seem artificial at first and clients may tell you they feel like they are simply parroting back what they hear or stating the obvious. However, with practice, most people find that summaries can help them clarify and enrich their communications and can be powerful communication tools.

You may have clients who think that listening to and accepting someone else's perspective indicates that they somehow endorse or support it. But the point of encouraging others to express their views is to listen to understand. Hearing and understanding a person's opinion does not mean that you agree with it. Emphasize that hearing and understanding a person's opinion is a starting point for further discussion. Make sure you coach clients to listen first and then demonstrate that they understand what was said. Then, if it is important, the speaker and listener can state any disagreement. Too many dead-end conversations consist of two people explaining and reiterating their own perspectives because neither has acknowledged having heard and understood what the other is saying. The following example demonstrates the importance of listening to both sides of an issue.

PERFORMANCE PREFERENCES
Communication Encouragers: Introverts and Extraverts

Individuals with a preference for Introversion (I) tend to listen to others without interrupting. When interacting, they may need to use more communication encouragers to provide stimulation and feedback, especially when listening to Extraverted types.

Individuals with a preference for Extraversion (E) tend to share their opinions immediately. They may rush in with comments, interrupt, and not provide silence to allow others to formulate their thoughts. They may need extra coaching to demonstrate active-listening cues, especially when interacting with Introverted types.

POINT NOT TAKEN

An ISFP construction supervisor was concerned about subtrade workers' losing morale because they were working long hours and weekends. The ESTJ manager was concerned about results because projects were behind schedule. Neither one initially listened to the other's concerns, although the solution was in the listening. Once the supervisor and the manager were able to acknowledge each other's concerns, the solution was easy. Timelines were relaxed somewhat and workers were given some breaks. Immediately morale improved and the workers became more productive. In a short period of time construction projects were back on schedule.

Empathic Responses

You can further encourage others to communicate using empathic responses. These responses demonstrate the listener's consideration and compassion and are important for establishing rapport and building relationships with others. People will already be beginning to show consideration when they listen to understand the perspectives of others. Empathic responses are a more active way to encourage others to express their views.

Have your clients practice sharing comments demonstrating that they can imagine what it must be like to be in a certain situation or to have a certain feeling. Watch out for the tendency of listeners to tell the speaker they know exactly how the speaker feels or to come across as overly sympathetic. Role modeling and rehearsal are helpful tools to use when coaching empathic responses. People often find these types of responses artificial at first; they sound stilted and insincere when trying out empathic responses. Demonstrate how empathic responses are the opposite of communication shutdowns, responses that can discourage others from expressing themselves. Nonjudgmental, neutral responses are much likelier to encourage a speaker.

Many organizations, families, and peer groups engage in communications such as teasing, sarcasm, jokes targeting specific groups, and other put-downs. These types of communications then become accepted and expected. However, newcomers and outsiders often find these types of communications make them uncomfortable. You may need to discuss communication habits within the work group. Establish norms and clarify what types of interactions are seen as acceptable and unacceptable.

Awareness, understanding, and appreciation of individual differences will help people avoid making tactless remarks. If the organization has people from diverse cultures, religions, races, or other types of background, you may need to provide information so your clients can begin to be aware of and accommodate individual differences.

Have clients rehearse their communications with a peer or coach. Point out and explain comments that are inappropriate and have clients come up with alternative ways to express themselves. Thinking before speaking is a challenge for some people. They may need strategies to help them avoid foot-in-mouth problems.

Many people find it difficult to see the difference between empathy and sympathy. Empathy can be seen in comments and actions that demonstrate an understanding and appreciation of the situation a person is in. It is an ability to see a situation from the other person's perspective. Sympathy tends to have more of a tone of feeling sorry for someone's situation or plight. It is appropriate to express sympathy when someone experiences a loss. However, an inappropriate use of sympathy can come across as condescending and even deprecating. There are not many situations where people want to hear comments that have a "Poor you" or

"I feel so sorry for you" tone to them. These distinctions are clear to the person hearing them, but sometimes not so clear to the person giving them. Modeling and role-playing concrete examples can help clients distinguish between these two types of comments. People want to be understood and acknowledged, but they usually don't want others to pity or feel sorry for them.

Clarifies and Acts on Communications

While active listening and empathic responses provide a good start to establishing rapport and ensuring that others are comfortable expressing alternative opinions, there is a further need to clarify and be able to act on what others say. Clarification goes beyond listening to and accepting a person's perspective and begins to focus on what the speaker might expect or need from the listener. Sometimes people express themselves simply because they are interested in sharing their perspective. More frequently, though, speakers want the listener to do something in response. These communications may include purposes such as asking for or giving directions, stating expectations, or asking for assistance. The speaker may be seeking information or clarification, or providing feedback. Once the listener has listened, understood, and acknowledged what the speaker is saying, the time has come to clarify and act on what is being communicated. The amount of time spent on each of these facets of communication varies widely with the message and the purpose. However, each part of the communication needs to be considered.

When clarifying it is essential to focus on the purpose behind the communication—and to do so without being overly sensitive, suspicious, analytical, or critical. When listening, it is essential to mentally assess what the reasons for this particular communication might be. This will help listeners clarify, confirm, and act on the message. Active listeners confirm what they are hearing and check to see if there are some things the speaker has forgotten to add.

Why Do People Communicate?

People may communicate for a number of reasons. When you listen, assess the reasons behind the communication so you can respond appropriately. Here are some potential reasons for a communication:

DETECT & DESCRIBE
Clarifies and Acts on Communications

. . . .

Don't see high performance

Evidence of misinterpreting communications:

○ Finding it difficult to follow instructions

○ Failing to change a course of action when given new information

○ Failing to summarize or repeat information

○ Failing to ask clarifying questions about information

Do see high performance

Evidence of clarifying and acting on communications:

○ Following instructions

○ Changing a course of action as a result of additional information

○ Summarizing what the speaker has said

○ Asking clarifying questions

• Sharing an emotion

• Complaining about other people or their situation

• Sharing information or an opinion

• Expressing enthusiasm and building support for actions or ideas

• Telling you about a change that will affect you

• Trying to convince you of something

• Trying to make you more sensitive to or aware of something

• Looking for your input, opinion, or feedback

• Giving you directions or instructions

• Wanting you to take action or solve a problem

• Giving you positive feedback or corrective feedback

• Asking you to make a decision

• Asking for information, assistance, or support

• Wanting to connect with and learn more about you

• Trying to persuade you to change your opinion

- Looking for agreement on an issue

- Wanting to align with you (perhaps for or against something or someone)

- Trying to impress you

- Thinking out loud, using your presence to see how the message sounds

Obviously, the listener needs to make a response that is aligned to the purpose of the communication. Sometimes it might be easy to see the purpose, whereas at other times the purpose might be obscure. This is where clarification is essential. Listeners need to check with the speaker to determine the purpose and then react accordingly. When communications are misinterpreted, inappropriate responses occur. For example, if someone simply wants to express an emotion, offering a solution is not likely going to be a helpful response. Here is an example that demonstrates the importance of understanding the speaker's purpose.

WHAT DO YOU WANT FROM ME?

An ENTJ described the following communication dilemma with an ENFP coworker. The ENFP would go to the ENTJ to discuss a problem. After the ENFP described the problem, the ENTJ would offer a solution. However, after the solution was offered, the ENFP would become frustrated and comment that she didn't want a solution. She found it rather condescending to have "the answer" given to her. The ENFP simply wanted to air the problem, think it through, and consider possibilities. Once the communication mode was defined, the ENTJ was able to be less solution oriented in her communication with the ENFP. The ENFP also learned to clarify what she was looking for in the interaction.

Some people have difficulty understanding and following directions or processing information. Many factors can affect the ability to process information effectively, and I cover them in more detail in the discussion of mindfulness in Chapter 5. If your client seems to have difficulty processing information, review that chapter to assess the need for some remedial strategies.

Incorporates Corrective Feedback

When you are coaching the feedback process, provide strategies for both giving and receiving feedback. When feedback is given in a calm, respectful way it is a lot easier to listen to and acknowledge. This section focuses on the listening and responding aspects of the feedback loop. Later in the chapter, I present strategies for giving effective feedback.

When receiving feedback, people need to be able to respond in an objective way. This can be a challenge for many, especially if they feel threatened, incompetent, or unappreciated. Some find it difficult to admit their mistakes. Personal reactions will come across as defensive responses, disbelief, arguments, disengagement, denigrating comments, or disappointment. You will need to recognize these unproductive reactions to feedback in clients and help them learn to set aside their personal responses so they can listen without making an overly emotional retort.

Another barrier to taking in feedback is closed-mindedness. For many reasons, people may not be open to or interested in hearing other perspectives. This will be especially true in situations where you are expecting clients to change the status quo or presenting feedback they disagree with. In these cases, they may need coaching to consider what they are hearing rather than immediately discard it.

You can teach clients a process to use when receiving feedback so as to avoid some of the problems they may have accepting the information. Get them to first check to make sure they understand the feedback. This needs to be done without arguing or debating. As with any situation where listening is required, the first need is to understand what is being said. As a second step, have them acknowledge what they have heard. Help them understand that when they acknowledge feedback, they need to focus on not reacting defensively—the whole purpose is to understand what the other person has said, not to explain it or to elaborate on reasons for it.

Once the feedback has been heard and acknowledged, the next step is to thank the speaker for giving it. Part of accepting feedback is for the individual to concede when they have made a mistake or acted

DETECT & DESCRIBE
Incorporates Corrective Feedback

Don't see high performance	Do see high performance
Evidence of rejecting or ignoring feedback:	Evidence of incorporating corrective feedback:
○ Arguing with feedback	○ Showing active-listening behaviors when feedback is given
○ Reacting emotionally or personally to the information	○ Reacting calmly and objectively to the information
○ Dismissing or undervaluing feedback	○ Reiterating or clarifying the feedback
○ Interrupting when being given feedback, or changing the subject	○ Asking for more information
○ Focusing on blaming others rather than acknowledging a personal part in a situation	○ Acknowledging the content of the feedback
○ Continuing to engage in behaviors after receiving feedback not to do so	○ Changing behavior as a result of feedback

inappropriately. However, some people may find it difficult to apologize when their actions have offended or created difficulty for others. Coach them to apologize for inappropriate actions. Too often apologies are conditional. Avoid statements that open with "I'm sorry, but—." In general, apologies are most effective when they are short, specific, and sincere.

Only after feedback has been given and acknowledged should the appropriateness of the feedback be commented on. At this point, if it seems appropriate to disagree with the feedback, the key is to do so in a calm, objective manner. People need to share their alternative perspective in a way that makes sense to and shows appreciation for the person who gave the feedback. What the recipient understands and believes is occurring in the situation needs to be balanced with the perspective of others. It is important for clients to learn to accept that if corrective feedback is being given to them, then the person giving the feedback does see the behavior in question as a problem. That is their reality. Denying someone else's reality will only create additional conflict or disagreement.

A QUESTION OF BALANCE
Objective and Subjective Reality

Probably one of the most difficult ideas to teach is the desirability of seeing things from multiple perspectives. People often assume that the way they perceive the world and the things they value are common to everyone. It is a major learning step to simply see the diversity of ways situations are perceived. Any event that occurs or thing that exists appears different to each person viewing it. What one person sees as appropriate can seem completely inappropriate to someone else. These differing interpretations can create many misunderstandings and potential conflicts. Be sure to coach clients to see things from as many perspectives as possible, so they can accommodate the intent of others. Reality is not a totally objective set of occurrences that everyone can see and agree on. Rather, reality exists inside the head of every person who is involved in the situation. This may seem like a theoretical and rather impractical concept. However, no one will be able to communicate effectively with others until they can see the subjective nature of all events and interactions.

Here is a summary of the process you can share to help others incorporate corrective feedback in their communications. You may need to coach clients on the entire process or target specific parts if clients are doing some things but ignoring others.

1. Listen carefully to what is being said.

2. React calmly and be objective.

3. Acknowledge and clarify what you heard.

4. Thank the speaker for the feedback.

5. Assess whether you need to share your perspective at all, and, if so, do so in a respectful way.

6. Assess whether it would be helpful to apologize, and, if so, do so in a short, specific, and sincere manner.

7. Think about and make a decision about what to do in response to the feedback.

8. Take appropriate action as a result of the feedback.

PERFORMANCE PREFERENCES
Accepting Corrective Feedback: Thinking and Feeling

People with different preferences face different challenges when accepting feedback. Those with a Thinking (T) preference tend to take an analytical approach to their performance. They can be self-critical and quick to point out their own flaws. However, they often find it more difficult to accept feedback from others, especially if the feedback they hear does not agree with their self-evaluation. Thinking types will be quick to analyze feedback. If the source is not highly credible and competent, the Thinking type may discount the feedback altogether. Thinking types want to hear clear, frank, corrective feedback from a competent source. Their development challenge is to accept feedback not presented in a strictly logical manner.

Those with a Feeling (F) preference tend to be more focused on appreciating and validating themselves and others than on carrying out a critical analysis. When others provide corrective feedback, Feeling types can struggle to separate a critique of their behaviors from their personal worth. Because they tend to take feedback to heart, they can become easily upset. Feeling types want to hear corrective feedback presented gently. They prefer to accept feedback that emphasizes positive attributes as well as problem areas. Their development challenge is to accept feedback not presented in an entirely nurturing manner.

SHARES INFORMATION EFFECTIVELY

As well as mastering listening, skilled communicators are also able to share information effectively with others. This is accomplished by customizing messages to a specific audience, giving appropriate feedback and resolving issues as necessary.

Customizes Messages to Show Purpose, Planning, and Precision

Messages that are not well thought out can create several problems. When people want to get information across to others, it is essential that they plan ahead to ensure the message will be well received. Such planning makes it possible to avoid all kinds of miscommunications that can occur with impulsive, unfocused, unclear, or possibly incomplete messages. To coach clients about communicating effectively, you may find it helpful to show them how to make a communication plan. This might be a form to fill out or a series of questions to think about or answer verbally. No matter what you use to help the client make a plan, the considerations are the same. Communication planning gives people an opportunity to think before they speak and to organize their thoughts. Communication planning also provides a focus to help customize the message to meet the needs of the specific audience.

DETECT & DESCRIBE
Customizes Messages to Show Purpose, Planning, and Precision

Don't see high performance	Do see high performance
Evidence of impulsive, unfocused, or unclear messages:	Evidence of customized messages:
○ Being vague about the purpose of the communication	○ Describing the purpose for the communication
○ Providing information others find difficult to understand	○ Explaining information clearly and succinctly
○ Being unable to answer questions clearly or clarify information	○ Answering questions and clarifying content easily
○ Using inappropriate language, jargon, or vocabulary	○ Considering the characteristics of the audience by adjusting vocabulary and jargon
○ Being unaware of cues that indicate others don't understand	○ Looking for cues to assess how well others are understanding what is being said
○ Providing information that is off topic or irrelevant	○ Providing information that is important and relevant

To help your clients set up a communication planning process, focus them on thinking about what they want to say. Here is a sample of useful questions to consider:

- Who is your audience—that is, who do you want to communicate with?

- What, exactly, do you want to communicate?

- Why do you need to communicate this?

- How can you customize the message to enhance the audience's understanding?

- Is the audience likely to be receptive to this message?

- How can you present the message so the audience will be more receptive?

- Are there emotional components of the message?

- How will you manage the emotional components?

- Have you considered the words you need to use to be objective about this topic?

- What is the best setting for this message?

- How much time do you need?

- How might your audience respond to this message?

- How will you handle these responses?

Discuss these questions with clients to help them think about and plan for an important communication. Or, if a client prefers to plan first and then discuss, assign some questions to answer before you meet and discuss them. Select the questions that are most important for the situation at hand. You will want to focus on an important communication that the client needs to make, such as providing a significant piece of feedback, making a major request or recommendation, or sharing information that is important to others.

This may seem like a tedious process to go through every time someone is considering sharing information, thoughts, or feelings. However, much of it will become automatic—there's no need to write down or extensively discuss all the questions every time. Your goal is to ensure clients know how to send purposeful and targeted messages. By encouraging them to stop and plan their communications, you can help clients avoid potential conflicts and miscommunications. A behavioral rehearsal of the communication may be helpful if the situation is especially important or difficult for the client.

Instructing others is a specific type of communication that requires a transfer of specific knowledge and skills to another person or group of people. Here are some points you can share with individuals who need to speak in front of a group:

- Focus on your audience.

- Evaluate background knowledge—find out what your audience already knows.

- Accommodate the interest level and learning style of your audience.

- Prepare your ideas and gather all the facts you need before you begin.

- Use guided questioning to walk the audience through the content.

- Share expert information at the level and amount the audience can retain.

- Provide written or visual aids.

- Avoid telling people what to do unless it is absolutely necessary— many people resist this.

- When you do need to direct others, be clear, specific, and concise.

- Check for understanding without being condescending.

- Have a vision of what you want to accomplish, and data, principles, and logic to back up your perspective.

- Anticipate and prepare for questions or criticisms.

- Answer questions in a direct, clear, and organized way.

- If you don't know, say so.

Personality type can also affect an individual's ability to send a message. It is especially difficult to share information when the target audience or type of message is different from the sender's own preferences. Here is how one Intuitive type described this situation.

GETTING THE DETAILS RIGHT

Part of our work role is to write technically detailed requirements and specifications documents for the software implementations for our clients. Our Sensing account managers tend to excel in this role, especially two ISTJs who are stars at this. On the other hand, the account managers who prefer Intuition find this task difficult and painful. They tend to use coping behaviors, such as having another colleague double-check their work to ensure the documents are accurate and detailed enough.

Many people are so focused on being sure they get to say what they want to say that they forget to think about how the message will be received. Learning when to not say anything is as important as learning how to say something. Perhaps the most critical questions when planning a communication are "What do you want to say?" and "Why do you want to say it?" If the purpose of the communication is to make the speaker feel better about something, and the information will not be particularly helpful for the audience, perhaps the information need not be shared. However, not communicating feelings, thoughts, or reactions that are influencing a relationship can be as big a disadvantage as expressing too much. Determining how much to communicate is an important first step in the plan.

Once someone has decided what they want to communicate, they need to consider their audience and how receptive the audience will be to the message. People show significant individual differences in how they take in information, so the would-be communicator needs to consider how much and what type of information to provide. Some audiences will want to hear all the details; others will be more interested in a general overview. Some respond well to a personal, encouraging approach; others will be more interested in a logical, objective communication. Some will prefer formal, written communications; others would rather discuss information and have it presented informally. It is important to learn to use relevant language and to be careful not to overwhelm others with too much information or intimidate them by using inappropriate jargon or vocabulary. Good communicators learn to tailor each message to the needs of the audience.

While communicating a message, the speaker needs to be aware of body language cues that indicate the audience understands and is being

PERFORMANCE PREFERENCES
Self-Expression: Extraversion and Introversion

Some people are naturally open and expressive and share whatever thoughts and emotions come to mind. This is often characteristic of individuals who have a preference for Extraversion (E). These people may talk more than listen and may express things without carefully thinking them through. This communication style does have advantages. Others tend to know exactly where expressive people stand on issues, which improves the chances that their opinions will be used as input when making decisions or taking action. However, sharing too much information has its disadvantages as well. Others may tune an overly expressive person out and may not listen carefully to the high volume of output. Thoughts that are not well formulated may be shared. This can provide a potential for misinterpretation and foot-in-mouth experiences.

Other people tend to be more selective when sharing information. They will think carefully before they speak and tend not to share unless they can see a reason to do so. This is often characteristic of people who have a preference for Introversion (I). This communication style has its own advantages. It reduces foot-in-mouth problems, and other people will (hopefully) tend to listen carefully, since they recognize the careful, well-thought-out nature of the communication. However, it has disadvantages too. The reserved person's opinions may not be heard or applied in decisions and action plans. Areas of conflict that need resolution may be avoided.

By using the advantages of both styles, a good communicator will be able to speak and write carefully and openly. When working with clients, see which side of the continuum they tend to start on. Highlight the strengths of their approach and help them see ways to build in the advantages of the other side to complement and balance their communication approach.

engaged by what is being said. If someone tends to talk too long, you may need to show them how to tell that the audience is getting restless. If someone tends to use a lot of jargon, you may need to alert them to the meaning of puzzled facial expressions. Also, speakers can check for understanding by evaluating the types of questions and responses the listeners are giving—rather than simply plowing ahead with their message and ignoring this feedback process. You need to help them increase their focus on the audience rather than on the message. No matter how interesting and important the message is to the speaker, if the listener is not receiving it then effective communication is not occurring. Here is an example that shows how it is sometimes necessary to coach contextual cues.

FITTING IN

An employment counselor was coaching a client in a work placement setting. This ESFJ client was friendly, outgoing, and interested in discussing personal issues and interpersonal relationships. She had been placed in a work setting where the norm was quiet and harmonizing. Others commented to her counselor that they found her to be overly direct and intrusive in her communication. The ESFJ client was unaware there was a problem and thought she was building rapport and relationships. The employment counselor coached her to pay more attention to the cues indicating others were uncomfortable. By paying attention to the cues, the ESFJ client began to notice that, for much of the day, the office was quiet and calm—when she was not initiating communications. She realized she needed to tone down her interactions.

People are often unaware of how much a specific comment or way of speaking can affect others. They need to understand that others can misinterpret comments that seem innocuous to them. Also, help clients take the specifics of the situation into account and watch for factors that may affect the way they need to communicate. These situational factors can range from the relationship they have with the audience to the time of year or how much of a surprise the message will be. Show clients how to customize the amount of detail and the way they express themselves to the audience and the situation.

It is also important to choose an appropriate time and setting when planning for communication. Of course, this will relate to the purpose for the communication. Teaching a skill may be appropriate in a different time and setting from that appropriate for sharing information about an organizational change. Respect for privacy and minimizing distractions are key considerations for choosing a time and place for communicating.

This stepping outside of self to accommodate others is a huge lesson in individual development. Whenever possible, find ways to help clients consider who they are communicating with. Understanding factors that do affect communication, such as personality preferences, learning styles, background knowledge, interests, and values, will help people consider the needs of their audience and present messages in a way that the audience will be able to understand.

Although it is important to show clients how to customize their messages, some general tips apply to communications in general. Usually it will be most appropriate to be specific, calm, honest, direct, positive, and sincere when stating a message. Show clients how to present their information clearly and concisely using a moderate voice that is neither too quiet nor too loud. Make sure they don't expect others to pick up the point by mind reading. Challenge clients when they start to hint or are indirect rather than communicating directly. Most of all, be sure to coach them to walk their talk. People lose credibility at once if they talk one way and act another. Emphasize that they need to do what they say they will.

When clients are expressing emotions, encourage them to take ownership rather than blame or attribute their emotions to others. The statement "You upset me when you don't listen" is likely to be taken more personally than the statement "I feel upset when I think I am not being heard." When clients first encounter it, this kind of change may seem like a trivial word game, but the way personal feelings are framed can have a significant influence on the way another person responds. Coach clients to focus on stating what they are feeling and avoid prescribing what others need to do.

These useful tips can help individuals customize communications:

- Plan what you want to say and why.

- Choose an appropriate time and setting.

- Think before you speak.

- Organize your thoughts.

- Assess the probable effects of your message before you speak.

- Tailor your message to the audience.

A QUESTION OF BALANCE
Enthusiasm and Calmness

When sharing important messages with others people must find a balance between enthusiasm and calmness. Presenting information in a calm, objective way ensures that a minimum of emotional negativity is attached. Certainly we have all experienced the destructiveness of negative comments made in highly charged moments. Many remarks uttered in emotional situations create misunderstandings. However, it is also possible to present information or respond to others too calmly. Someone who comes across as too unenthusiastic can give the impression of being detached or uninterested.

When someone has enthusiasm for a topic, their commitment and interest can inspire others. However, if they present a point in an overly enthusiastic way, others can interpret their viewpoints as exaggerated or overly idealistic.

When balancing enthusiasm and calmness, be sure to help your clients consider the audience the message is intended for. This will help ensure that their message is perceived as having the right tone.

- Customize the amount of detail included.

- Be specific, calm, honest, direct, positive, and sincere.

- State your point clearly and concisely.

- Use a moderate voice—not too quiet or too loud.

- Use relevant language.

- Walk your talk—do what you say you will.

- Don't expect that others can read your mind.

- Avoid hinting or being indirect.

- Be careful not to overwhelm others with too much information.

- Don't intimidate others by using inappropriate jargon or vocabulary.

A QUESTION OF BALANCE
Humor and Seriousness

Consider how your clients balance humor and seriousness when communicating with others. Assess whether they are typically more humorous or serious in their approach and see if they would benefit from balance in this area.

Humor can be an uplifting addition to communication. Laughter is energizing and in some situations can help cut through tension. However, people have different ideas about what is funny and have different levels of tolerance for humor. As well, humor can be cutting and may poke fun at certain groups and people. Humor takes time and others may become frustrated with a series of humorous responses when they are attempting to address an important issue.

Using a serious approach to communication emphasizes the importance of a topic. Information is usually shared in an efficient, focused manner. Serious communication will be necessary for discussing important issues, making decisions, and planning actions. However, others may find it unenjoyable to communicate with a person they see as too serious. The level of tension may rise at meetings and creative ideas may not emerge. Someone who is typically serious may not know how to respond in more open-ended discussions focused on using humor to brainstorm or imagine possibilities.

Gives Positive and Corrective Feedback

One of the most critical communication areas—and one often fraught with difficulty—is giving feedback to others. People seek feedback, yet they may take feedback very personally. Clients may need assistance determining the amount and type of feedback to give. They may also need help in presenting feedback in a way that others are likely to accept.

The balance between positive and corrective feedback is important to consider.

People who are unskilled at giving feedback tend to label or generalize rather than describe behaviors. The person who comes to work late can be labeled as *irresponsible* or *undependable*. The person who has a

DETECT & DESCRIBE
Gives Positive and Corrective Feedback

Don't see high performance	Do see high performance
Evidence of giving unsuitable types or amounts of feedback:	Evidence of giving appropriate positive and corrective feedback:
○ Failing to offer positive comments and encouragement	○ Offering positive comments and encouragement
○ Avoiding discussing problem behaviors directly	○ Being direct and open when discussing problem behaviors
○ Being overly critical	○ Being constructive and not destructive when offering feedback
○ Giving feedback at an inappropriate time and place	○ Choosing the appropriate time and place to give feedback
○ Offering only positive and not corrective feedback to others	○ Balancing the amount of positive and corrective feedback given
○ Being vague or unclear	○ Using clear, objective language
○ Labeling or blaming others	○ Avoiding labels or blame

conflict with a customer is *grouchy* or *unfriendly*. These labels are not helpful for many reasons. They can alienate or demean the person getting feedback and are not a good starting point for improving performance.

People are much more receptive to specific information. When you are coaching someone on providing feedback, encourage them to focus on and describe specific behaviors. Coach clients to avoid making judgments, labeling, or blaming. Clients will be much more receptive to and able to understand feedback when it is made up of specific, concrete, information and examples. It is also helpful to provide feedback as immediately as possible. Over time, memories of events become distorted and it can be much more difficult to describe and assess what actually happened.

As with any communication, someone with feedback to offer needs to assess when the person will be most receptive to hearing it. The time and place for the communication will be important. Privacy and confidential-

A QUESTION OF BALANCE
Appreciation or Analysis

To perform effectively, people need to hear a balance of positive and corrective feedback. Positive feedback allows people to see what they are doing well and, for many, is highly motivating and encouraging. Many people thrive on appreciation. Corrective feedback is useful also to help people understand what they are not doing well. Corrective feedback provides the basis for problem solving and performance enhancement. People need this analysis to help them see areas for improvement. Purely positive feedback may make people feel good, but it won't provide any information to help them develop. Purely corrective feedback will show individual areas to develop, but it doesn't add to morale or provide encouragement. Worst of all, no feedback provides no encouragement or information for development.

Individuals need to learn to provide others with both types of feedback in appropriate amounts. Have clients assess their need to provide feedback to others and whether they tend to be more appreciative or analytic when providing feedback. Have them consider whether they are providing adequate feedback that is both appreciative and corrective. If not, help them develop a plan to provide both kinds of feedback. Clients must also be aware of the preferences of the person they are providing with feedback and tailor the balance of feedback to what will be most useful in the specific situation.

ity issues must be considered when choosing a time and place for communications the recipient would prefer not to have anyone overhear.

Have clients assess their motivation or reasons for giving feedback. At times, people want to give feedback to make themselves feel better rather than to help the other person. If this is the case, perhaps the feedback need not be given. Help individuals analyze why they think it is important for them to provide feedback. Ensure that the purpose of the feedback is to help or improve situations. Coach individuals to avoid giving feedback when they are emotional.

A QUESTION OF BALANCE
Consideration and Directness

. . . .

It is important not to hint or give indirect feedback. People may not accept or even recognize feedback when it is given in an indirect way. Clients need to learn to give open, honest, and direct feedback. At the same time, feedback that is given too directly can be seen as overly impersonal or blunt. This is another fine line you must coach clients to manage. If their current style of giving feedback is overly cautious or indirect, help them find ways to express what they need to say more directly. If their style leans more toward being overly direct, help them find ways to incorporate careful consideration. Show them how to balance frankness and direct-ness with compassion and caring.

QUICK TIPS
Providing Feedback

. . . .

The following tips can help individuals provide feedback:

- Describe specific behavior.
- Provide specific, concrete, information and examples.
- Provide the feedback as immediately as possible.
- Assess when the hearer will be most receptive.
- Avoid general labels or comments.
- Be direct and clear.
- Don't hint or give indirect feedback.
- Assess your motivation or reasons for giving feedback.
- Be sure your purpose is to help the recipient, the organization, or both.
- Balance frankness and directness with compassion and caring.
- Avoid making judgments, labeling, or blaming.
- Avoid giving feedback when you are emotional.

Resolves Issues

Virtually all work relationships involve differences of opinion and conflicts. People need to have a strategy to deal with these issues. Listening and information-sharing skills are basic tools in this process, but it is also helpful to have a concrete set of steps people can use to resolve differences. It is important to share a conflict resolution process with clients and use it regularly. When clients begin to approach conflict using a positive model, it will be rewarding. It will be essential for the organization to model the approach and use it across levels of authority. If a conflict between a supervisor and someone on the staff is resolved by using positional power, it is unlikely that other conflicts will be resolved using mutual respect. This is a systemic issue that must be dealt with on an organizational level and is one of the many examples where it is important for an organization to walk the talk.

DETECT & DESCRIBE
Resolves Issues

Don't see high performance

Evidence of avoiding or ignoring issues:

- Avoiding or ignoring conflicts, situations, or people
- Complaining to others rather than approaching a conflict directly
- Expressing excess negativity and frustration
- Failing to engage in a conflict resolution process
- Being unwilling to see situations from other perspectives
- Focusing on a solution that is best for one side
- Having difficulty letting go of past conflicts

Do see high performance

Evidence of a focus on resolving issues:

- Addressing conflicts
- Speaking directly to others who are involved in the conflict
- Being calm and reasonable
- Engaging positively in a conflict resolution process
- Listening openly to the perspectives of others
- Looking for a solution that benefits everyone
- Letting issues go when they have been resolved

The following section outlines some concrete steps clients can use when they become involved in conflicts. Throughout the conflict resolution process, it is important to coach people to use their listening and information-sharing skills. Share the conflict resolution steps with clients and guide them through the process. Avoid becoming personally engaged in the process yourself, however; your task is to be an objective third party. As you help individuals resolve conflicts, be careful to assess your own biases so as to avoid sharing them or influencing the process, especially as individuals are identifying their needs.

Before you explain the steps in the conflict resolution process, make sure all parties involved are willing to be engaged in the process. Here is a checklist to help assess willingness to work together to solve the problem.

○ Are all the involved parties interested in and willing to put energy toward solving the problem?

○ Is everyone able to see and validate alternative perspectives and needs?

○ Are they all willing to negotiate and compromise?

○ Will they all treat others with respect and equality?

○ Do they see others' needs as equally important as theirs?

○ Is everyone objective and calm?

○ Is everyone focused on the problem, not the person?

○ Is everyone focused on a positive outcome for all parties?

Conflict Resolution Steps

Once you have a group of people who are involved in and have expressed some willingness to approach the conflict, here is a four-step process you can use.

1. *Identify the needs of each individuals involved.*

Be sure all individuals express their needs, wants, and fears. Encourage people to use effective listening and information sharing to focus on understanding and appreciating the various perspectives in the situation. The broader the perspective each member in the conflict can see, the likelier the issue is to be resolved to meet the needs of everyone. This is not a time for judging or arguing perspectives. The focus is on listening to understand.

Keep clients focused on attacking the problem and not the people involved. Coach them to avoid expressing their needs in terms of solutions, since this will limit the ability to generate creative, win-win outcomes. For example, consider the effect if someone says, "I need the boardroom every Thursday." This statement has a solution implicit in the way the need is stated (that is, the only way to fill the need is to hand over the boardroom every Thursday). Compare the effect of addressing the purpose rather than the solution: "I need a space to meet with a group of six people, preferably in the morning on Thursdays." This is a more open-ended way of expressing the need and can lead to a variety of win-win solutions.

As you are mediating this part of the process, help people think outside the box by looking carefully at what their needs really are. Help them separate needs from wants. This will help them more clearly define the problem. At the same time, focus on their fears and emotions as well. Someone may have been embarrassed and at risk of losing a customer when they went to use the boardroom for a scheduled meeting and found it already occupied. Perhaps they were also concerned that the customer saw them as incompetent or inefficient. If you can coach your clients to share these negative feelings in a calm and open manner, you will be able to help those involved in the conflict understand and appreciate the other perspectives and situations. By the end of this first step, the needs of each involved party should have been heard, understood, and validated. If this does not occur, the involved parties are not likely to come to a satisfactory solution.

2. *Take a win-win approach to generating possible solutions.*
Once the needs are on the table, help the involved parties think of creative options that allow all of them to meet their needs. Show everyone how to see the situation as an opportunity that will have positive outcomes. Make sure the power is shared and each participant is respected as an equal in the process.

Taking a win-win approach may require that clients are willing and able to shift from a competitive to a collaborative framework. You may need to do considerable coaching if one or all of the parties tend to approach situations in a competitive way. In a competitive mind-set, one person will lose and one will win. Situations are seen as including a limited amount of resources to be won or lost in their resolution. With this mind-set, conflicts can turn into power struggles. In a collaborative mind-set, situations are assumed to have unlimited possibilities and options. So in a collaborative mind-set, instead of competing for a specific boardroom, the involved parties may look for ways to maximize and capitalize on all possible meeting spaces within the organization to meet a variety of interaction needs.

This collaborative approach is a totally different mind-set from the highly individualistic focus that is often found in North American business culture. You may need to champion this different way of thinking before addressing a specific conflict in need of resolution. Some individuals may need paradigm shifting before they will be able to think in a win-win framework. For effective conflict resolution to occur, all parties must want everyone to benefit. Mutual gain is the expected outcome. Once this is established, involved parties can brainstorm and explore options. People may need assistance finding common ground and being inventive. It may be difficult for some to change their position without feeling they are losing face or giving in. Encourage everyone to appreciate others who are willing to accommodate and show flexibility. Participants should see themselves as partners rather than competitors as they move through this process. If there is a significant difference in positional power between two parties in conflict, it will be especially important to address respect and equality issues.

3. *Reach agreement on a solution.*
After exploring options, the parties need to choose a solution that provides the best outcome for everyone involved. This may involve some negotiation. People may want to explore what trade-offs and compromises might be acceptable. Proposed solutions can then be easily evaluated on the basis of how well everyone's needs are being met. Be sure that the solution chosen is clear and well understood by all parties so as to avoid misunderstandings.

Sometimes problems can arise that the parties are not able to solve themselves. This can be especially true if the issue is extremely important or the level of trust between parties is extremely low. If the needs of the involved parties do seem highly conflicting without any collaborative aspects, you may need to participate in the process as a neutral third-party mediator. Try to coach clients to move forward on their own as much as possible whenever they can, or you may find that people begin to see you as the one who solves their problems. Your goal is to transfer the process so participants are able to address and solve conflicts independently. Help clients use and move through the process effectively. Avoid adding to any specific content, making judgments, or offering solutions. Ask open-ended questions and encourage the participants to add input that will facilitate each of the steps.

4. *Move together toward a solution.*

Once a solution is determined, it will be key to ensure that follow-through occurs. Depending on the circumstances, it might help to have a written plan or agreement. Even if the agreement is not written, it is essential that the steps to be taken and desired outcomes are clear to everyone. Again, try to encourage the participants to put their plan into place rather than have them expect an external party to fix the situation. If things don't go exactly as hoped, help focus everyone's attention on what each side has learned. Then the parties will be able to use the information to fine-tune the situation and improve their future conflict resolution efforts.

QUICK TIPS
Developing Communication

Throughout the chapter you have seen many aspects of communication factors that will influence whether someone will be able to communicate effectively. Here is a quick overview of the main chapter points to help you assess what areas of intervention will be most applicable in your situation.

- Promote the use of active listening.
- Show clients how to encourage others to communicate.
- Help clients avoid communication shutdowns.
- Encourage clients to see situations from multiple perspectives.
- Teach strategies for comprehending and clarifying what is heard.
- Coach clients to send a clear message that shows purpose, planning, and precision.
- Show clients how to give and receive positive feedback.
- Show clients how to give and receive corrective feedback.
- Teach clients how to use an effective conflict resolution model.
- Emphasize conflict resolution using collaboration rather than competition.

TLC FOR ALL TYPES: COMMUNICATION

All personality types can demonstrate effective communication. Here are some of the special challenges of developing this competency that relate to personality preferences. As you choose an intervention, be sure to take the personality type of your client into consideration.

RESPONDERS (ESTP AND ESFP)

Responders prefer communications that are short and to the point. They often send clear, practical messages and focus on the facts and realities in their explanations. As with all Extraverts, Responders may need coaching to listen without interrupting. When showing them how to improve communications, use humor, sensory stimulation, and playfulness. Relate the communication competency to real-life examples and situations.

Responders learn best when they are shown or can do rather than being told. Role playing, trying out new behaviors, and practical applications of the communication competency will be more helpful than theoretical or abstract explanations. Because Responders are focused on the here and now, they often do not see the value of looking at underlying dynamics of conflict. Because of this, they may benefit from coaching to help them deal with long-term or complex conflicts or issues.

Logical Responders (ESTP) often do not see a practical or logical reason for developing rapport and acknowledging feelings in the work setting. They may find it helpful to focus on appreciating and providing positive feedback to others. Compassionate Responders (ESFP) can find it difficult to give corrective feedback and may benefit from coaching in this area.

EXPLORERS (ENTP AND ENFP)

Explorers tend to communicate with enthusiasm and energy. At times they can seem overly enthusiastic and may need to learn to tone down their excitement for ideas when talking to others. Explorers may become distracted by ideas rather than listening carefully. They may interrupt or change topics rapidly, which can be confusing and can also come across as disrespectful to others or others' ideas.

Explorers are often focused on ideas and the future. Because of this, their communications can seem global, abstract, and lacking in detail. Explorers can benefit from learning to be more sequential and detailed when they communicate with others. Work with them to ground their abstract ideas into a form they can communicate to others.

Logical Explorers (ENTP) often do not see a practical or logical reason for developing rapport and acknowledging feelings in the work setting. They may find it helpful to focus on appreciating and providing positive feedback to others. Compassionate Explorers (ENFP) can find it difficult to give corrective feedback and may benefit from coaching in this area.

EXPEDITORS (ESTJ AND ENTJ)

Expeditors tend to use a direct and concise approach to commu- nication. They will respond best when you focus on competencies, goals, actions, and results. When coaching the communication compe- tency, explain logical reasons why they need to develop in this area. This can be a challenge when explaining the importance of developing rapport and demonstrating empathy.

Expeditors are more comfortable understanding and appreciating feelings and values when they are presented in a logical, fac- tual way. They also tend to use communication shutdowns. Expeditors are comfortable debating and competing and can be surprised when others see these behaviors in a negative way. Present conflict resolution as an opportunity to solve a problem.

Practical Expeditors (ESTJ) will see the details and may need coaching to understand or communicate big-picture information. Insightful Expedi- tors (ENTJ) will see the big picture and may overlook or not communicate about specific facts and details.

CONTRIBUTORS (ESFJ AND ENFJ)

Contributors tend to communicate in a warm, friendly, empathic, and appreciative manner. They seek to understand people's values, opinions, and reactions. Contributors find it easy to develop rap- port and are quick to offer positive feedback. These parts of the communication competency come easily to them. They may find it difficult to provide corrective feedback to others and hesitate to express opinions that may disrupt the harmony of the group.

When Contributors are working in settings where people feel unappreciated or undervalued, they can become discouraged. In these situations they may work issues too much, finding it hard to ignore differences of opinion linked to personal relationships and values. A negative organizational morale or culture will weigh heavily on Contributors and they will find it difficult to perform their tasks. You may need to help them let some interpersonal issues go and focus on the work at hand. When resolving conflicts, Contributors are quick to focus on collaboration, cooperation, and inclusion.

Practical Contributors (ESFJ) like to share practical information on details and may need coaching to see patterns and possibilities. Insightful Contributors (ENFJ) tend to be global in their approach and may need coaching to focus on and share immediate, practical facts and details.

ASSIMILATORS (ISTJ AND ISFJ)

Assimilators tend to be accurate and precise when communicating with others. When coaching them to develop the communication competency, focus on facts, real-life examples, and what is known to be true. Others may perceive Assimilators as overly detailed in their communications. You may need to show them how to summarize and generalize information so they can explain their comprehensive expertise and experience concisely.

When Assimilators communicate with other types, they may not show their engagement in a form others can recognize. They may need to learn to demonstrate their attention by means of nonverbal and verbal cues. Assimilators present information in a step-by-step and structured manner. They may need to ask for clarification when presented with global, abstract, or unstructured information. Provide enough information for them to get a comprehensive understanding. Also avoid surprises and ambiguity; provide them with detailed information as soon as possible, especially regarding changes.

Logical Assimilators (ISTJ) want to see logical reasons for developing communication skills. They tend to contain their emotions in the workplace and may not see a practical or logical reason for developing rapport and acknowledging feelings in the work setting. They may benefit from learning skills in empathic responding. Compassionate Assimilators (ISFJ) are interested in maintaining harmony. They tend to do so in a quiet and unassuming way. Because they may find it easier to avoid conflict than to confront it, you may need to coach them to express their personal needs and opinions.

VISIONARIES (INTJ AND INFJ)

Visionaries are big-picture thinkers who focus on communicating complex concepts and theories rather than facts and details. They tend to communicate using models and by showing the overall framework of their ideas. Visionaries usually like to build complexity and may need coaching to help them explain their ideas simply. This will require them to focus on practical realities, facts, and details in a sequential manner. They may also need to minimize their use of metaphors, symbols, and other figures of speech.

One of the greatest communication challenges for Visionaries is to remember to share ideas before they become too entrenched in their own thoughts. Since Visionaries tend to think about their ideas in a comprehensive way, once they have processed an idea thoroughly it can be difficult for them to accept new input. At the same time, they are uncomfortable sharing an idea until they have thought it through. This is an important area for them to find a balance in so they do not come across to others as closed-minded to new input.

Logical Visionaries (INTJ) may struggle to show rapport. They can be impatient with small talk. Compassionate Visionaries (INFJ) may benefit from coaching to assert their thoughts and feelings because they naturally seek harmony and avoid conflict.

ANALYZERS (ISTP AND INTP)

Analyzers tend to be direct, frank, and concise in their interactions. They are able to deal with almost any situation in a calm and objective manner. Analyzers usually will not take things personally, except perhaps when their competence is being challenged. When helping them develop the communication competency, focus on logical reasons and explanations for what you are teaching. Then provide detailed concepts, information, or data and allow time for them to evaluate what they are hearing.

Analyzers find small talk, developing rapport, and sharing feelings especially unappealing. They need to see logical reasons for engaging in these behaviors. They may also use sarcasm or be cynical or critical in their communications. Although Analyzers mean no harm and enjoy arguments, debates, and challenges, other types may respond negatively to this interaction style. When working with Analyzers, offer challenges and opportunities to try ideas and test conclusions. This will help them see the logical reasons for engaging in communication behaviors such as developing rapport.

Practical Analyzers (ISTP) focus on facts, details, and current realities. They are not highly motivated to explore underlying dynamics and relationship issues when resolving conflicts. Insightful Analyzers (INTP) communicate using concepts and models. They tend to first analyze and critique situations rather than see the personal perspectives. They may benefit from coaching to look at personal and situational factors when communicating with others.

ENHANCERS (ISFP AND INFP)

Enhancers prefer to communicate in a comfortable, quiet, one-on-one setting. When helping them develop the communication competency, be sure to be supportive, empathic, quiet, and sensitive. Enhancers are comfortable establishing rapport, usually show listening skills, and approach communication in a personal, appreciative way. When working with them, avoid being overly critical or analytical. Be careful and thoughtful, and provide any critical feedback gently.

When possible, identify and avoid challenging Enhancers' personal values. They tend to react personally to what is being said and it can be hard for them to be objective, especially in situations of challenge or conflict. Enhancers often change from being accommodating to being withdrawn and stubborn when their core personal values are challenged. They may benefit from coaching to help them assert their feelings. This can be difficult because they are committed to maintaining harmony and want to avoid creating a situation that might result in conflict.

Practical Enhancers (ISFP) like to communicate facts and details. They are interested in hearing real-life examples that demonstrate the importance of the communication competency. Insightful Enhancers (INFP) focus on the bigger picture of human experience and want to communicate in a way that is consistent with their values. Respect and appreciation of individual differences is often important to Insightful Enhancers when they are communicating.

Chapter 5
Mindfulness

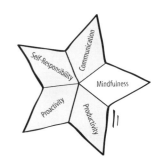

Mindfulness refers to the process of thinking about and evaluating the effectiveness of thinking, strategies, and behaviors. This may sound rather abstract, but the results of mindfulness are actually very clear to see. Individuals who use mindfulness well are able to monitor and adjust their behaviors and strategies to ensure they are successful. For example, a mindful individual who is trying to solve a problem and has become stuck will think about why the blockage has occurred and what needs to be done to move forward. Perhaps mindfulness can be best described as a process that selects the right thinking approach, strategies, and tools for working on a task, making a decision, or solving a problem. Depending on what thinking processes are being used, a mindful person will appear resourceful, strategic, creative, analytical, or practical.

Cognition refers to thinking and information processing and includes the mental processes people use when learning and carrying out activities. Examples of cognition include comprehending, summarizing, integrating, analyzing, evaluating, and synthesizing. Mindfulness is a process by which an individual is able to organize and plan when to use the appropriate cognitive process. You cannot see someone being mindful; all you can see are the results. For example, when someone is critiquing mindfully, they will spot flaws; when summarizing, they will

> ## COMPONENTS OF MINDFULNESS
>
> **Knows How to Learn**
>
> - Accesses and uses relevant or new information
> - Critiques and evaluates information sources
> - Integrates and transfers new information across situations
>
> **Knows How to Apply Thinking**
>
> - Systematically solves problems and makes informed decisions
> - Consciously applies different modes of thinking

be able to share a large volume of information concisely. The easiest way to see how these mental processes translate into concrete applications is to take a look at the types of questions someone might ask when engaged in mindfulness. These questions show how and what an individual is thinking while working toward understanding work tasks, solving problems, and making decisions.

Questioning is an especially powerful tool for coaching others to use the mindfulness competency. By using thoughtful questions, you can help clients focus on aspects of their thinking that they are not currently aware of. You can gradually stop asking questions and encourage clients to question and formulate their own thinking strategies. Here are a few general questions someone might ask when using the mindfulness competency effectively:

- Is this strategy working? Why or why not?

- Am I on the right track?

- Do I need more information before I proceed?

- What do I need to do next?

- Why am I having difficulty with this?

- What could I do differently?

When people use mindfulness they employ the appropriate thinking skills in the appropriate situations and in a systematic way that maximizes effectiveness. As a result, they will take in, analyze, and integrate new information with what they already know so as to make informed decisions, solve problems, and adjust their responses to situations.

People who don't use mindfulness will use and then continue to use thinking processes that are inappropriate to the situation. For example, when stuck on a problem, they may continue to rely on trial and error rather than look for a more effective systematic approach. They may not take in new information that is important to doing their work or making a decision. Because of this they may repeat mistakes or continue to do work in an ineffective way when a more effective option is available.

The mindfulness competency consists of two distinct groups of components. I call the first group "Knows How to Learn"; it includes behaviors individuals require to take in and apply new information effectively. The second group, "Knows How to Apply Thinking," explores an individual's ability to select and adjust thinking processes. Note the list of the components of mindfulness in the order in which they will be covered in the chapter (see page 161).

GAP ANALYSIS
Mindfulness

The pairs of statements that follow represent the endpoints of a continuum of possible performance in mindfulness. Place an X on each line at the location that best describes the current level of performance.

Knows How to Learn

Relies exclusively on prior learning $\longleftrightarrow$ Accesses and uses relevant or new information

Accepts information at face value $\longleftrightarrow$ Critiques and evaluates information sources

Does not transfer learning across situations $\longleftrightarrow$ Integrates and transfers new information across situations

Knows How to Apply Thinking

Uses a haphazard or passive approach to problem solving and decision making $\longleftrightarrow$ Systematically solves problems and makes informed decisions

Is not aware of or does not use a full range of thinking modes $\longleftrightarrow$ Consciously applies different modes of thinking

Take time to reflect on mindfulness. Use the space below to write down any specific information or insights you, your client, or others may have regarding your client's ability to apply mindfulness in the course of daily work activities.

_____

_____

_____

KNOWS HOW TO LEARN

People who apply thinking processes effectively find new information and then comprehend and apply it when performing their work. They logically analyze, critique, and summarize the information they are exposed to and integrate and link new information to what they already know and understand. As a result, they are lifelong learners.

Accesses and Uses Relevant or New Information

To use mindfulness effectively, people must first find and take in new information. Then they can apply it. You cannot see inside someone's head, of course, but a number of clues can indicate that a client may not be accessing or applying new information.

Because mindfulness reflects internal processing, it can be helpful to consider some of the questions your clients will ask themselves when they are engaged in accessing and applying information. You can initially coach clients by asking them questions. Then coach them to ask their own questions. Here are some mindful questions regarding accessing and using information:

- What do I need to know?

- Where can I find this information?

- Is this information helpful to me?

- Would I understand this information better if it were in a different form?

- Is this information relevant to my work?

- How can I use this information?

- Is there someone else who could use this information?

- Should I remember or store this information?

People who exhibit mindfulness will usually seek out sources of information without any coaching or assistance. Learning new information to help them improve their work is a behavior they endorse and engage in without coaching. Be sure to provide such clients with access to, and time to learn and apply, information. Employers vary widely in the time and

DETECT & DESCRIBE
Accesses and Uses Relevant or New Information

Don't see high performance	Do see high performance
Evidence of reliance exclusively on prior learning:	Evidence of accessing and using relevant or new information:
○ Lacking resources (such as dictionaries, manuals) in the workspace	○ Using resources (such as dictionaries, manuals) in the workspace
○ Not asking questions or seeking new information from others	○ Asking questions or seeking new information from others
○ Ignoring appropriate periodicals or updates	○ Subscribing to and reading appropriate periodicals or updates
○ Neglecting to access on-site resources	○ Finding and using on-site resources
○ Neglecting to use the Internet to access information	○ Being comfortable with Internet search engines
○ Using computers and technology ineptly or unwillingly	○ Showing computer and technical literacy
○ Using outdated or older information when completing work tasks	○ Using new information when completing work tasks
○ Staying out of discussions about new ideas or information	○ Discussing new ideas or information
○ Being ignored by others when they need a source of information	○ Being acknowledged and sought out by others as a source of information

other resources provided for engaging in research and professional development activities. These resources are essential to help people stay current in the work they are doing. Some clients may not know what sources of information they can access to help them do their work. You may need to both familiarize these clients with information sources and encourage their use.

Does the organization provide adequate learning resources? Match the existing resources to the following list to see if relevant information is being provided.

- Newsletters
- Association memberships
- Library
- Information services
- Periodical publications
- Magazines
- Conferences
- Trade shows
- Print resources
- Internet sites
- Mentors
- Opportunities to talk to colleagues or customers
- Workshops
- Courses
- Literature on certification processes
- Networking opportunities
- Computer tutorials
- Videos, CDs, DVDs
- Radio and television

It is possible for people to be willing and able to seek new information but to lack the time or other resources to do so. They may also lack incentives for learning, especially if new ideas are not usually accepted or encouraged. Ask yourself the following questions to help assess how well the organization promotes the learning of new information:

- Does the organization encourage professional development activities?

- What types of professional development activities does it encourage?

- Does it provide funds for workers to attend learning events?

- Is it easy to access professional development funds?

- Are the funds adequate for the types of learning people need?

- Has the organization created ways for workers to share information with their colleagues?

New technology can be an area of skill gap, especially for older workers. Being unable to work with new technology can be a barrier to accessing information. Younger workers may have learned how to search for information, especially on the Internet, through school assignments,

PERFORMANCE PREFERENCES
Accessing Information: Extraversion and Introversion

. . . .

Extraverted (E) types tend to prefer breadth to depth when exploring a topic. They may prefer to discuss or apply new information before taking time to read, listen, and reflect on details. They are drawn to resources that are quick to use and highlight main points without troubling them with details. They prefer learning opportunities that provide them with occasions to interact with others.

Introverted (I) types tend to prefer to understand a topic in depth. They may prefer to read, listen, and reflect before discussing and applying information. Complete and comprehensive resources are attractive to them. They prefer learning opportunities that provide them with time and space to reflect on new information.

whereas those without previous experience may not have the confidence or skill to use the Internet effectively and may need to be shown how. Assess carefully whether clients are skilled at and comfortable using the current technology. Consider individual learning needs when you upgrade to new technologies. This will help minimize some of the gaps in technological expertise.

Information Overload

Individuals can be intimidated or overwhelmed by the sheer volume of information available. This information overload can create a situation where individuals avoid looking for information. Many clients find it helpful to recognize that in our rapidly changing work world it is sometimes more important to be able to find and access new information than it is to memorize and retain the information. Accessing information effectively can be as useful as remembering it in some situations. However, in other situations the information must be immediately available. Help clients separate what must be known from what can be looked up. People not only need to find and understand information, they need to decide whether to memorize it, use it, store it, remember where to access it, or discard it. Help clients identify and separate what information must be known and recalled immediately and what information can be accessed from external sources.

Memory strategies can be key to information retention. Too often people in helping or supervisory positions expect that giving information to someone once means they will retain it. This assumption is unrealistic, given the mass of information workers are expected to take in. When people are expected to apply a number of key pieces of information, it is more helpful to find ways to make the information easily accessible than to expect it to be recalled accurately and completely. Information sheets, procedure manuals, and other written or visual cues can be effective memory aids. Does the organization provide key information in a summary form? Are there ways you can assist your clients in summarizing, storing, and accessing day-to-day essential information?

E-mail is an information-sharing tool that has exploded in volume of use, especially in large organizations. This instant communication channel has some advantages and some disadvantages. Many people receive a large volume of e-mail on a regular basis. This can be a problem, especially when someone is away from the computer for any period of time. Scanning and then dealing with e-mail is a new information management skill that is only starting to be taught. As with any other type of information, people need a concrete strategy to deal with, store, or delete e-mail messages. Does your organization have policies or guidelines about what types of information are best shared through e-mail? Many companies have a preponderance of For Your Information (FYI) e-mail sent out to a wide range of workers, many of whom are not affected by or interested in the information. Changing some types of information overload then becomes systemic rather than an individual's problem.

Information overload easily occurs when people attempt to use the Internet as a resource but don't know how to customize their search. Those who do know a bit about searching the Internet often find themselves overwhelmed by the enormous number of sites available, and even the variety of search engines and directories available for research seems too large to remember. When clients seem to avoid Internet use, show them how to focus a search to produce less numerous and more relevant information links. Instruction in the use of search engines can be a very helpful tool in this regard. In addition, depending on your clients' learning style and time constraints, you may choose to advise them to try any or all of the following steps:

- Take a course about the Internet (there are a variety of courses you can take online and offline).

- Practice *surfing* (following lines of interest from site to site); many of the search engines have self-directed instructions for customizing or refining a search.

- Get help from an experienced Internet surfer.

- Find a reference (book, magazine, list of Web sites).

Learning Style

People who demonstrate mindfulness focus on and access the specific information resources that fit their learning style and meet their learning needs. If clients are unsure of how they learn best, you may want to discuss learning preferences to help them choose the type and depth of resources that will be most useful for them.

Some learning preferences are based on the mode of information input. Carefully consider what sensory channels your client prefers. Some people are visual learners: They learn best when they can see what they are learning. Videos, diagrams, illustrations, and other visual learning aids will facilitate their learning. Others are auditory learners and learn best when they can hear or discuss information. Still others prefer hands-on learning and are most successful when they can try tasks and work with the actual materials. When setting up learning opportunities, try to incorporate all three modes: seeing, hearing, and doing. This will ensure that you are accommodating the different learning preferences. When working with clients, help them assess their preferred mode.

PERFORMANCE PREFERENCES
Taking In Information: Sensing and Intuition

Sensing (S) types prefer practical information that has an immediate application. They trust what they know to be true from their own experience and relate well to specific facts and activities. When searching for and applying information, they work best if they have a practical process for finding the facts. They may need you to show them how to ground and apply metaphorical and abstract information.

Intuitive (N) types first see connections and relationships between information and ideas. Links and possibilities intrigue them. When searching for and applying information, they work best if they are exposed to ideas and possibilities as well as facts. They may need you to show them how to focus on and retain the facts and details rather than skim over them.

Learning Skills and Abilities

Once information is available, a person must be able to take it in, remember or store it, and then use it. This information-processing loop must be complete. If the loop is interrupted, the information can become lost or distorted. People need to be able to assess their learning needs, weaknesses, and strengths in this information-processing loop. For example, someone may have difficulty paying attention, recalling a sequence, understanding verbal directions, interpreting visual information, or memorizing facts. Most people tend to have some information-processing areas that are easier and more difficult for them. A corporate executive may be articulate, brilliant, and innovative, yet may need to carry a pocket spell-checker. Using mindfulness, people can identify and maximize their learning strengths and minimize their weaknesses. One fairly easy way to assess difficulties is by analyzing the types of errors clients make when completing their work.

Error analysis is a powerful learning tool that many people underutilize. Consider the following situation.

WHAT DID YOU LEARN?

A young man walked into the motor vehicle operators licensing office and wrote an exam to obtain his learner's permit. He turned in the exam, which was immediately marked; he did not pass. The examiner asked if he would like to see his results. The young man said no and walked away. He complained to a friend on the way out that he had now failed the exam three times.

This young man was given the chance to learn from his mistakes and dismissed it. Had he made an effort to understand what he didn't know, he would have been able to focus on those areas and prepare for his next try at the exam. The same is true for our everyday work duties. If someone makes a mistake, it is important to look for the reason the mistake was made. This is different from assigning fault, which is a way to detach from or avoid accountability for the error. Analyzing the cause of the error provides information that allows the worker to compensate for the problem.

When working with someone who has information-processing difficulties, think about how they are currently processing information. This helps you spot weaknesses, try strategies, and evaluate the results to see if the strategies are helping. Ask and answer questions such as these:

- Is the client motivated to learn?

- Is this information useful and important for them to learn?

- Is the information provided in a mode that they can easily understand?

- Are they able to focus and concentrate on the information?

- What specifically does the client have difficulty doing?

- Are they repeating errors at work?

- What seems to cause the errors?

- Have they tried to correct the problem? What helped? What didn't help?

Identifying an area to address puts a person in a position to think of practical ways to compensate. Problems always have many possible causes—and many potential solutions. For example, someone who has problems paying attention can learn active-listening and note-taking strategies. Someone who has trouble remembering sequences can learn to summarize and write down the steps in the sequence. If someone struggles to remember what they hear, they can learn to take written notes. For example, if they tend to forget names in a meeting, they can make a diagram of the table and jot down the names of the people during the introductions. You can help with all these learning processes. Be practical and specific when designing ways to get around difficulties.

Reading is especially important for taking in information. Before starting to read, it's essential for someone to have clear expectations about what they need to accomplish through their reading. A detailed description of essential operating procedures needs a different kind of reading than a global statement of business objectives does. A training manual may be part of a formal learning process that requires memorization of specific details; an operating manual may call for no more than familiarization with the table of contents. E-mail describing an organizational change may simply require the reader to change some phone numbers and contact information. The mindfulness competency is what allows people to put incoming information in the context in which it needs to be used. To help clients codify the mindful approach to reading, you may wish to share the SQ3R reading strategy (below) with them. This approach is especially useful with those who have difficulty dealing with essential written resources.

SQ3R: Survey, Question, Read, Recite, Review

The SQ3R reading strategy helps people focus on and retain information from what they are reading by means of advance preparation and follow-up work. The following sections go through the steps in this reading process—survey, question, read, recite, and review—and provide questions designed to help your clients think about and thus more deeply process their reading material.

SURVEY

Before starting to read, people should preview or survey the material. This will help them identify ways of organizing and using the information. Surveying materials also helps people get the most out of their reading by defining a purpose for and developing an awareness of the overall structure and content of the materials. When readers keep the purpose and structure of reading in mind as they work through the material, they find it easier to focus on the reading process. Readers should survey the entire reading and then survey the specific sections of the materials. Ask your clients to look through all the material and consider the following questions:

- Does the reading material provide a focus on what is important, such as objectives, summaries, overviews, and so on?

- Are there any learning aids such as a table of contents, headings, charts, graphs, diagrams, illustrations, worksheets, italicized words, glossaries, appendixes, indexes, bibliography, underlining, summaries, and so on?

- What content is being covered in the material?

- Why do I need to read this?

- What do I want to get out of the reading?

- Is it necessary to read all of the material or only certain parts?

- Does the material have familiar terminology and vocabulary or is a dictionary necessary?

- Are there other materials that go with this reading to make it clearer or more complete?

QUESTION

When previewing and preparing to read, the reader can ask questions to keep focused and enhance understanding of the material. Here are some questions you may want to have your clients consider:

- What is this section about?

- What is the main idea here?

- Is this an example, illustration, or supporting detail?

- What will I need to know?

- What depth of detail do I need to know?

- Should I take notes?

- Do I already know this information?

- Will I need to remember this?

- How could I rephrase this information using my own words?

- Does this relate to anything I already know? How is it the same? How is it different?

READ

Now the reader is ready to read the material in depth, answering the questions listed in the preceding step in the process. This will enable to reader to keep the context and purpose of the reading in mind and will promote understanding.

It may be necessary to refer to other sources of information if the reader is having difficulty with the materials. Readers may find it helpful to take notes to summarize main points and important details. Note taking is most effective when readers focus on what is important and then use their own words.

Help clients choose one of the following options for noting or recording important information:

- Write summary notes in the margins of the material.

- Use a highlighter or underline important points. Highlight only 10 to 20 percent of the material.

- Use index cards with questions or cues on one side and information on the other. Many learners find such cards especially helpful for learning terminology. If keeping the cards organized is a problem, punch holes in them and put them on a binder ring.

- Make notes with questions on one side of the page and information on the other, then cover up the information and use the questions as a self-test.

- Create a written summary.

- Organize appropriate types of information as tables, graphs, pictures, flow charts, illustrations, maps, or outlines.

Think back to the clients' personality preferences when helping them choose an effective note-taking strategy. For example, readers who like to integrate information might use a map or picture. A step-by-step outline or table is effective for readers who prefer sequentially organizing information. Logical thinkers may find some concepts clearer if put in a flow-chart. Whatever note-taking strategy the reader chooses, make sure it includes a strategy for learning and remembering new terms.

RECITE

Repeating information ensures that the reader is paying attention and retaining information while reading. After about fifteen to twenty minutes of reading, it is useful to stop and test to see how much information has stuck. Readers can facilitate self-testing by setting up notes in a way that allows them to test themselves by writing down or repeating the information. Too often readers simply read the words on the page without putting in the effort to understand or remember the information. The Recite step ensures that readers are concentrating on and processing the material. Readers should recite only key information.

REVIEW

Studies of learning effectiveness indicate that people remember best when material is studied repeatedly. It is most effective to review material within twenty-four hours of first reading it. The best strategy for most people seems to be short, frequent review sessions. However, few readers recall sufficient information simply by reading and rereading. Readers need to make sure they have strategies in place to actively check memory of the material rather than simply rereading. Self-testing is one of the best strategies to check what is being remembered. People can do this by testing themselves from their notes, writing down what they remember, or having someone ask them questions.

Reading Difficulties

Clients who find reading difficult can be skilled at covering up the problem and may avoid learning activities that require them to study printed materials. If you suspect that someone has a reading difficulty, first assess the possibility of a visual impairment. If a client has any of the following symptoms, consult a professional who can assess the particular problem.

- Difficulty seeing words clearly may mean lack of visual acuity.

- Difficulty moving eyes easily and smoothly across the page may mean lack of eye movement skills or an eye muscle problem.

- Pain while reading may indicate eyestrain.

- Difficulty processing or discriminating between specific letters or words may point to a learning disability.

Like basic reading skills, reading comprehension and vocabulary levels vary greatly. If the materials people are expected to learn from are beyond their reading comprehension level, they will not be able to understand or apply the information. The type of language and level of vocabulary you use when working with clients will influence their ability to comprehend and apply the information. Many topics have their own specific terms, or jargon. Be especially aware of acronyms and technical terminology in reading materials, which can be confusing to anyone unfamiliar with them. Some companies use so many acronyms that they list them in the orientation package handed out to new workers.

If reading materials have so many complex or unfamiliar words that content becomes difficult to follow, readers need to use some sort of strategy to make sense of them. Here are some strategies to help people deal effectively with jargon or other unfamiliar vocabulary:

- Use a glossary or index if one is provided.

- Learn a new word every day. Study it. Find a way to use it.

- Use a dictionary often. Have dictionaries available.

- Invest in a pocket dictionary.

- Write down definitions. Include examples, illustrations, and applications.

- Use your own words to define unfamiliar terms.

If you suspect that someone has learning difficulties, you may want to consider arranging for assessment by a psychologist specializing in learning. A learning specialist can assess specific areas of difficulty and provide concrete, work-related accommodations. Before consulting a specialist, however, use your mindfulness competency to assess the situation yourself.

Critiques and Evaluates Information Sources

With so much information readily available, people need to be able to evaluate the source of the information to determine potential biases and inaccuracies. Without this focus, they are apt to act on incorrect or inappropriate information. This ability to critically analyze what is seen and heard is essential when taking in and managing information. To evaluate information requires critical thinking.

To use critical thinking effectively, people need to be aware of factors that can influence the accuracy and objectivity of the data. Information becomes useful only when it is understood, analyzed, and evaluated. The following questions will help you teach clients how to understand, analyze, and evaluate an information source.

DETECT & DESCRIBE
Critiques and Evaluates Information Sources

Don't see high performance

Evidence of accepting information at face value:

- ○ Making no effort to evaluate the source of information
- ○ Failing to assess credibility of information sources
- ○ Using information from a single source
- ○ Treating opinions as equivalent to facts

Do see high performance

Evidence of critiquing and evaluating information sources:

- ○ Seeing and evaluating biases in information
- ○ Asking questions to determine the credibility of information
- ○ Seeking multiple sources to confirm information
- ○ Separating facts from opinions

- How old is the information?

- Is the information opinion or fact?

- Who collected the information and why?

- Who wrote about the information? Are they credible? Are they biased?

- What is the point of view of the author?

- Who published the information? What biases or assumptions might they have?

- Why was the information published? Who was it published for?

- Is this promotional material? (Are they trying to sell a product, service, concept, or candidate?)

- Do the authors or speakers use emotionally loaded words?

- Can the conclusions be logically drawn from the evidence at hand?

- What are your own biases on this topic? Do they affect what you will accept?

- What assumptions are being made?

- If relationships are being shown, are they cause and effect?

- Who was included in the data and who was not?

- If it is research, does the researcher use a sample that represents the group?

- Do facts or research support the main idea?

- What information is not included?

- Is there any reason to question the information?

- How does this information compare with other information you have on the topic?

- Where might you get information on the same topic with a different bias or perspective? (There is no unbiased information, only information with different biases.)

- Who might be able to use this information?

- How might this information be relevant to you?

- What conclusions or evaluations can you make about the information?

- Do you need more information on this topic?

- How can you get more information?

In the age of information it is important to evaluate information sources critically. Be sure your clients are able to find out the date the information was collected. Information that is outdated can create more problems than no information at all. This is especially true if the information is related to procedures, regulations, or other requirements. Watch out for the temptation to use older print resources that have not been updated or revised. Information can change quickly and out-of-date resources are, at best, inaccurate and misleading. If the organization does rely on print documents, be sure mechanisms are in place to keep the library current. This process of updating information can be time and resource consuming. Does the organization recognize the need to update key resources? You may need to decide the life span of resources and have plans to revise or replace them. As an alternative, it may be possible to use the Internet as a source of more recent information—bearing in mind that the dates of Internet information also need to be checked.

People need to evaluate the credibility of the source of any information. They can do this by checking out the credentials of the authors, identifying biases or affiliations, and researching the background of the sources. When assessing data, they need to find out who collected it and why. Show clients how to determine the purpose of the information and the point of view of the author. This will help them identify bias.

Accessing multiple sources of information is an effective way to further evaluate information, although multiple sources often provide confusing or contradictory information. Sorting out the contexts, sources, and biases in the different perspectives can be a daunting task. Often various credible sources will focus on different aspects of a topic and thus provide different conclusions. People must be able to identify the assumptions that underlie the reasoning in the arguments. In addition, they need to understand their own assumptions and biases and be careful to be open-minded when gathering information.

People also need to separate opinion from fact and speculation from research. They must analyze facts and research to determine if the context and specific findings are applicable to their work situation. Facts can be proven. Predictions, guesses, and opinions are individual reactions to a topic. It is important to separate these sources of information and consider their nature when making a conclusion. It is also helpful to identify underlying assumptions made by authors when evaluating information. It is important that clients learn to recognize and evaluate evidence supporting an argument or position.

A QUESTION OF BALANCE
Facts and Opinions

Facts and opinions are both helpful sources of information. Facts are data. Make sure your clients understand the context of a fact before they interpret it. Often when information is used to persuade others, only specific facts are included while others are purposefully left out. Opinions are personal views. They may initially seem less reliable, but it can be informative to gather the opinions of experts in a subject area. Be sure clients are aware of the experts' biases.

You can coach clients to see what conclusions might be logically drawn from the evidence at hand. Cause-and-effect relationships need to be explored and understood if someone is expected to evaluate information. Events may simply occur together but not be causally related. Sales and promotion brochures tend to use such timing of events as evidence to support their products and services. Make sure your clients bear in mind that events have both direct and indirect causes—and most events have multiple causes. These relationships must be understood when analyzing information. People often jump to a conclusion, allowing themselves to be influenced by erroneous arguments rather than carefully considering all of the facts at hand.

The facts are especially difficult to sort out when information sources are biased toward marketing or promoting something. Help individuals see how promotional materials can be misleading. Find examples of brochures for products and services. Have clients analyze the content. Discuss how testimonials, guarantees, promises, and other sales strategies may be designed to promote rather than inform. It is essential to recognize and critique these persuasive strategies for what they are. When clients have authority to make purchases and recommend vendors and services, they need to be especially aware of sales and marketing techniques. A checklist or set of criteria for evaluating options can be a helpful tool. Creating such a tool in collaboration with the client will clarify the underlying purchasing needs and focus the client on thinking about the purchase in an analytical way. Even if people are not in a purchasing role, using critical thinking can help them make logical connections.

People can also be emotional or biased when evaluating information. Show your clients how to watch for emotionally loaded words and emotional biases in resources. Remember that people are much likelier to accept and remember information that is consonant with their belief system. Everyone needs to be aware of this tendency. Help your clients explore their biases.

Integrates and Transfers New Information Across Situations

As well as being able to access, evaluate, and apply information, people must be able to summarize and synthesize what they are learning. This

PERFORMANCE PREFERENCES
Analyzing Information: Thinking and Feeling

Thinking (T) types naturally tend to spot flaws and evaluate what they see and hear. They are often quite drawn to the process of analysis and evaluation. Feeling (F) types tend to appreciate rather than analyze. They may need more coaching to see the necessity and value of critical analysis.

process enables them to find the main ideas in what they are learning and combine pieces of information into themes. They also must be able to relate what they are learning to what they already know. Without this integrative processing, there is little transfer of learning from one situation to another. For example, imagine a customer service course that teaches a strategy for developing empathy and rapport with a customer. Ideally, the students will link the information learned in this context to situations where they are interacting with colleagues or leaders.

When learning a new strategy, people should think about past experiences and make links between the new learning and other situations. For example, say that in the practice session in the customer service class, a student finds it difficult to listen without making judgments or offering solutions. This experience, for someone who is thinking about their strategies and performance as a whole, can stimulate a number of associations: better understanding of a time when they received feedback about being too directive in their leadership approach, or of the way their teenage child has lately stopped expressing opinions on the grounds that the parent wasn't really listening. These links allow people to transfer their learning across specific contexts and situations. However, such transfers will only occur when someone uses mindfulness to think about what they are learning.

Here are some examples of questions that can help someone link and integrate new information. Remember, the questions are simply cues. The mindfulness competency itself is found in the planning and organizing of the thinking process underlying the learning process.

DETECT & DESCRIBE
Integrates and Transfers New Information Across Situations

Don't see high performance	Do see high performance
Evidence of a lack of transfer learning across situations:	Evidence of integrating and transferring new information:
○ Having trouble finding the main ideas in new information	○ Being able to summarize the main ideas in new information
○ Failing to apply information from one context to another	○ Applying information to different contexts
○ Overgeneralizing information	○ Being careful not to overgeneralize
○ Failing to link what is being learned to what is already known	○ Linking what is being learned to what is already known
○ Not seeing alternative uses of learning	○ Finding diverse applications for learning

- What parts of this information are most important?

- Do I know something about this already?

- How does this relate to what I already know?

- Does this relate to other situations?

- How can I use this information in other situations?

- Does this fit with what I already know?

- If this doesn't fit with what I know, what specifically doesn't fit?

This is another situation where it is essential to integrate new information and avoid information overload. People are easily overwhelmed by volume unless they can develop strategies to summarize and integrate information. One of the first things they must be able to do is capture the main idea in what they see, read, or hear. Finding main ideas in a stack of information is not always easy.

You can use any of several strategies to help clients pull out main ideas. When working with people, it is most helpful to use materials already have on hand such as policies, procedures, technical guides, or handbooks. You can help them look for one central idea by working through a specific page or a few pages in one of these resources. Show them the difference between details and supporting information and central ideas. Have them state one or two central ideas that the details can fit within. Watch for the tendency to get too broad or too specific when completing this process. Have clients think about the material and decide how important the information is.

It can be helpful to take notes when finding main ideas. Show your clients how to use an outline, sequence, or mapping strategy to organize and summarize what they are reading or hearing. Highlighting is also a useful tool when reading for information, as long as the reader doesn't highlight more than 10 to 20 percent of the material. Some people find it helpful to use a variety of colored highlighter pens to cue them to different aspects of the material. Classifying and categorizing information is another helpful way to synthesize information, as is linking or charting relationships within the information the reader is expected to understand. These strategies are also part of the SQ3R active-reading strategy to help focus on and recall information. Further summarizing and processing will build on the initial reading strategy. The same process can be applied to information that is provided verbally in contexts such as meetings, seminars, training, workshops, and courses.

PERFORMANCE PREFERENCES
Integrating Information: Sensing and Intuition

Sensing (S) types find it easier when integrating and summarizing information to start with the facts and details. From this practical starting point, they can build a framework to organize and integrate tangible information in a step-by-step manner. When working with Sensing types, show them the facts and details first and then help them move into a larger framework.

Intuitive (N) types tend to see connections and links first. Once they have a broad framework of links, they can start to attend to and organize the details into the framework. This organization will likely be more global and random in structure than step-by-step. When working with Intuitive types, focus on the overall framework first and then have them process the facts and details.

Although it is important to be able to summarize, it is just as important to learn to not overgeneralize from a small number of examples. Encourage clients to look for exceptions and understand the limits of summarizing as well as the benefits. Summarizing information too broadly can also mask important details. People must be careful to consider what depth and breadth of information they are required to absorb. If the details are more than the client can store in memory, suggest creating some form of job aid or information storage system that makes it possible to find the required information quickly and effectively. A pocket-sized booklet containing key information can be an invaluable job aid. Here is an example of how one worker used a cheat sheet to help recall a frequently used sequence.

REFERRING, NOT REMEMBERING

One INFJ individual was having considerable difficulty recalling the correct sequence of steps required for translating a document from one software form to another. Rather than tax his sequential memory, he simply created a small sheet listing a brief summary of the required steps. He then photocopied the steps onto a heavy sheet of paper and stored the job aid near the computer. The problem was immediately solved.

KNOWS HOW TO APPLY THINKING

People need to apply the information they have taken in to systematically solve problems and make informed decisions. As well, they must be able to incorporate long-term and systemic factors into their thinking process. Someone using the mindfulness competency evaluates and consciously adjusts the use of thought processes to increase their effectiveness.

Systematically Solves Problems and Makes Informed Decisions

Many people can benefit from learning systematic strategies for solving problems and making informed decisions. Some work performance issues can be attributed to impulsive or irrational decisions. Decisions that are not well thought out and balanced can create a variety of negative consequences. In a similar way, a trial-and-error or unsystematic problem-

DETECT & DESCRIBE
Systemically Solves Problems and Makes Informed Decisions

Don't see high performance

Evidence of a haphazard or passive approach to problem solving and decision making:

○ Taking little time or energy to assess a problem

○ Using a trial-and-error approach

○ Neglecting causes of problems

○ Being uninformed regarding possible options and the logical consequences

○ Lacking follow-through when deciding or implementing a solution

○ Neglecting to evaluate or adjust solutions or decision

○ Attempting several solutions or making several decisions that are unsuccessful

Do see high performance

Evidence of systematic problem solving and informed decision making:

○ Taking time and energy to focus on a problem or decision

○ Using a well-defined, systematic approach

○ Seeking the root cause of problems

○ Becoming well informed about options and logical consequences

○ Making and following through with a well-thought-out plan

○ Evaluating results

○ Adjusting the plan to improve results if necessary

solving strategy can result in ineffective work practices. There is considerable overlap between the decision-making and problem-solving processes. Both require systematically working through a process to choose a course of action.

To minimize the results of poor problem solving and decision making, make sure clients have systematic approaches to these processes. Does the organization have and share a decision-making and problem-solving approach that people can apply when carrying out their work? Are these approaches clear and simple enough for use in any situation? If systematic approaches to problem solving and decision making are in place, be sure these approaches are publicized in a practical format. Post them on the wall or share them as a summary sheet.

Wall posters and summaries may not be enough for some workers, who will need assistance until they learn their way through the processes. Work through a real problem with them and help them use the steps in the process to define the problem, generate options, and choose, implement,

A QUESTION OF BALANCE
Problems and Possibilities

People do need to address and deal with problems. However, it sets up a negative frame of reference when deviations from the norm or unexpected events are seen as problems. It can be helpful to see challenges and roadblocks as possibilities, not problems. It is these unpredicted or not-planned-for events and results that allow an organization to find new approaches and improve situations. When you reframe situations positively you can look for alternative ways of operating that will enhance your results. Although I refer to the process being used as problem solving, you can also move through the same series of steps with the mindset of capitalizing on an opportunity rather than solving a problem.

and evaluate a solution. Different people will focus on and miss different steps in these processes. While you are assisting someone, assess which steps seem more difficult and more natural, and then coach them on using their strengths and minimizing their blind spots in the processes. Personality type can help you identify which components of problem solving and decision making the client is likely to focus on and which components may be blind spots.

If the organization does not have a clear, systemic problem-solving process in place, you may want to suggest a plan customized to its specific needs. The next section describes a generic model you can use as a starting point for creating a problem-solving approach.

Problem-Solving Process

Here is a generic problem-solving process you can share with clients. This quick overview is not designed as a comprehensive approach to problem solving (you will be able to find many resources that focus on the process). This process has been defined through a questioning phase to emphasize and highlight the mindfulness aspects of problem solving.

STEP 1: DEFINE THE PROBLEM

This first step ensures that you will work on identifying root causes for a problem rather than simply focusing on symptoms.

- How do I know there is a problem?

- How can I specifically define this problem?

- Is this problem important?

- Does the problem need to be solved?

- Do I need to solve this problem?

- Who else is involved and how much ownership do they have in this problem?

- Am I considering all aspects and possible causes of the problem?

- What is the root cause of this problem? Is there more than one cause?

- What root cause is most important to address?

- Am I getting distracted or sidetracked by other related problems or issues?

- How can I separate this problem from related problems or issues?

- Do I need to deal with any other related problems or issues?

- Is there an opportunity in this problem?

- What will be the result of solving this problem?

- How will I know if I am successful in solving the problem? What will I measure?

STEP 2: GENERATE AND RESEARCH SOLUTIONS

Once the problem is clearly defined and a root cause has been hypothe-sized, the next step is to generate and research options.

- What are possible solutions to this problem?

- Can I look at this problem from a different perspective?

- If I change my perspective, might other solutions be possible?

- Am I being sufficiently open-minded when generating possible solutions?

- Have all the parties engaged in this problem been able to share their perspectives?
- How will I determine whether a particular solution will work?
- What further information do I need to gather and how will I find it?

STEP 3: CHOOSE A SOLUTION

This is a decision-making step. (More information on decision making is included in the next section.)

- What constraints and resources do I need to consider when choosing a solution?
- What biases do I have that might influence my decision?
- What criteria should I use for making the decision and why?
- Am I considering both short- and long-term effects and consequences?
- Am I balancing the needs of the people with the needs of the task?

STEP 4: IMPLEMENT THE SOLUTION

This is the step when the solution is put into action.

- What steps do I need to implement?
- Are the resources being used as effectively as possible?
- What roadblocks might get in the way and how can I circumvent them?
- Am I getting distracted or sidetracked by other problems or issues?
- Do I need to deal with any other related problems or issues before resolving this one?
- Are mechanisms in place to ensure follow-through?

STEP 5: EVALUATE THE RESULTS

This step ensures the problem has been dealt with successfully.

- Has the problem been solved?
- Was the solution achieved in the best way possible?
- What lessons were learned?

- What might I do differently next time?

- Am I capitalizing on potential opportunities?

- Do I need to do something to keep this problem from happening again?

- Are there parts of the problem-solving process I do well?

- Are there parts of the problem-solving process I need to improve?

Some workers who lack a systematic approach to problem solving may end up in situations with negative consequences. A construction supervisor describes the approach used by an apprentice.

WHAT HAPPENED?

An apprentice was installing a shower enclosure on the second floor of a house. His supervisor noticed a leak in the ceiling directly below where the apprentice was working. When the leak was pointed out to the apprentice, he commented that he couldn't have caused the leak because he had not changed any of the plumbing. When the supervisor explored the situation more thoroughly, he discovered the apprentice had fastened a screw into a water line inside the wall. The apprentice was surprised; he had not considered the possibility of a link between leaking water and his actions even though there was no other logical explanation. The supervisor used this teachable moment to encourage systematic problem solving.

Decision-Making Process

Individuals also need a systematic approach to making a decision. The decision-making process summarized here can be used at any single decision point no matter what the scale of the decision. Again, the process focuses on the mindfulness aspects of decision making.

STEP 1: CLARIFY THE SITUATION AND IDENTIFY ALTERNATIVES

The first need is to clearly define your possible courses of action.

- Do I need to make a decision?

- What will happen if I don't make a decision?

- What are my timelines and are they adequate?
- Am I using a broad perspective to ensure I am identifying all possible options?
- Do I need to complete any preliminary research to be sure I am identifying additional options?
- Have I sought the input of other people who will be affected by the decision?

STEP 2: SET AND EVALUATE THE DECISION-MAKING CRITERIA

Once options are identified, it is important to evaluate what criteria will be used to decide among them.

- Have I established clear criteria for making this decision?
- Have I considered all the criteria that are important to this decision?
- Have I ranked or otherwise prioritized my criteria?
- Have I considered the needs and criteria of others affected by the decision?
- Have I considered including both objective and subjective criteria?

STEP 3: EVALUATE THE ALTERNATIVES AND MAKE A CHOICE

Once criteria have been established, the next step is to choose an alternative based on the decision-making criteria.

- Do I have a way of measuring how well each option meets the criteria?
- Have I done enough research to ensure I can evaluate each alternative accurately?
- Have I followed each option through to its consequences and implications?
- Am I taking enough evaluation time to ensure my decision is well informed?
- Does my choice accurately reflect the prioritized criteria?

STEP 4: REFLECT AND REVISIT THE DECISION-MAKING PROCESS

Each decision is a learning experience as well as a chance to get something done.

- Did I get the expected results from my decision?

- If I didn't achieve the expected results, why not?

- What might I do differently next time?

- Are there parts of the decision-making process I do well?

- Are there parts of the decision-making process I need to improve?

You can introduce some of these questions when helping your clients make better decisions. Assess what steps of the decision-making process they are doing well and identify steps they can improve. Following are some common decision-making blind spots you might see in clients.

People sometimes suffer from tunnel vision when they set out to clarify the situation and identify alternatives. This is a step in the process when it is important to think outside the box and consider the decision from broad perspectives, which can enable people to generate options they did not immediately see. People may also need help in assessing who else needs to play a role in the decision-making process. Decisions that are made with too little or too much consultation can create problems. It is also important to assess when decisions need to be made quickly and independently. Workers need to be given the autonomy and authority to make these choices.

Your clients may need help in developing criteria for evaluating options when making a decision. Have them list and prioritize their criteria. To help them evaluate the appropriateness of the list, ask them to explain how they determined and prioritized each criterion. By clarifying their choices verbally, you can assess and discuss the appropriateness of each criterion. Your goal here is to help clients incorporate a logical, objective perspective as well as a consideration of the situations and needs of the other people involved. This is an important balance. Overemphasis on either side can create problems.

When evaluating and choosing an alternative based on the decision-making criteria, people need to focus on the logical consequences of each option—and may need your help in doing so. Some clients may need to be shown how to slow down and mentally work an option through to its outcome before taking action. In a similar way, others may need assistance seeing both short- and long-term consequences of options. The following section discusses how clients can use a variety of thinking modes while they are solving problems and making decisions.

Consciously Applies Different Modes of Thinking

To work independently, people need to think about how, when, and in what context to use different modes of thinking. For example, when someone is responding to an emergency, it is not a good time to engage in a strategic thinking process. Also, people need to be able to determine when to stop using a creative thinking process to generate alternatives and move into an evaluative process to select the one likeliest to succeed. In the same way, they must learn when to turn off their critical analysis so they can be more open-minded about alternatives that may not appear completely reasonable at first glance. This conscious evaluation and adjustment of the thinking processes is a key component of mindfulness.

Many people have written on the various aspects and ways of thinking, but for the purposes of this book it will be enough to discuss five basic modes of thinking. Increasing clients' awareness of these modes will help them assess when and why they need to shift from one to another. It will also help them balance and refine their information processing, problem solving, and decision making. Each mode has many aspects and skills associated with it. You may want to use additional resources to explore the thinking modes in greater detail. These are the five modes:

- Practical thinking
- Creative thinking
- Global thinking
- Logical thinking
- Humanistic thinking

The following sections provide strategies for using each of the five modes.

DETECT & DESCRIBE
Consciously Applies Different Modes of Thinking

Do see high performance

Evidence of the use of practical thinking:

- ○ Observing and inventorying facts related to a specific situation
- ○ Choosing realistic and practical solutions to problems
- ○ Making efficient decisions that take minimal effort to implement
- ○ Making use of conventional wisdom and personal experience
- ○ Adapting processes and strategies to the specific situation at hand

Evidence of the use of creative thinking:

- ○ Sharing many ideas and possibilities
- ○ Contributing ideas that are distinctly different from what others are sharing
- ○ Finding alternative uses for common objects
- ○ Presenting many alternative solutions for problems
- ○ Providing many possible choices when making decisions

Evidence of the use of global thinking:

- ○ Identifying trends and patterns
- ○ Describing long-term implications and consequences
- ○ Finding links and connections between pieces of information
- ○ Synthesizing information into an integrated, holistic form
- ○ Focusing on whole systems and interactions rather than specific pieces

Evidence of the use of logical thinking:

- ○ Analyzing and evaluating information
- ○ Using objective reasoning to reach a conclusion
- ○ Weighing the pros and cons of options
- ○ Focusing on logical consequences and implications
- ○ Describing cause-and-effect relationships

Evidence of the use of humanistic thinking:

- ○ Weighing information using personal, subjective beliefs and values
- ○ Assessing the effects of decisions and actions on the well-being of others
- ○ Focusing on how harmony and morale will be affected by decisions
- ○ Accommodating the likes, dislikes, and commitments of people in a situation
- ○ Acknowledging the motivation and needs of others

Practical Thinking

Some of the alternative terms used to describe practical thinking are *everyday thinking, realistic thinking, common sense,* and *conventional wisdom.* Practical thinking involves considering the realities of a situation and selecting the easiest and most pragmatic approach. Reality checks are key to this mode of thinking. Some people will need assistance to see the facts and details of a situation.

Here are some of the questions people might ask when engaged in practical thinking:

- Is this a practical solution or decision?

- Is there an easier way to do this?

- Is there a way I can expend less energy?

- Will this really work?

- What has worked before?

- What have I learned from past experiences in this type of situation?

- How can I adapt what I know to deal with this specific situation?

Practical thinking grounds the individual. It provides the reality check for ideas and a concrete link to the facts and details related to a particular situation. Sometimes people who are seen as highly intelligent lack this mode of thinking. They can become lost in theories and ideas and fail to link these abstractions to the immediate realities.

Practical thinking requires a focus on the here and now. If clients find this connection difficult, you will need to work toward grounding them slowly. If they are focused on ideas and theories, have them make a step-by-step plan to move from the current situation toward their ideas. Create a Gap Analysis between what is and what they envision. This will focus them on present realities as well as clarify how large the gaps are. Focus them on details such as timelines, costs, and resources required. You may need to illustrate ways to observe and research current realities and past attempts at solutions. Have your clients make observations or record specific data in the areas in which they need to demonstrate practical thinking.

Creative Thinking

Some of the alternative terms used to describe creative thinking are *divergent thinking, thinking outside the box, generative thinking,* and *unconventional thinking.* Individuals are encouraged to use creative thinking in processes such as brainstorming, which involves suspending critical thoughts to come up with as many ideas as possible. Creative thinking is often measured by the ability to come up with many alternatives, especially alternatives that are original and show flexibility of thought. Flexibility of thought is seen through responses such as finding unusual uses for objects, changing and redefining the contexts of problems, and seeing things from diverse perspectives. Here are some of the questions to ask when engaged in creative thinking:

- What other things might be connected to this topic?

- How can I look at this differently?

- What is the second, third, or fourth right answer?

- What haven't I thought about?

- What other options might there be?

- How can I sidestep restrictions that are limiting my thinking?

Creative thinking enables people to see new and different ways of approaching situations and solving problems. By using creative thinking, organizations are able to envision changes and new ways of doing things. Not everyone is comfortable using this mode of thinking. Some may see the creative thinking process as unrealistic and rather "head in the clouds." Others may struggle to see outside the practical thinking mode and find it difficult to imagine what they have not experienced. It is important to show clients practical reasons for suspending considerations of reality. For example, if they see that creative thinking is a useful step in a process of evaluating and choosing options, they may be more willing to engage in it. Those who are grounded in practical thinking may find it easiest to move into creative thinking by considering a series of incremental changes or thinking about changes that have occurred in the past that might be appropriate to the situation at hand. They can use their previous experience with change and new ideas to help them create ideas in the present situation.

A QUESTION OF BALANCE
Practical and Creative Thinking

Encourage clients to be both practical and creative in their approach to situations. It is important to balance the realities with the possibilities. If the realities are minimized, it will be impossible to implement the decision. If the possibilities are not considered, the individual and the organization may miss out on opportunities.

Global Thinking

Some of the alternative terms used to describe global thinking include *futuristic thinking, systems thinking,* and *integrative thinking.* Global thinking is focused on the future and on integration of components and systems into a holistic framework. It is a long-term, big-picture approach. Many may see this global thinking as an exclusive responsibility of top management, but the organization will benefit if everyone understands and works toward its broader goals and visions. Global thinking allows you to see situations from broad perspectives. When you look at a small piece of something, it is easy to miss many of the interactions and links to other parts of a system. This can result in shortsighted problem solving and decision making. Here are some of the questions to ask when engaged in global thinking:

- What are the long-term effects and consequences of actions?

- What parts of the whole system will be involved?

- What are our long-term goals?

- Are our current actions moving us toward our long-term goals?

- What is the vision for the future?

- What will the organization look like when we implement our vision?

- How do the systems and processes within the organization interact and interface?

When using global thinking, it is necessary to choose from unlimited possibilities and see implications beyond the current situation. This mode of thinking interfaces with creative and logical thinking. For example, some creative thinking is involved when formulating a vision, and some assessment of logical consequences is involved when looking at long-range effects. However, the defining element of global thinking is the integrative, long-term aspect.

Some people focus on the practical, immediate facts and details of a situation and will not automatically take a longer-term or more strategic approach. You may need to help them by pointing out patterns and trends they know to be true from experience. Once they are comfortable doing this, they can start to extrapolate into the future from current data.

Other people focus on global aspects only when they have a practical reason to do so. When introducing or expecting others to create models and integrate information, remember that some people are more comfortable with a practical, sequential framework. It will be helpful to incorporate these preferences when teaching clients how to think globally. Figurative language can be a barrier to understanding. Some people do not quickly see the relationships between symbolic or figurative stories, examples, and current realities. They may need to be shown how to create these links by working through a number of examples.

PERFORMANCE PREFERENCES
Practical, Creative, and Global Thinking: Sensing and Intuition

Sensing (S) types tend to use practical thinking. They are often observant and focused on taking in and considering the realities of a situation. You may need to coach them when to use creative and global thinking by showing them practical reasons for engaging in these modes.

Intuitive (N) types are often attracted to creative and global thinking. Practical thinking may be more of a stretch for them. You may need to coach them to consider the practical aspects of a situation and to ground their ideas in reality.

Logical Thinking

Some of the alternative terms used to describe logical thinking include *analytic thinking, critical thinking, objective thinking,* and *strategic thinking.* Logical thinking involves analyzing, evaluating, and making judgments about information. This mode of thinking may result in a critical evaluation or in a more positive logical plan or solution. Here are some of the questions to ask when engaged in logical thinking:

- Why is this happening?

- What is causing this situation?

- What will be the logical consequences of action or inaction?

- What are the pros and cons of various objectives?

- What is the logical thing to do?

- What solution matches the criteria most closely?

Logical thinking allows people to evaluate situations. This mode of thinking requires minimizing personal biases and seeing situations as objectively as possible. Some clients may have difficulty carrying out the logical thinking process, making errors when they try to use this mode. To use logical thinking well, people must make accurate assumptions and recognize faulty arguments. You may need to coach logical thinking by asking clients questions about their thinking process. Find out how they come to their conclusions by exploring what assumptions they make. You may need to challenge or point out conclusions that do not flow logically from the information at hand. Some clients may find the logical thinking process too objective and not personal enough. In this case, you will need to coach them to balance the logical thinking mode with the humanistic thinking mode.

Humanistic Thinking

Some of the alternative terms used to describe humanistic thinking include *emotional intelligence, values-based thinking,* and *subjective thinking.* In humanistic thinking, human values and feelings are key factors to consider and accommodate. Humanistic thinking considers how people feel about information rather than simply focusing on the information itself. Here are some of the questions to ask when engaged in humanistic thinking:

PERFORMANCE PREFERENCES
Logical and Humanistic Thinking: Thinking and Feeling

Thinking (T) types are naturally drawn to logical thinking and may need coaching to balance their analysis of situations by also using humanistic thinking. Feeling (F) types are naturally drawn to humanistic thinking and may need coaching to balance their subjective consideration of people by also using logical thinking.

QUICK TIPS
Developing Mindfulness

Throughout the chapter you have seen many aspects of mindfulness and factors that will influence whether people will demonstrate mindfulness effectively. Here is a quick overview of the main chapter points to help you assess what areas of intervention will be most applicable in your situation.

- Provide information resources for clients.
- Encourage clients to learn and use new information.
- Help clients manage information overload at a personal and organizational level.
- Consider clients' learning skills and style.
- Ensure clients are able to read effectively.
- Identify learning difficulties and show clients how to compensate for them.
- Coach critical thinking.
- Ensure clients can transfer learning into different contexts and situations.
- Provide and coach systematic processes for solving problems.
- Provide and coach systematic processes for making decisions.
- Coach clients to recognize their use of different modes of thinking.
- Coach clients to adjust and evaluate their thinking to maximize effectiveness.

- Who is affected by this issue?

- How will people feel about this decision?

- Will anyone be hurt?

- Is this fair to everyone involved?

- Will this make things better or worse for the people involved?

- How will this affect morale?

- How will this affect relationships?

When individuals are aware of these distinctly different modes of thinking, they can consciously begin to adjust and evaluate their use in specific situations.

TLC FOR ALL TYPES: MINDFULNESS

All types demonstrate mindfulness. Here are some of the special challenges of developing this competency that relate to personality preferences. As you choose an intervention, be sure to take the personality type of your client into consideration.

RESPONDERS (ESTP AND ESFP)

Responders are interested in learning new information that is practical and immediately useful. They usually prefer hands-on or active learning to sitting and reading or listening. When solving problems and making decisions, Responders tend to place less emphasis on global thinking. They are attracted to practical thinking and focus on short-term solutions to problems. Responders use their creative thinking in the world

around them to adapt information to new situations. They may need some coaching when engaging in global thinking.

Logical Responders (ESTP) are attracted to using logical thinking and enjoy solving practical problems. Humanistic thinking may be less comfortable for them than looking at logical aspects of situations. Compassionate Responders (ESFP) are attracted to using humanistic thinking and finding practical solutions to help people meet their immediate needs. Logical thinking may be less comfortable for them than looking at personal aspects of situations.

EXPLORERS (ENTP AND ENFP)

Explorers are interested in learning new ideas and finding new ways of doing things. They enjoy learning about theories and models. When solving problems and making decisions, Explorers tend to use creative and global thinking to find unusual solutions. They may avoid closure, preferring to keep options open and explore possibilities. You may need to coach them to come to closure more quickly. They may also need coaching to incorporate practical thinking, since they are more focused on the possibilities than on the realities of a situation.

Logical Explorers (ENTP) are attracted to using logical thinking and enjoy solving problems, especially problems related to systems and processes. Humanistic thinking may be less comfortable for them than looking at logical aspects of situations. Compassionate Explorers (ENFP) are attracted to using humanistic thinking and finding solutions to help people develop their potential. Logical thinking may be less comfortable for them than looking at personal aspects of situations.

EXPEDITORS (ESTJ AND ENTJ)

Expeditors are interested in learning expedient ways to reach goals and objectives. They are attracted to developing competencies. When solving problems, Expeditors tend to use logical thinking and seek the most expedient solutions. They prefer closure and are attracted to making decisions as quickly as possible. You may need to coach them to broaden their consideration of options. Expeditors are not naturally drawn to humanistic thinking. They may benefit from coaching that shows them how to logically incorporate the personal side into their thinking process.

Practical Expeditors (ESTJ) attend to the facts and details of a situation. They are attracted to practical thinking and may not want to take additional time to use the creative and global thinking modes. Insightful Expeditors (ENTJ) are attracted to creative and global thinking. They may need coaching to attend to the details and practical aspects of situations.

CONTRIBUTORS (ESFJ AND ENFJ)

Contributors are interested in learning new information that will have a positive effect on people's lives. They prefer to learn in a supportive environment that provides positive feedback. Contributors are attracted to humanistic thinking and are naturally interested in understanding how situations affect individuals. They like to collaborate and cooperate when solving problems. Contributors may need coaching to balance their preferences with a more logical analysis of a situation.

Practical Contributors (ESFJ) attend to the facts and details of a situation. They are attracted to practical thinking and may not want to take additional time to use the creative and global thinking modes. Insightful Contributors (ENFJ) are attracted to creative and global thinking. They may need coaching to attend to the details and practical aspects of situations.

ASSIMILATORS (ISTJ AND ISFJ)

Assimilators want to keep learning information that is relevant to their experiences. They are highly observant and tend to build up a rich experiential base to which they constantly add new facts and details. This learning process may take time, since Assimilators carefully examine and incorporate new information with what they know to be true from their experience. Be sure to provide them with in-depth, accurate information. Assimilators focus on practical realities and may benefit from coaching to help them make generalizations and find main ideas. Practical thinking is attractive to them and they may benefit from coaching to develop their thinking in the creative and global modes.

Logical Assimilators (ISTJ) are attracted to using logical thinking and enjoy solving problems, especially problems related to their expertise. Humanistic thinking may be less comfortable for them than looking at logical aspects of situations. Compassionate Assimilators (ISFJ) are attracted to using humanistic thinking and are able to find solutions to solve immediate problems and help others in a practical way. Logical thinking and evaluation may be less comfortable for them than looking at personal aspects of situations.

VISIONARIES (INTJ AND INFJ)

Visionaries want to learn about complex ideas and are drawn to theories and models. They need time to process and integrate information. They are especially drawn to global thinking and see links and connections. Visionaries may benefit from coaching to help them use practical thinking to focus on realities. When solving problems and making decisions, Visionaries want to be sure a long-term perspective is being considered.

Logical Visionaries (INTJ) are attracted to using logical thinking and enjoy solving problems, especially complex problems. Humanistic thinking may be less comfortable for them than looking at logical aspects of situations. Compassionate Visionaries (INFJ) are attracted to using humanistic thinking and are especially motivated to find solutions to solve complex problems and help others develop their potential. Logical thinking and evaluation may be less comfortable for them than considering personal aspects of situations.

ANALYZERS (ISTP AND INTP)

Analyzers are interested in analyzing new information. It is important to provide them with opportunities to critique what they are learning. They are drawn to logical thinking. Analyzers may benefit from coaching to use humanistic thinking to process the personal aspects of situations.

Practical Analyzers (ISTP) attend to the facts and details of a situation. They are attracted to practical thinking and may not want to take additional time to use the creative and global thinking modes. Insightful Analyzers (INTP) are more attracted to creative and global thinking. They may need coaching to attend to the details and practical aspects of situations.

ENHANCERS (ISFP AND INFP)

Enhancers are interested in learning new information that is personally meaningful. When coaching their learning, be sure to take time to understand their values and interests. They are attracted to using humanistic thinking and are careful to consider the needs and situations of others when they are solving problems and making decisions. Enhancers may benefit from coaching to use logical thinking to assess situations objectively. This will balance their tendency to focus on the personal side of situations.

Practical Enhancers (ISFP) attend to the facts and details of a situation. They are attracted to practical thinking and may not want to take additional time to use the creative and global thinking modes. Insightful Enhancers (INFP) are attracted to creative and global thinking. They may need coaching to attend to the details and practical aspects of situations.

Chapter 6
Productivity

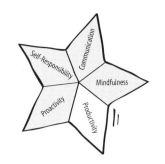

Productive people focus on and achieve exceptional results. To accomplish this they prioritize, plan, and organize their time and activities. They persist on tasks at hand and efficiently complete work that meets a high standard. Highly productive people are continuously looking for ways to be more effective at completing their work as they work toward and exceed the expectations that have been laid out for them.

Productive workers are seen as results oriented, goal oriented, productive, task oriented, persistent, conscientious, good at follow-through, well organized, efficient, and effective. They show pride in their work and strive to do the best job they can. They show initiative and are high achievers. Others are able to trust them to do their work well.

If workers are not productive they will be seen as disorganized, easily distracted, or low achievers. Employers are not confident that such individuals will work toward and achieve high standards, expecting them instead to coast through their days without really giving their work the time and energy it requires and deserves.

Lack of productivity is often seen as the problem area when someone is having work performance issues. For example, failing to complete a report or close a deal with a customer can look like a productivity problem. However, other factors also may be involved. When you are working with someone who is not generating results, assess the reasons for the problem. Perhaps the person didn't complete a report because they lacked competence in the mindfulness area and didn't know how to find and analyze the necessary information. Or perhaps they are not closing deals with customers because they lack the communication skills necessary to develop rapport and

COMPONENTS OF PRODUCTIVITY

Focuses on Obtaining Results

- Prioritizes, plans, and organizes time and tasks
- Persists on tasks

Achieves Exceptional Results

- Completes work to a high standard
- Continually improves work processes and exceeds standards

listen to customer needs. Focus on the productivity competency when the difficulties are directly related to the ability to prioritize, plan, organize, and persist on tasks. Addressing the productivity competency will also be relevant with clients who are not able to set and maintain standards for their work. Again, when assessing difficulties meeting standards, you may find that lack of other competencies is affecting performance. For example, someone who is giving substandard presentations may need coaching in communication as well as productivity.

The productivity competency consists of two distinct groups of behaviors. I refer to the first group as "Focuses on Obtaining Results"; it includes behaviors individuals require to be attentive, planful, and persistent in their approach to work. The second group of behaviors, "Achieves Exceptional Results," explores the ability to meet and exceed expectations. Note the list of the components of productivity in the order in which they will be covered in the chapter (see page 205).

FOCUSES ON OBTAINING RESULTS

Productive people approach their work by establishing priorities. This provides an opportunity to assess what is most important. Once it is clear what their most important priorities are, they can plan and organize their activities. By persisting on their plan, they set the stage to accomplish results.

Prioritizes, Plans, and Organizes Time and Tasks

To achieve results, workers must accomplish tasks. Those who do not plan and organize their work well are at a disadvantage. They may be unsure about what work needs to be done first. People who are unorganized tend to rush from one task to another, always seeming to be behind or unprepared. Although at times everyone feels rushed and unable to meet all their obligations, effective individuals tend to use the tools of prioritizing, planning, and organizing.

Prioritizing

Establishing priorities has many advantages. For one thing, simply taking the time to inventory the various tasks and objectives at hand makes it easier to see the responsibilities that need to be addressed.

GAP ANALYSIS
Productivity

The pairs of statements that follow represent the endpoints of a continuum of possible performance in productivity. Place an X on each line at the location that best describes the current level of performance.

Focuses on Obtaining Results

Has an unorganized and inefficient approach to work ⟵————————⟶ Prioritizes, plans, and organizes time and tasks

Gives up easily ⟵————————⟶ Persists on tasks

Achieves Exceptional Results

Work is incomplete or substandard ⟵————————⟶ Completes work to a high standard

Works to minimally accepted standards without improving processes ⟵————————⟶ Continually improves work processes and exceeds standards

Take time to reflect on productivity. Use the space below to write down any specific information or insights you, your client, or others may have regarding your client's ability to be productive in the course of daily work activities.

_____

_____

_____

DETECT & DESCRIBE
Prioritizes, Plans, and Organizes Time and Tasks

. . . .

Don't see high performance

Evidence of an unorganized and inefficient approach to work:

○ Being unsure of priorities

○ Spending significant time or energy on unimportant activities

○ Missing deadlines

○ Completing tasks in a last-minute rush that reduces quality of results

○ Being unprepared for meetings

Do see high performance

Evidence of prioritizing, planning, and organizing:

○ Identifying and working on most important tasks first

○ Making and following a plan to accomplish important goals

○ Meeting deadlines

○ Completing tasks on time while maintaining quality of results

○ Being prepared for meetings

A QUESTION OF BALANCE
Responding Immediately and Establishing Priorities

. . . .

A client sitting down to list and prioritize all tasks, including small items, may be losing an opportunity to act in the moment. Items that can be dealt with immediately turn into items on a list that is rewritten and revisited. Sometimes the most effective approach is to simply make a call, complete a task, or otherwise deal with a simple item rather than take the time to integrate the activity into a planning process. However, if people continually respond to immediate requests, they can become caught up in the moment and find the more important but less urgent tasks are not getting the attention they deserve. Knowing how to balance the immediate with the planning process requires careful consideration. For example, say your client reads e-mail but doesn't plan to respond to it immediately. As a consequence, the backlog of e-mail requiring response piles up. Now the e-mail has become a larger task and is more difficult to fit into the schedule. Perhaps it is more effective to coach someone to read and respond to e-mail immediately, so this type of problem does not occur. However, someone who is constantly checking and responding to e-mail is not able to focus on other tasks. Your challenge is to help your clients maximize their efforts in the moment while also establishing and being sure to focus on priorities.

People can use any of a number of strategies to set priorities. Systems for prioritizing focus on ways to consider what is important and then on ways to list tasks at hand and then rank them using numbers, letters, or systems of lists. Individuals can make priorities by reflecting on their goals, aligning activities with their values, thinking about their mission, or sequencing tasks and assessing timelines. The specific system used to prioritize tasks is not as important as the fact that an effective individual does use a system.

When assessing clients' ability to prioritize, ask them what they see as important and why. You may find that their expectations and priorities regarding their role differ from those of their leader or customers. If you suspect this is the case, have others describe what they see as most important for the individual to do. This provides a platform to discuss what is seen as important and why. When working with clients, it is essential to ensure their priorities are aligned with the priorities of their supervisor, customers, and organization. Aligning expectations can go a long way toward ensuring that workers are setting priorities that link to the needs of their organization.

When it seems that expectations are aligned, explore the way your clients currently establish priorities. They may need to fine-tune a process or find a new system for setting priorities. Setting priorities does not tend to be done as an isolated event. It is usually the first step in a planning and organizing process. When identifying systems that will work for your clients, consider the time and task management aspects of planning discussed in the next section. It will be helpful to consider both short- and long-term priorities when working with individuals. If only short-term priorities are considered, people may miss out on opportunities to work toward broader goals and objectives.

Time and Task Management

Once someone has decided what is most important and what needs to be done first, they need to make a plan to organize their time and tasks. Planning tools range from paper-and-pencil systems to software programs and electronic organizers. There are planning systems to help individuals manage their day, week, month, year, and life. There are also project and contract management systems. Again, the system itself is less critical than the decision to use some systematic process to manage time and tasks. When working with clients, always assess what (if any) system they are

PERFORMANCE PREFERENCES
Setting Priorities: Sensing and Intuition

Sensing (S) types are attracted to acting in the moment and tend to be practical when setting goals and establishing priorities. They may benefit from setting longer-term goals. This will help them balance their practical approach by seeing the broader perspective. Activities that need to be done to work toward long-term goals tend to not have the immediacy that more pressing short-term goals have. Because of this, Sensing types may not see them as important.

Intuitive (N) types tend to enjoy visioning and making long-term goals. They find it stimulating to work on activities that are aligned with these visions and goals. They may benefit from coaching to be more in tune with the demands of current situations and to address immediate priorities.

currently using to manage their time and tasks. Go through the paper and to-do files of clients to see how they are currently managing their activities. Find out what is working for them and what is not working well in the system they are using. Further assess their current strategies by observing and working with them as they engage in planning and organizing. Remember that people will have different strategies for organizing, as the following example illustrates.

METHOD TO THE MADNESS

An ENTP office manager was labeled as disorganized by coworkers. She did not use a filing cabinet to store files until projects were completed; instead, she had "project piles" of files in various locations around her office. Rather than accept the negative label, she encouraged others to see her as a "conceptual organizer." Everything she needed for a project was grouped together. When she had time to work on that project, she would bring out the project pile and work on tasks effectively. With this insight into her method, others were able to see that there was order in the apparent disorganization.

Several time wasters can get in the way when someone is trying to become organized. A major one is poor information management. People lose a lot of time trying to find pieces of paper that contain information. They are deluged with memos, circulated articles, agendas, files, reports, customer or client information, and so on and on and on. This information needs to be managed so the holders can access it when they need it while not being distracted by it at other times. Paper information is not the only time waster—nonpaper sources of information such as e-mail, Web site addresses, and voice messages all demand time to manage. You can tell this is a problem for someone if they can't find important information, miss meetings or opportunities to respond to timely issues, or ask for or complain they were not aware of information that has already been distributed.

You may need to coach clients on creating a process for dealing with information. If e-mail contains the date of a meeting, the most expedient action may be to immediately input the details into a planner. Perhaps the organization has software that can add meetings to individual schedules to help in this area. Teach your clients to deal with pieces of paper immediately whenever possible, avoiding the temptation to sort them into piles that will simply need to be dealt with at a later time. Have clients adopt or create a system for organizing time and tasks and coach them to use it regularly. Here are some tips to help people manage their time and materials:

- Have clients put materials and resources in designated spots. Coach them to use notebooks, folders, or a briefcase if they tend to lose pieces of paper.

- If your clients have to deal with a lot of information, help them establish a filing system. It will minimize the time they spend looking for things.

- When you work with someone who likes to make lists, have them make a list of their daily activities, including only the things they need to complete that day. Some people make lists that could take weeks, even months, to complete. These lists become frustrating because people rarely feel like they've completed much.

- Make sure the tasks on your client's daily to-do list are specific and achievable. Then prioritize them in order of importance.

- Encourage clients to reward themselves with a short break when they complete a task.

- Remember to coach follow-through. It isn't enough to buy a planner or set up a scheduling system. You have to encourage their use and help clients evaluate whether the approach is working for them.

- Rather than changing many things at once, try one or two organization strategies that you think will work best for your client.

Workspace Organization

Finding, using, and storing supplies and other types of workplace resources can be an enormous source of distraction. "Things" need to be organized as well as paper and information. How much time does your client spend looking for a stapler, staples, pens, paper, and other supplies? Regular maintenance of resources individuals use frequently will ensure that tools are kept in an optimal state. In the long run this will save time and energy that are often lost fixing things or waiting for things to be fixed.

You can observe and then coach clients on organizing their workspace. Help them minimize the distraction of searching for items, especially those they use regularly. Are the tools and equipment they need handy? Do they have comfortable and ergonomically sound chairs, desks, and workstations? Is there anything the organization can do to make the workspace more comfortable and efficient? Here are some practical suggestions to share with clients when assessing and improving their workspace:

To make a space quiet

- Shut a door.
- Use earplugs.
- Talk to the noisemakers.
- Unplug the phone or turn on the answering machine.

To make a space comfortable

- Change or adjust the chair.
- Change or adjust the table or desk.
- Control the heat, light, and glare if possible.
- Place or change posters or pictures on the walls.
- Lose clutter—especially stuff unrelated to the work at hand.

To make a space practical

- Ensure work materials are available and accessible.
- Place computer, desk, chair, and other furniture in the most efficient places.
- Organize materials.
- Keep the materials used most often close at hand.

Procrastination

We all procrastinate for different reasons in different situations; it isn't necessarily a problem. And sometimes leaving a task incomplete is not a sign of procrastination. The individual may have chosen not to complete it because its priority is low. It is important to know the difference between effectively setting priorities and procrastinating. If, for example, someone reports a strong urge to sort their rarely used bottom drawer before finishing a lengthy inventory report due tomorrow morning, they are probably procrastinating. If you are working with a client who is procrastinating regularly, you may want to explore why and then deal with the reason directly. Here are some common reasons for procrastination:

- Not knowing what to do or how to do it
- Lacking the skills, tools, or information to proceed
- Being distracted from the task
- Being uninterested in the task
- Feeling too tired or stressed
- Feeling ill, unfit, or lethargic
- Fearing failure
- Fearing success
- Being indecisive
- Failing to establish clear priorities
- Being unwilling to start something that there isn't time to finish
- Being unwilling to start something for fear it won't get done perfectly

Choose ways to help people avoid procrastination and organize their time, information, and resources more effectively. Do this on a regular basis and your clients will see you as someone who is interested in helping them accomplish their goals. By listening to what roadblocks they experience when they try to prioritize, plan, and organize, you can identify ways to help clients become more focused and planful in their approach.

Prioritizing and planning are the first steps toward focusing on obtaining results. People must be able to follow through with their plans. This requires persistence.

Persists on Tasks

No one will be highly productive unless they can persist on tasks. Persistent people are resourceful, find solutions to problems, and maintain their attention on tasks. This can be an especially difficult behavior for some people to master. Some find it a struggle to persist and lose interest when tasks are routine and repetitive. Others become frustrated or tempted to give up on tasks that are highly complex, difficult, or challenging. In either case, workers require the persistence to stick to a task when it becomes uninteresting or unpleasant. Without persistence, tasks remain uncompleted and difficult problems remain unsolved.

DETECT & DESCRIBE
Persists on Tasks

Don't see high performance	Do see high performance
Evidence of giving up easily:	Evidence of persistence on tasks:
○ Shifting focus from one task to another without completing the initial task	○ Working on a task for an extended period of time
○ Avoiding or procrastinating on certain tasks	○ Finding ways to maintain interest on tasks that are not highly motivating
○ Becoming stuck or unable to proceed when barriers to progress occur	○ Using resourcefulness to find ways around barriers
○ Using an ineffective problem-solving approach	○ Taking a systematic problem-solving approach to problems
○ Failing to follow through on obligations and responsibilities	○ Following through on obligations and responsibilities

PERFORMANCE PREFERENCES
Completing a Task: Judging and Perceiving

People with a preference for Judging (J) tend to be focused on task completion and will often naturally persist to complete tasks. However, they are less likely to persist on tasks that are not directly linked to a result. When working with them, you may need to ensure the tasks they are expected to complete are necessary. As well, they will want to be given the autonomy and tools to complete their tasks efficiently.

People with a preference for Perceiving (P) tend to prefer to initiate rather than complete tasks. They can easily become bored with any task and may switch to something else rather than complee the task at hand. Perceiving types tend to find highly structured and routine tasks especially difficult. When working with them, strategies to enhance follow-through will be especially helpful.

To help people develop persistence, you need to define and measure specific behavioral expectations. When clients are developing this competency, make sure the way you measure success reflects specific improvements in performance. For example, if someone simply stops working on a repetitive task when bored, you might measure success by the volume of work done. If the difficulty is related to inability to solve a problem, you will need to measure persistence by a different criterion than simply volume of work accomplished. In this case, successful solutions to problems may be a more relevant outcome to measure.

Assessing the reasons for lack of persistence is the first step toward improvement. If you are unsure why someone is not persisting, walk through the task with them to see where they become stuck. This will help you clarify the specific barrier to persistence you need to address. The following sections discuss some common reasons and some strategies to promote improved persistence.

Concentration and Attention

Some people must struggle to maintain their attention. This can be an enormous block to persistence. Clients with concentration and attention difficulties often benefit from specific strategies that help focus them on the task at hand. Here are some suggestions you can try:

- Notice what clients are doing when they are concentrating well. For example, does it help when they write things down, look at a speaker, or avoid looking at the clock? Help them identify their concentration behaviors and then practice them.

- Notice what causes distraction. Discuss with your clients what things they find most distracting. Is it sights, sounds, sensations such as uncomfortable clothes or hunger, or mental vacations? Once the distractions are named, people can be more conscious about noticing when they are becoming distracted and when they need to refocus their thoughts.

- If someone fidgets, encourage the use of an object to manipulate, but be sure to recommend something that doesn't distract them or others from the task.

- Have clients vary their activities, take short breaks, and reward themselves for progress.

- Evaluate the workspace and experiment with changing the environment. For example, music may be more helpful than silence for people who have trouble concentrating. Music masks small sounds that might otherwise be distracting. Windows, hallways, and art on the wall are possible sources of distraction to consider.

- Avoid common distractions: people, telephones, radio, and so forth. Perhaps your client can move to a different workspace or use an answering machine to take calls.

- Help clients assess their physical readiness to work. Monitor hunger, fitness, time-of-day rhythms, and tension. Try to schedule tasks that require the most concentration when the client can expect to be alert and energized.

- People need to focus on their work rather than on other issues. Explore any issues that might be distracting. Coach them to do what they can about minor problems. Major problems need to be dealt with outside the workplace. Consider providing referrals to assistance programs targeting problems that are interfering with work and are beyond clients' ability to resolve.

- Encourage clients to organize their workspace and resources to minimize time spent looking for things.

- Look for underlying causes of the concentration and attention problems and then help people deal directly with these. For example, if clients find it hard to concentrate on a manual because the vocabulary is unfamiliar, they will need to slow their pace and reach for the dictionary or other supplementary materials. If clients cannot listen during a meeting because they have a serious personal problem or situation on their mind, they may need to be referred for assistance.

- If clients are taking any medications, have them check with their doctor to assess side effects. Some medications can affect the ability to concentrate.

Boredom

Clients may feel bored or unmotivated to continue on specific tasks. Most people dislike some aspects of their work. They tend to be less persistent on these tasks and will give them a low priority. When people are not interested in the tasks they need to do, they can either do them anyway or change the type of work they are doing. Someone who is not suited to the work at hand is unlikely to become highly engaged or motivated. Assessing a client's suitability for a particular type of work may provide recognition that the current role is not a good fit. If so, your client may want to consider a career or role change. Here is an example where a client's dislike for tasks created a performance issue.

SITTING ISN'T FITTING

An ESTP was reassigned from warehouse work to data management after an injury. His work habits degenerated almost immediately. He was not used to sitting and did not like the highly detailed computer work. After completing a career planning process, he was able to describe his preference for active, practical work with opportunities to be flexible and adaptable. The organization was then able to move him into a demonstration-based safety-training role. His performance immediately improved.

PERFORMANCE PREFERENCES
What Is Interesting?: Extraversion and Introversion

Everyone gets bored at times, regardless of personality type. Nonetheless, it is useful to consider the personality type of the people you are working with when assessing how to help them persist on tasks that they find uninteresting.

Individuals with a preference for Extraversion (E) tend to find it especially tedious to work with highly detailed and complex tasks. They can become impatient in these situations and will want to seek variety and change activities frequently. Individuals with a preference for Introversion (I) can get bored when tasks are overly simple and don't have enough depth to engage them.

It is not always realistic to match someone to an ideal type of work—and even the most ideal work will involve tasks that are not highly interesting. In any case, people need strategies to persist on uninteresting tasks. As coaches, we can first identify the tasks that are particularly uninteresting and then work with the client to develop motivators for completing the tasks. It often helps to suggest that clients take frequent small breaks or reward themselves for accomplishing all or part of a task. Some people may want to focus on the most uninteresting task first and get it over with, a worst-first approach. Others may find it motivating to challenge themselves to do the task faster or better.

Repetition

Some people respond poorly to repetitive tasks, whereas others seek out and enjoy this type of activity. Someone who does not concentrate well or loses interest when doing repetitive tasks may begin to make errors or may decrease the speed at which the task is accomplished. Some people will simply abandon or avoid doing the repetitive aspects of their work and focus their attention on the variable tasks. You may need to first assess how comfortable and suited to repetitive tasks your client is. If someone is not comfortable with this type of work, you may need to consider a transfer to another role.

A QUESTION OF BALANCE
Speed and Accuracy

Speed and accuracy are both important. This can affect all types of work productivity, but is especially critical when workers are engaged in repetitive tasks. There is a trade-off between these two important factors: As a task is completed faster more work is accomplished, but the likelihood of errors increases. People who work more slowly often have lower error rates but also get less done in a fixed period of time. In a similar way, speed may affect how thoroughly a task is completed. A task that is accomplished quickly may not be as thoroughly done as a task that is completed more slowly and perhaps more carefully.

When assisting workers, discuss this trade-off. Ideally, work will be accomplished with the maximum of both quantity and quality. However, a balance will need to exist between these two factors. Assess accuracy by counting the number of errors made. Assess how important the errors are and analyze the cause of the errors. This analysis will help determine the most appropriate balance between speed and accuracy. Set and agree on reasonable standards for both the quality and the quantity of work to be accomplished.

Someone who is required to engage in highly repetitive tasks may need strategies to help maintain interest and accuracy. Opportunities to engage in different types of tasks throughout the day may be helpful. For repetitive physical tasks, giving attention to the ergonomics of the work setting will be especially important to minimize the possibility of repetitive strain injuries. Keep personality type in mind when considering strategies to help clients deal with repetitive tasks. The following example illustrates how one woman was able to persist on and complete tasks that were not well suited to her personality.

DEALING WITH THE DETAILS

An ENTP was working in a human resources office. She was responsible for a number of detailed, repetitive tasks requiring data entry and verifying accuracy of data. She found these tasks uninteresting

PERFORMANCE PREFERENCES
Repetition and Inspiration: Sensing and Intuition

People with a preference for Sensing (S) are comfortable with some repetition, as long as the results are useful and the task is done in a manner that makes practical sense. They can get bored completing tasks that do not have an immediate usefulness. When working with Sensing types, be sure to show them the practical and immediate benefits of persisting on a task.

People with a preference for Intuition (N) tend to have a work style of starts and stops. They may work hard at something for a while and then lose their inspiration. Intuitive types may not maintain interest in a task unless they can see a meaningful long-term result of their actions. When working with Intuitive types, be sure to show them how persisting on the task will result in a long-term benefit.

and difficult to persist on. After some discussion with her leader, she was able to add other, less detailed, tasks to her workload. Then she could balance the amount of time she spent on the tedious work with time spent on more conceptual and stimulating tasks. Setting up this multitasking approach allowed her to pay attention to the detailed tasks, knowing that she would soon switch to a more rewarding activity.

Lack of Problem-Solving Strategies

People tend to lack persistence when faced with problems they don't know how to solve or obstacles they don't know how to deal with. If workers do not have a good strategy for solving problems, they can get frustrated and give up.

One of the major cues that people are unsure of how to proceed is when they start to use a trial-and-error approach. In some of these situations you may need to teach and coach a strategic problem-solving approach. Use focusing questions: "What have you tried?" "What might be causing the problem?" "What can you try next?" These questions will help the client focus on solving the problem systematically. Problem-solving strategies are covered in greater depth in the discussion on mindfulness in Chapter 5.

PERFORMANCE PREFERENCES
Solving Problems: Thinking and Feeling
· ·

People with a preference for Thinking (T) tend to become bored with simple tasks that do not provide them with an opportunity for problem solving or troubleshooting. When working with Thinking types, be sure to engage them in the process of logically analyzing and solving problems.

People with a preference for Feeling (F) tend to get bored when the tasks they are doing are not related to helping people or serving them in a positive way. When working with Feeling types, be sure to show them how solving a problem will have a positive effect on the people involved.

Lack of Knowledge or Information

In some situations, when people are not persisting on a task, it may be because they are unsure of what to do next. They may have good problem-solving skills but lack the skills or information they need to complete their tasks. It is important to teach the task to them in a way that allows them to work through it independently. Make sure they have clear procedures to follow. Reference materials in the form of process guidelines or standard operating procedures may be helpful tools to use in this case.

A QUESTION OF BALANCE
Persistence and Resourcefulness
· ·

We expect effective workers to persist on a task until it is completed. When the task becomes complex and difficult, people must be able to stick to their approach and continue to work through the roadblocks. If they give up too easily, or try a number of things without a concentrated effort, they are likely to be unsuccessful. However, too much persistence can be an issue when the approach being used in not working. In these cases people must be able to change course and try different strategies and approaches to accomplish their goals. Assess where the client you are working with fits on this continuum. Do you need to coach someone to be more persistent on a task by concentrating their effort or do you need to help them recognize when to change gears and not continue to put in unproductive effort? People succeed when they are both persistent and resourceful at the right times.

Interruptions

Interruptions can be a barrier to persistence. It is helpful for people to divide their work into interruptible and not-interruptible categories. When doing work that is not interruptible, they may need to set up certain parameters in their workspace. For example, they may need to close the door, turn off the phone, and let others know they are unavailable for a specific period of time. When this is not possible, people need to develop strategies to help them refocus quickly. See if there are simple things a client can do to minimize interruptions. For example, it may be possible to move the desk so as to face away from a hall or area where others tend to make eye contact and then engage in conversation.

Once you assess the reasons for a lack of persistence, you can focus on creating a plan to increase persistence. Ensure your interventions directly address the reasons.

ACHIEVES EXCEPTIONAL RESULTS

Being organized, efficient, and persistent is a good start toward productivity. However, this is not enough. People must also complete the work they are expected to complete. The work must be done well, ideally at a higher standard than expected. As well, highly effective people will be looking for ways to improve the way the work is being done. This will allow them to be more effective in the future.

Completes Work to a High Standard

Some work standards may be very simple and concrete, such as arriving on time, and others can be very complex, such as completing all phases of a multifaceted project within the scheduled timelines. No matter what the standards are, effective workers are aware of and strive to meet them.

Clarify Expectations and Standards

When you work in this behavior area, your obvious first step is to ensure expectations and standards are clearly defined and shared with your clients. Whenever possible, organizations should make concrete and specific roles and responsibilities, and the associated accepted standards, available to all workers. Initiate a discussion with the client to start defin-

DETECT & DESCRIBE
Completes Work to a High Standard

Don't see high performance	Do see high performance
Evidence of incomplete or sub-standard work:	Evidence of completion of work to a high standard:
○ Lacking specific standards for the work	○ Having clear standards and expectations for the work
○ Being unclear about what others expect	○ Showing a history of high ratings and compensation on standards-based evaluations
○ Focusing on being compensated for time rather than results	○ Focusing on achieving results, not just putting in time
○ Ignoring how lack of results might interfere with the work of others	○ Making sure results support the work of others
○ Failing to link personal results to the results of the organization as a whole	○ Linking results to organizational needs

ing specific outcomes. In a way similar to defining priorities, list criteria that specifically demonstrate the work is being completed to accepted standards.

These standards may exist in the form of job descriptions, but such write-ups often have a fair amount of ambiguity. They tend to list roles the individual is responsible for but lack specificity in the standards expected for the roles. Sometimes, clarifying the expectations is all that is necessary to improve performance. Workers may not be demonstrating a behavior simply because they are not aware it is expected. The following example demonstrates the importance of clarifying expectations.

THE NEW GUY

A plant operator saw himself as "the new guy" even though he had been doing the work for well over a year. He would consult the experts, workers who had been there for more than five years, when difficult problems arose in the work setting. He was surprised to learn that others thought he was not working up to standard. Once he realized he was expected to take more initiative in solving problems, he was immediately able to change his behavior. He still consults the experts when he has specific questions, but he has stopped relying on them to take a lead role in these situations.

Standards, like any desired outcome, are most effective when they are measurable. If you are expecting someone to demonstrate good customer service, spell out the criteria you use to define good customer service. In a gas station, this might be starting to pump gas and offering to check the oil within a minute after a customer drives into the station. In a restaurant, it might be making sure the customers receive exactly what they ordered 100 percent of the time. By using specific numbers to clarify amount and time, you let your clients know what they need to shoot for.

Behavior on the job is then measured by setting a clear standard and assessing work in comparison to the standard. When possible, engage the client in clarifying and specifying the standard to be met. People also need to be educated on standards that originate outside the organization, such as health and safety regulations and other mandatory requirements. Make sure people see examples of high-quality work. They may not realize the level at which they are expected to work. When possible, allow them to work from, observe, or refer to a sample of quality work.

Check to ensure the client has been taught the specific skills and knowledge needed to complete the task. People often cannot complete work to a high standard without additional skill development, no matter what the expectations are.

If the quality of someone's work declines, it is important to discern the underlying cause. For example, someone may be bored or distracted from the task by conflicting demands or by factors outside work. Discuss the decline with the client in order to understand the factors affecting performance.

Highly effective people tend to set and meet their own standards. To encourage this, engage clients in a dialogue regarding standards for their work. What do they see as top performance? How specifically do they define and measure it? Are they currently achieving that standard? What can they do to meet the standard 100 percent of the time? As people move ahead in this area, have them take greater responsibility for setting standards and describing and evaluating how well they are meeting them.

Measure Results, Not Time

Self-responsible, productive people tend to measure their days by work accomplished rather than by hours and minutes they spend at work. They will complete a task before they take a break or go home for the day rather than watch the clock and simply leave when their time is up. When clients are locked into clock watching rather than achieving results, you may need to encourage them to focus on completing specific pieces of work rather than simply putting in hours. This paradigm shift to work accomplished rather than time spent may need to be reinforced by adjustments in organizational policy.

Compensation systems, promotion systems, and reward systems are often based on seniority rather than performance. Someone who has been performing a role for a certain number of years will be reinforced by an increase in salary, benefits, or rank. They may even get a plaque, dinner, watch, or other reward. It is good to reward employees for long service. However, if longevity is the only thing rewarded, the system may be sending the wrong message.

Some long-term employees become complacent and unmotivated. They may tell new workers to slow down to avoid making workers who are "serving time" look bad. These practices discourage high performance. Some people put in time until they can retire or afford to leave the organization. You may have heard them counting the years, months, hours, or even seconds until their release. Others are careful to watch the clock to ensure they don't spend a minute more than their required time on the job. Although organizations do need to monitor the time individuals spend on their work, their compensation and supervision systems can create a clock-watcher mentality rather than encouraging personal responsibility for completing work. The following worker provides a clear example of this.

CLOCK WATCHING

A woman proudly described how, by using a flex system, she was able to come in six minutes early each day, take a slightly shortened lunch hour, and take every second Friday afternoon off. She spent considerable time and energy carefully monitoring her arrivals and departures to ensure she was able to meet the exact working requirements each week to the minute.

Perhaps workers think it doesn't matter what they accomplish during the day since their compensation is based on presence at work rather than productivity. Check to see if this dysfunctional norm is in operation in the organization and see if you can offer suggestions to change it. How does the organization manage individual performance? Is seniority more important than performance? If so, people may be encouraged to focus on time rather than results. Highly structured, time-focused organizations can actually discourage their workers from focusing on productivity.

To deal with this situation, more and more organizations are implementing performance-based evaluation and compensation systems. The organization might consider changing some reward systems and how to structure the workday. It might provide flexibility in the way people take breaks so they are able to complete tasks rather than stopping before completing a task. It might encourage workers to reward themselves when they reach certain milestones rather than focusing only on the time they have spent at work. Sometimes it is important to set specific consequences when results are not achieved and to set rewards when results are achieved. Bonuses and other incentives may help increase a focus on results.

Link Results to the Big Picture

Sometimes inconsistent performance indicates a sense that the efforts are not important. If this is the case, encourage people to list or describe specific ways their actions are benefiting or hurting the organization. If they are unable to see these links, provide some concrete examples. It may be useful to focus on logical consequences of not achieving results. Show what happens across the organization when results don't show up when needed. Emphasize how and why their actions are important.

If poor results do not have immediate negative consequences, focus on a bigger picture and show people how their behaviors may harm themselves and others in the future: work may need to be redone, customers may become dissatisfied, and the organization's products or services may be seen as substandard. Customers and dollars may be lost. People may need assistance to grasp the longer-term consequences. Many are not able to see past immediate results and rewards. They look for immediate gratification and easy solutions to problems. Encourage their performance by helping them focus on benefits and results of accomplishing a task.

Sometimes people see luck or fate as controlling their success. They do well on a task because it was easy or they get a promotion because there wasn't much competition. They don't connect effort to success. In this case it is important to solidify a link between completing tasks well and accomplishing future goals.

Continually Improves Work Processes and Exceeds Standards

Top-performing workers improve their effectiveness. They achieve high standards consistently and also look for ways to streamline the way their work is accomplished. Prioritizing, planning, and organizing time and tasks have already been covered as ongoing ways to improve efficiency. A direct analysis of the work itself can also lead to increased effectiveness. This component of productivity is probably your best target for clients who are already demonstrating the ability to focus on and achieve results. People who are willing to function at this level are of great benefit to an organization.

DETECT & DESCRIBE
Continually Improves Work Processes and Exceeds Standards

· ·

Don't see high performance

Evidence of working to minimally accepted standards without improving processes:

○ Completing work the way it has always been done

○ Failing to look for opportunities to improve results

○ Setting work standards at or just below the minimum

○ Using statements such as "That's good enough to get by"

Do see high performance

Evidence of continual improvement of work processes and standards:

○ Analyzing how the work is being done

○ Finding ways to improve results

○ Setting standards that are higher than what is expected

○ Implementing changes to improve results

Improving Results

You might argue that once someone has found a way to achieve results, it is not necessary to analyze and seek ways to improve the process. Although a company can certainly benefit from having workers who consistently accomplish goals the same way time after time, the twenty-first-century work setting requires process improvement. Equipment, situations, markets, and competitiors are always changing; to remain competitive, work processes must evolve as well.

Encourage clients to evaluate their process for achieving results. Sometimes people are so busy doing their work they don't take the time to see how they could change the way they are working to become more effective. Start by looking at short-term, practical aspects of their work. Challenge clients to find ways to do things more quickly or with less effort. Ask questions to focus them on the quality, timeliness, and usefulness of what they have done. Have them make comparisons with other things they have accomplished or work they have seen others do. Here are some questions you can use to stimulate thinking in this area:

- How can I do this more efficiently?
- Am I doing my tasks in the best order?
- Do I spend time waiting for anything? Can I avoid this?
- Am I repeating tasks rather than doing them right the first time?
- Did I anticipate likely problems and plan how to handle them?
- Does everyone involved in the process understand the tasks and timelines?
- Can I streamline any tasks?
- Can I omit any tasks without producing substandard work?
- Is the equipment I need to use well maintained?

As well as looking at short-term, immediate ways to improve a process, also encourage individuals to consider long-term improvements. Challenge them to see the results they are working toward as part of a larger system. Broader improvements may require additional time and energy and may not show immediate results. Discuss the chances that the long-term benefits will be worth the effort. If a work process is used often and has significant inefficiencies, improving it is likely to prove beneficial. Here are some questions you can use to stimulate thinking in this area:

- How does this result benefit the organization?

- Are there different ways to achieve this result?

- What effects do my results have on other processes in the organization?

- Am I receiving the inputs I need from others at the best time?

- Could I receive the inputs I need from others in a better way?

- Am I using the best possible equipment to do this work?

- Am I using the best possible process to do this work?

- Is the physical space set up to maximize achieving this result?

- Are the standards of achievement ideal for how the result is being used?

- Are appropriate resources assigned to accomplishing this result?

Exceeding Performance Expectations

Top-performing workers not only meet but exceed standards. Being high-achievers, they move beyond what is expected. They tend to set personal standards that are higher than the external standards set by others. They take on additional responsibilities and are both persistent and resourceful. These are exceptional workers. If your clients are focusing on performance issues or problems, this is unlikely to be the component of productivity you will be addressing first.

What motivates people to exceed expectations? Perhaps the performance standards are easy to achieve. In this case, workers may exceed expectations just to keep busy. The standards in the workplace should not be set so low that people are not challenged to perform; over time, they may become bored or dissatisfied with their roles. Ideally, work expectations should be achievable with effort. Then, as individuals master tasks and roles, they are able to exceed the initial expectations.

Over time, expectations need to be reviewed and adjusted to reflect ongoing learning and development. Remember too that people may reach a point where increased results are not likely. This is true when they are working to their full capacity or have little time to develop and grow. Some people will be satisfied working at this level, while others may gradually lose interest if the work they are doing does not provide them with additional challenges and opportunities to develop.

When working with clients in this area, help them look for ways to set and achieve higher standards. Have them consider what they could do to improve their results. Link this back to the questions they were considering when improving their process. Now rethink the questions with the results rather than the process in mind. Focus on how the results could be better. Here are some questions you can use to stimulate thinking in this area:

- Would any changes in my results make them more useful to others?

- Are there other results that would be more beneficial to the organization?

- Am I delivering results to others at the best time?

- Am I delivering results to others in the best possible way?

- Would upgrading my skills or knowledge lead to a better result?

Another way to exceed standards is to take on additional responsibilities. In many organizations it is expected that people will increase their scope of activities and responsibilities as necessary to ensure the work is completed—but this is not always the case. Clients may not take on any additional responsibility because they are not sure if it is acceptable to increase their scope. Some organizations have highly structured roles and may actually disapprove of attempts to take the initiative and step outside a specific set of activities.

If you encourage clients to exceed expectations by increasing their areas of responsibility, don't expect all of them to work outside their defined scope independently. Focus on incremental change. Plan one small action that shows their willingness to take initiative and broaden their role.

If clients are not increasing their scope when necessary, they may be unaware of how their work links to that of others. Sometimes you need to show clients the specific interfaces of their work. When they understand the work others are doing, they are better able to ensure their work is aligned so the entire process runs smoothly. Have them suggest additional things they could do to make the work of others easier.

Risk Taking

People take risks when they try new ways of accomplishing results. This risk taking is an essential step of improvement. Although systems and processes can be improved incrementally with little risk, improving them significantly often requires trying something completely different. Not everyone is comfortable taking risks. Many find it more comfortable to stick with what is known. Maintaining the status quo has its advantages, but sometimes to be competitive, organizations must revise the way they do their work.

Not all risk taking is good. Taking appropriate risks is not the same as acting impulsively. Good risk taking is well planned or thought out. A calculated rather than a casual approach is necessary. As well, some risks can have far-reaching consequences, both negative and positive. Other risks are smaller in scope and are less likely to have dramatic results.

Some organizations accept and even encourage risk taking. Others discourage it. It will be important to assess whether a given client is more comfortable maintaining the status quo or trying new ways of doing things and how that preference fits with the style of the organization.

Low confidence and self-esteem can be barriers to efforts to experiment with new behaviors. Clients who are unsure of their self-worth will not be confident trying new things or making mistakes. To build confidence, expand on strengths and offer encouragement and positive feedback when the client takes a risk. And don't expect people to take major risks initially. Focus on incremental change. Plan one small action they can start with to test the waters.

You may need to look for specific opportunities and then coach clients to try something new. Many people are afraid to try something new and fear negative consequences. When clients do take risks and demonstrate initiative, help them evaluate their success and capture the learning. Be sure to gradually move them toward identifying possible new behaviors themselves.

QUICK TIPS
Developing Productivity

Throughout the chapter you have seen many aspects of productivity and factors that influence whether someone will demonstrate productivity effectively. Here is a quick overview of the main chapter points to help you assess what areas of intervention will be most applicable in your situation.

- Help clients prioritize and plan.
- Help clients organize time, tasks, and workspaces.
- Assess time wasters and reasons for procrastination and lack of persistence.
- Help clients focus their attention and improve concentration.
- Explore whether the client is well suited for the tasks expected on the job.
- Encourage problem solving when clients are unable to achieve results.
- Set and share clear standards and expectations.
- Ensure the organization's work systems encourage accomplishing tasks, not putting in time.
- Show clients how their results align with broader organizational goals.
- Encourage and coach continual improvement.
- Reward clients who are exceeding standards.
- Encourage developmental risk taking.

TLC FOR ALL TYPES: PRODUCTIVITY

All types can demonstrate productivity. Following are some of the special challenges of developing this competency that relate to personality preferences. As you choose an intervention, be sure to take the personality type of your client into consideration.

RESPONDERS (ESTP AND ESFP)

Responders focus on what is most interesting in the moment. The most appealing tasks are those that produce immediate results. Coworkers and opportunities to have fun and interact may divert Responders from working independently. Alternative ways to prioritize tasks may be necessary for them in some work settings. They may benefit from learning to use longer-term planning.

Using resourcefulness and adapting to situations is much more attractive to Responders than persisting on tasks. Responders may struggle to complete routine or highly repetitive tasks and will likely benefit from coaching if they are required to persist for a long time on this type of task. They are usually willing to take risks and try new behaviors, as long as they are in familiar areas. Responders are less likely to try something new if the area is outside their experience.

Logical Responders (ESTP) seek practical reasons for completing tasks. Problem solving and troubleshooting to fix immediate problems are attractive tasks for them to engage in. They will question and may circumvent tasks that require them to follow rigid rules and procedures, especially when they can see alternatives or shortcuts. Compassionate Responders (ESFP) are interested in working toward practical and concrete results to help others. They may be less interested in completing tasks when they are not able to express themselves or connect with other people. Compassionate Responders are not attracted to completing tasks that require them to follow rigid procedures, especially if the procedures are uncomfortable or unpleasant for the people involved.

EXPLORERS (ENTP AND ENFP)

Explorers tend to underestimate the time and resources needed to accomplish tasks. As a result, they may promise to accomplish more than they can practically manage. Explorers may need your help learning to complete reality testing and drill down to detail before committing to deadlines. They tend to work in bursts of inspiration and may leave things to the last minute. It is usually unreasonable to try to convert them to a steadier approach, since they are spurred to action by the time pressure. Do help them plan to leave time available near deadlines to accommodate their work style.

Explorers find it difficult to maintain interest in repetitive tasks and are more interested in starting projects than in finishing them. They can become blocked if they are not highly engaged in or excited about the task at hand. They may need to talk to others to see the purpose for the task. Explorers can be distracted by the temptation to work on ideas that are not realistic. They may need assistance developing strategies for following through. Explorers are interested in achieving long-term rather than short-term results. They are comfortable taking risks and charting unfamiliar territory. Coach them to complete a reality check before spending time moving in an impractical direction.

Logical Explorers (ENTP) seek challenge and enjoy working in environments that reward competition, drive, and performance. They see the benefit in setting and achieving standards and are interested in working toward developing competencies. They want to create their own model and set their goals independently, perhaps with consultation from a competent helper. Compassionate Explorers (ENFP) seek to express themselves in their results. Often they enjoy providing a customized and unique way of achieving a goal. Their results are often focused on helping others develop their potential. Both types of Explorers have to struggle to complete highly structured, repetitive, or detailed tasks.

EXPEDITORS (ESTJ AND ENTJ)

Expeditors focus on accomplishing tasks and are highly motivated to accomplish goals. They are decisive, logical, and action oriented in their approach. Expeditors can be impatient when they must depend on others for input. In these cases, they tend to take control and organize not just themselves but everyone involved in the task. At times they may meet resistance to this, and thus they may benefit from understanding the different work completion styles when they are directing others.

Practical Expeditors (ESTJ) have a realistic focus and work efficiently toward short-term goals. Although both types of Expeditors can be in danger of being more efficient than effective, Practical Expeditors can be more at risk for being overly short term rather than long term in focus. Insightful Expeditors (ENTJ) are more interested in achieving long-term results. They want to put vision into action. They can become impatient if they are required to slow down and explain their visions to others or consider alternative courses of action.

CONTRIBUTORS (ESFJ AND ENFJ)

Contributors value completing tasks and are most motivated to do this in a collaborative setting. They want to be sure the tasks they are completing are aligned with the needs of and useful to others. If people are unhappy with processes involved, Contributors will stop to resolve conflicts. People are more important than tasks to them. To help them persist, be sure to consider and deal with interpersonal issues as they arise. At the same time, Contributors can benefit from learning to focus a little less on interpersonal dynamics and more on the task at hand. They will take risks and try new behaviors if the people around them and the norms of the organization support the risks. They work best independently when they see their work contributing to the goals of the larger group.

Practical Contributors (ESFJ) focus on achieving immediate goals and may not always turn their attention to the long-term or more global results. They tend to use a step-by-step, planful approach. Insightful Contributors (ENFJ) focus on achieving long-term goals, especially changing processes and systems to make them more useful and validating for people. Their approach to task completion is less step-by-step and more global than that of their practical counterparts.

ASSIMILATORS (ISTJ AND ISFJ)

Assimilators are persistent and strive to complete tasks. They are reality based and practical in focus, and they concentrate on attending to and organizing details and following procedures. They may need some encouragement to focus on longer-term goals and results. Assimilators may get stuck if they are unsure of specific procedures to follow. This often happens when they are required to do unfamiliar tasks or asked to complete tasks in rapidly changing situations. Assimilators prefer to be given clear and specific expectations regarding what they are required to do and how they are to do it. Whenever possible, provide them with concrete, real-life examples to illustrate the results they are to accomplish. If this is not possible, Assimilators may need permission and assistance to define their own processes and standards for results. Assimilators are unlikely to initiate risk taking and need to be encouraged to take small, incremental risks.

Logical Assimilators (ISTJ) need to see logical reasons for completing tasks. They will analyze a situation thoroughly and then decide on the best course of action. They need time to plan and organize the work logically before they start. Once they have decided what to do and how to do it, they tend to be highly determined in their approach. Compassionate Assimilators (ISFJ) tend to want to take time to reflect before they begin to work toward achieving results. They want to ensure that things run smoothly and that there is a sense of connection and appreciation within the organization. They can be distracted from accomplishing tasks when these things are not in place.

VISIONARIES (INTJ AND INFJ)

Visionaries will persist on tasks once they have been able to conceptualize a plan for their actions from start to finish. They are less motivated to complete tasks that are not related to their vision. They dislike routine tasks or tasks that require them to deal with detailed facts. They may need some assistance with follow-up when they are required to engage in these types of tasks. Visionaries focus more on long-term goals and may not be as tuned in to the immediate needs of a situation. They may need coaching to ensure they are not spending a lot more time planning than acting.

Logical Visionaries (INTJ) need to understand the reasoning behind completing tasks. They will create a logical framework for their work and will analyze the importance of tasks in relation to this broader outlook. Compassionate Visionaries (INFJ) will assess the importance of tasks in relation to a broader framework as well, but will create their framework based on people's needs, ideas, and values.

ANALYZERS (ISTP AND INTP)

Analyzers are resourceful and tenacious when analyzing and solving problems. However, when they have figured out a cause for the problem they may lose interest. Analyzers may be motivated to move on to finding the cause for another problem rather than persisting on the tasks required to implement changes to fix the first problem. They seek challenge and tend to logically analyze what tasks to take on. Analyzers are comfortable taking risks and can sometimes be seen by others as too quick to step outside of and circumvent the rules. They may benefit from coaching to help them recognize the effects their unconventional behaviors can have on others.

Practical Analyzers (ISTP) want to create efficient, immediate solutions. They look for the easiest way to get the work done and are adaptable in the moment. Practical Analyzers are more short-term than long-term in focus. Insightful Analyzers (INTP) are interested in analyzing and finding ways to improve systems. They are more long-term than short-term in focus. They prefer to conceptualize and create long-term solutions to complex problems. Following through and implementing their ideas can be less attractive to them.

ENHANCERS (ISFP AND INFP)

Enhancers want to accomplish results that will make things easier for the people who are important to them. They prefer to complete their tasks in a way that meshes with their personal values and will resist completing any task that is not aligned with what is important to them. Enhancers are more likely to start than complete tasks and may need encouragement to follow through on tasks that are not personally meaningful or helpful to people. They are less driven to achieve results in settings where others do not appreciate their efforts or results.

Practical Enhancers (ISFP) seek to achieve results that will have an immediate positive effect on others. They are more short-term than long-term in focus. Insightful Enhancers (INFP) want to achieve results that will benefit others in the longer term. Both types of Enhancers find their ability to focus on their work negatively affected by interpersonal conflict. They also struggle to achieve results in settings where others are impersonal, critical, or highly logical rather than personal in their approach.

Chapter 7
Proactivity

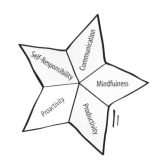

Our world is changing rapidly. If we do not pay attention, we may miss valuable opportunities. Proactive individuals use a heads-up approach to work, observing patterns and trends and anticipating change. They adjust quickly when they need to do so and are able to position themselves for success.

Proactive people come across as curious, creative, flexible, future oriented, imaginative, innovative, versatile, and insightful. They explore new options and take risks. In contrast, those who do not demonstrate proactivity seem inflexible, rigid, or overly conservative.

The proactivity competency consists of two distinct groups of behaviors. I summarize the first group as "Anticipates and Adjusts to Change"; it includes behaviors required to see patterns and trends and adjust to accommodate change. This group also covers how to help people adjust their behavior and position themselves to cope with unexpected changes. The second group, "Fulfills Career and Life Goals," explores the ability to capitalize on opportunities. Note the list of the components of proactivity in the order in which they will be covered in the chapter.

COMPONENTS OF PROACTIVITY

Anticipates and Adjusts to Change

- Looks for patterns and trends from diverse perspectives
- Adjusts behavior to accommodate change

Fulfills Career and Life Goals

- Sets career and life goals
- Uses self-development and self-promotion to capitalize on opportunities

Proactivity

The pairs of statements that follow represent the endpoints of a continuum of possible performance in proactivity. Place an X on each line at the location that best describes the current level of performance.

Anticipates and Adjusts to Change

Focuses on current reality from a single perspective	⟵——————————⟶	Looks for patterns and trends from diverse perspectives
Responds to new situations in old ways	⟵——————————⟶	Adjusts behavior to accommodate change

Fulfills Career and Life Goals

Is unsure of career and life direction	⟵——————————⟶	Sets career and life goals
Does not seek self-development or self-promotion	⟵——————————⟶	Uses self-development and self-promotion to capitalize on opportunities

Take time to reflect on proactivity. Use the space below to write down any specific information or insights you, your client, or others may have regarding your client's ability to be proactive in the course of daily work activities.

_____

_____

_____

ANTICIPATES AND ADJUSTS TO CHANGE

Before you can help others develop proactivity, they will need a good reason to look ahead. Your clients may argue that—unlike the more obvious competencies such as communication and productivity—proactivity is not a necessary competency for carrying out day-to-day work activities. However, the world is changing so fast that those who maintain the status quo end up falling behind. Even work that has remained the same over long periods is now changing. Workers need to look ahead to get ahead.

You'll find it useful to present concrete reasons for proactivity that relate to each client's specific situation. Consider the client's personality type and the kind of work the client is engaged in to focus on the reasons that will prove most important to them. Here is a list of general reasons that may help explain the need for proactivity:

- Increase awareness of the changes that will affect clients and their work

- Facilitate clients' ability to move in the direction they want

- Avoid surprises or being caught unprepared

- Focus energy on enhancing performance in the right direction

- Have something to look forward to

- Get into position for upcoming opportunities

- Develop new processes and methods

- Accomplish tasks in innovative ways

- Create new results to benefit the business in the short and long term

Looks for Patterns and Trends from Diverse Perspectives

People cannot be proactive unless they anticipate changes in the world around them. To accomplish this, they must actively seek information and then look for patterns and trends. Researching advances and leading-edge practices and processes within their scope of endeavor will help them stay current in their field. To use new information effectively, individuals must examine and evaluate what they hear, see, experience, and think about from a variety of perspectives. By processing the information through

DETECT & DESCRIBE
Looks for Patterns and Trends from Diverse Perspectives

Don't see high performance	Do see high performance
Evidence of focusing on current reality from a single perspective:	Evidence of looking for patterns and trends from diverse perspectives:
○ Arguing from a single viewpoint	○ Summarizing or analyzing situations using more than one viewpoint
○ Seeing only a narrow range of effects and consequences	○ Acknowledging diverse effects and consequences
○ Using outdated materials	○ Seeking out new information related to the field of endeavor
○ Being unaware of new developments in the field of endeavor	○ Exploring or discussing cutting-edge developments or new ideas
○ Avoiding conferences or trade shows	○ Attending relevant conferences or trade shows
○ Ignoring current publications	○ Reading current publications
○ Failing to link news and current events to business implications	○ Tracking news and current events and discussing business implications

broad perspectives, they can see the maximum number of possible effects, consequences, and opportunities.

Open-Mindedness

Collecting all the information in the world is useless for someone who is unable to switch perspectives. It is easy for clients to dismiss information that doesn't fit with their worldview and accept information that does. However, this won't help them adapt to change. To increase open-mindedness, your challenge is to find ways to help your clients become more aware of, open to, and accepting of alternative perspectives.

As with proactivity in general, you will need to convince your clients that open-mindedness has advantages. To convince clients of the need to change perspectives, use practical examples that demonstrate difficulties that emerged when someone became stuck in an accepted or comfortable way of doing something. Also find examples to show how viewing the situation from a different perspective provided essential new information.

When you are helping a client think about something in a new way, list points that demonstrate the new or different way of thinking. For example, the new work relationship can be compared with the traditional work relationship by describing specific changes, such as an increase in contract workers and a decrease in permanent positions. When clients can see concrete examples of change, they may more readily understand the overall framework of the alternative perspective.

Encourage your clients to imagine how other people act in the situations in which they find themselves. As well as helping them become more open-minded, this exercise will increase their ability to respond with empathy to others.

Sometimes people are strongly invested in their way of thinking about things and resist exploring alternative perspectives. In these cases you would be wise to listen carefully to understand how and why they are wedded to their viewpoint. The reasons may be practical, idealistic, logical, or value based. Acknowledge clients' perspectives before trying to add to them. Assure them you are not dismissing their way of seeing the situation but adding other perspectives to provide a broader view. Whenever possible, link these additional perspectives to the clients' existing perspectives using the clients' own line of thought. For example, if their way of seeing the situation is practical, show how an alternative perspective also has some practical components.

To be open to diverse perspectives, people must be able to tolerate ambiguity. There is rarely one right answer when you view something from many perspectives. Some people prefer clear-cut answers and are uncomfortable switching their way of thinking. They tend to be committed to one viewpoint and judge other perspectives through that lens. Help such clients become less overwhelmed in situations with multiple interpretations and many possible courses of action. They may want to choose one course of action and move forward at once. Have them explore more than one possibility. They may see this as a waste of time, but assure them this type of thinking will enhance their ability to deal with change. This exploration of multiple possibilities will also help clients think outside the box.

A QUESTION OF BALANCE
Firm-Mindedness and Open-Mindedness

A firm-minded, unyielding point of view is often seen as a positive characteristic. When people are firm-minded, they are not likely to bend or be swayed by other opinions. They will stay the course and persist until the task is completed. This is indeed a helpful characteristic in some situations, but firm-mindedness can have its disadvantages as well. Sometimes it is not wise to stay a chosen course, especially when additional information or changing situations make it wiser to move in another direction.

In these cases open-mindedness has an advantage. By being open to changing a position on a topic or a way of doing something, people are better able to adapt to changing circumstances. When old ways of responding are not appropriate, an open-minded person is able to adapt quickly.

Outside-the-Box Thinking

When looking at a situation, clients can be most proactive when they see possibilities such as events that might happen, alternative solutions to problems, or new ideas about contributing factors. They can find original ways of thinking about a situation, which opens the door to new possibilities. Perhaps a client can generate a more effective way to accomplish a task or use a new idea in a proactive way to improve an existing process.

Your clients may also adapt existing things and ideas to create a new result. For example, they may use resources the organization already has to create an alternative and practical solution to an old problem. Broad ways of seeing situations allow clients to be more proactive in their approach. Encourage creative activities such as free association, brainstorming, and other forms of outside-the-box thinking. Here is an example of how one worker in the finance industry thinks outside the box to meet customer needs.

PERFORMANCE PREFERENCES
Thinking Outside the Box: Sensing and Intuition

. . . .

Sensing (S) types and Intuitive (N) types are both able to think outside the box, but they tend to differ in the way they use innovative thinking.

Individuals with a preference for Sensing can be very adaptable in the moment and use their innovation in a practical way. For example, a Sensing type thinking outside the box may be able to use materials at hand to jury-rig a gas line so a stalled car can get to the garage.

Individuals with a preference for Intuition tend to focus on coming up with new and different ideas. Although they may work with the materials at hand, they are likelier to focus on the ideas themselves rather than on practical applications. An Intuitive type is likelier to invent a totally new and different way of doing something.

MAKING THE IMPOSSIBLE HAPPEN

An ENFP describes how he is setting a company sales record. Unlike his coworkers, he spends considerable time and energy finding creative solutions to his customers' needs and problems. He makes impossible things happen by looking at the possibilities. He does this by listening to the clients and then finding alternative ways to help them meet their needs. His workplace was, at first, concerned about his approach because he didn't always follow conventional procedures. However, he was able to show his company how his adaptive approach consistently achieves results. He was even able to negotiate flexible work hours, which really fit his personality type.

Futurist Thinking

Work with each client to think like a futurist, someone who predicts the future. Futurists observe present and past events and technology and then use the information to make an educated guess about the future. Clients need to focus on the internal and external forces that affect their current work and their company as a whole. Most people are able to make some predictions about what will happen next in their work environment, foreseeing different futures depending on the information they have as well as on their biases and interpretation of the information. Of course, having a large volume of information from a variety of sources will help clients make more accurate predictions. Using critical and creative thinking skills will also be helpful.

Different futurists use a variety of sources of trend information, so they often predict different things. Some make predictions using population data, which tell them how many people live in an area, their age, and other characteristics such as income and marital status. Others use economic data or market trends, or they search printed materials for references to certain topics. Whatever data they use, the concept is the same: Learn about what is going on and, from those data, make predictions. Here are some common sources of information futurists find helpful:

- Census data or demographics
- Historical data
- Conferences and trade shows
- Professional publications
- The Internet
- Interviews

- Market data
- Newspapers
- Magazines
- Personal experiences
- Experiences or ideas of others
- Surveys

Identify which of these sources of information are readily available to and most useful for your clients. Consider which sources tend to have specific information relevant to the work your clients do. Once the information is gathered, clients will need to process it by analyzing, evaluating, forming opinions, identifying themes or relationships, and then making predictions.

Today we face a glut of information and a shortage of knowledge. Information by itself is not always helpful. We need to use our thinking skills (critical and creative) to form a view of the future that helps us set goals, plan, and solve problems. In much the same way, futurists' effectiveness depends on their ability to interpret data.

Following are some global changes that have been predicted by various well-known futurists and reported in a variety of sources. Help your clients practice mindfulness by asking questions about each trend. For example, is this trend affecting the client's work? How? Are there new opportunities that might result from this trend? Will this trend have any negative effects on the work your client is doing? What might the client be able to do to minimize any negative effects? Are there new skills the client needs to learn to benefit from this trend?

- Emergence of a global marketplace—a rapid global sharing of products, capital, technology, and ideas. Rapid growth of communication technology.

- Establishment of the Information Age and spread of knowledge work, where output is information rather than goods. Rapid turnover of new information and technologies.

- Technological boom in advanced manufactured materials in areas such as expert computer systems, artificial intelligence, robotics, nanotechnology, and biotechnology.

- Niche marketing and increased customization. Increased power and influence of specialized consumer groups such as youth and women.

- Aging of baby boomers and growing numbers of elderly as life expectancies increase.

- Increased numbers of lifestyle options. Increased pace of living and desire for speedy services among some groups, as well as increasing numbers in other groups looking to slow down, simplify, and find meaning.

- Increased numbers of small businesses and self-employed workers. More contract and part-time work options.

Specific trends affecting your clients will occur at the local, regional, national, and global levels. Help them look for new ideas, new points of view, and scientific and technological breakthroughs. Be careful not to overwhelm them with details, but help your clients find ways to make watching the future a regular part of their daily or weekly activities. Here are some tips for increasing awareness of current trends and future possibilities:

Read, listen, or watch

- Review a variety of media sources.
- Review local, regional, and global news.
- Read nonfiction best-sellers.
- Subscribe to newsletters and association publications.
- Pay attention to trend reports.
- Read from a variety of disciplines.

Relate

- Take note of the views of a variety of other people.
- Form a strong personal network.
- Join or monitor associations.
- Work with various clubs or groups.
- Attend conventions and trade shows
- Talk to potential customers or employers.
- Visit schools and businesses and ask for information.

Reflect

- Observe your reaction to information.
- Note your assumptions and biases.
- Be aware of your needs, likes, and dislikes.
- Challenge yourself to take in new ideas.
- Use critical thinking to evaluate information.
- Use creative thinking to imagine new possibilities.

Respond

- Volunteer in new areas.
- Experiment.
- Try different things.
- Go different places.

Future watching will help you guide your clients toward developing a vision of their future. This vision will be unique for each client. It will serve as a guide in decision making regarding work, learning, and career development. Some clients, especially those who prefer structure and practicality, will find it difficult to move into futurist thinking. In the following example, an INTJ manager explains how some people are required to change their way of thinking.

SHIFTING GEARS

People who like and excel at structured and detailed tasks often reach a stage where they get promoted and have to deal with more open-ended, fluid, future-oriented, visioning types of issues. They like the clarity of practical, realistic work and are put off by less-structured conceptual work. A key individual in our department is struggling with this right now. She is great at executing using existing processes and standards, but she is miserable at creating or implementing changes. Her boss is pushing her in that direction, but she doesn't really understand what is being asked of her.

It is important to help people who love predictable structure move toward change gradually. This is when it is especially important to link future thinking with concrete evidence and processes that have worked well in the past. A gradual extrapolation into the future will be much more comfortable for a structured, practical type than an abrupt conceptual leap of faith.

Adjusts Behavior to Accommodate Change

People who have become aware of potential changes can adjust their behavior accordingly. Proactive people will take action to improve their current situation and to position themselves for anticipated changes. Perhaps the most difficult part of adjusting to change is being able to respond quickly to the unexpected. This section will consider how to accommodate changes, both anticipated and unexpected. By teaching your clients how to anticipate change and see things from multiple perspectives, you can help them minimize the amount of unexpected change. Even so, everyone will occasionally get caught off guard by change and will need strategies to manage such situations.

PERFORMANCE PREFERENCES
Thinking Like a Futurist: Sensing and Intuition

Sensing (S) types are oriented toward realities and practicality. Because of this orientation, it can be somewhat difficult for them to focus their attention on future possibilities. They may need your assistance to see reasons and develop a plan for future watching.

Intuitive types (N) tend to find it easier to turn their focus to the future. Making links and seeing possibilities comes naturally to them. When working with clients in this group, acknowledge and support this preference. Ensure they have data to support their views.

DETECT & DESCRIBE
Adjusts Behavior to Accommodate Change

Don't see high performance	Do see high performance
Evidence of responding to new situations in old ways:	Evidence of adjusting behavior to accommodate change:
○ Being unable to describe what is needed in times of change	○ Describing what is needed in times of change
○ Staying frozen in denial, anger, or other negative emotions	○ Acknowledging losses and reactions to them
○ Refusing to discuss or deal with work and personal effects of change	○ Taking action to help deal with work and personal effects of change
○ Continuing behavior as if the change has not occurred	○ Taking action after a change that will make it easier to move forward

Unexpected Change

You may have a number of roles when you are helping someone adjust to unexpected change. If you are working within an organization, you may be the person responsible for announcing changes. At times you may be able to consult with or involve people in the change process. At other times decisions will have been made and you will simply be the messenger. If you are working outside an organization, you may be dealing with clients who have experienced change already and are trying to cope. Change is constant and ongoing and you will be helping people who are experiencing a number of changes that affect them in a variety of ways. Whatever your role in the change process, you can do some basic things to assist individuals who are coping with change.

People require different types and amounts of information and support when they are trying to cope with unexpected change. Many will seek more information or opportunities to participate in or discuss the change. Obviously, every situation is different and you will not always be able to provide everything that might be useful to everyone you are working with. For example, if a change is finalized and already imposed, you will not be able to offer a chance to be involved in conceptualizing and deciding. You may still be able to provide opportunities to discuss and implement the change depending on the circumstance. As you read through the following list, consider what points your clients might benefit from and how (or if) you might be able to provide each one. If you have influence within an organization, you may be able to help plan how changes will be made and implemented in a way that takes the needs of the various participants into consideration. If so, use this list of the things people commonly seek in times of change as a starting point for a change plan:

- Facts and details about the changes
- A chance to discuss what is happening
- An opportunity to be involved in the conceptualization
- A chance to participate in the decision making
- A chance to be involved in the implementation
- A specific role or action to carry out
- Time to reflect on the changes
- Time to get used to the changes
- A timeline for the changes
- A structured plan to implement the changes

- A vision of the changes

- Access to support

- Logical reasons for the changes

- Opportunities to preserve what is already working

- An emphasis on how the changes affect people

- The future implications and possibilities associated with the changes

- Reassurance and emotional support during the changes

- Options and flexibility during the changes

People can react to unexpected change in a number of ways. Unexpected change can be devastating, especially to those who are highly invested in the way things were. However, some people find that when a significant change has occurred, they are relieved or actually pleased that the situation is changed. You can try to anticipate how each client will react to the change by assessing how invested the individual is in the old ways of doing things. Observation and listening are the best tools to use initially when helping someone through the change process. Be prepared to answer questions and strive to understand how your client perceives the change.

All changes, good or bad, entail losses. To thrive in times of change, people need to recognize their losses. Accepting and dealing with the thoughts and emotions associated with loss will help them move ahead. It is useful to share information about the process everyone goes through when experiencing loss so that clients can recognize and deal with their reactions to change. These reactions can include a variety of emotions, thoughts, and defense mechanisms—shock, denial, worry, self-doubt, anger, frustration, sadness, and betrayal. They may also include acceptance, excitement, and relief. When helping clients deal with change, provide opportunities for them to recognize and acknowledge what they are losing and what they will miss.

Once clients have dealt with their losses, they will need an opportunity to reflect on how they will position themselves after the change. They have lost the old ways, but they may not yet know what the new ways will look like. William Bridges refers to this as the *neutral zone.* The neutral zone can be an uncomfortable place to be. However, it is also the place

PERFORMANCE PREFERENCES
Unexpected Change: Extraversion and Introversion

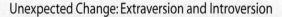

People with a preference for Extraversion (E) often seek interactions when they need to deal with unexpected change. They want to discuss the change. Depending on their other preferences, they may want to talk about various aspects of the change such as why, how, what, when, and who will be involved in it or affected by it. These individuals want to take action and are most comfortable when they have a part to play so they can do something concrete to respond to the change.

People with a preference for Introversion (I) seek a chance to reflect on the change internally. They also want information, but they are focused on taking in and thinking about the information rather than immediately responding to it. If the change is implemented before they have had a chance to think about it and adjust to it, they will be very uncomfortable.

Consider both these orientations and design your interventions accordingly when you are helping clients deal with change.

where the greatest personal growth can occur. Help your clients manage their time in the neutral zone by having them think about the following questions:

- What information and support will help manage this change?

- What are the sources of information and support for managing this change?

- What can be done to further assess the situation?

- How could the change make life better?

- What opportunities for growth can come out of this change?

Thinking the change through by asking mindful questions can improve your clients' chances of making adaptive adjustments. This time to reflect on and speculate about what comes next will prepare them to move forward. As people adjust to change, they may need to take risks, try new things, or start again. They may need encouragement, coaching, or teaching as they explore and implement ways to adjust. This stage also encompasses a variety of associated feelings and thoughts, including optimism, uncertainty, satisfaction, anxiety, happiness, fear, and excitement.

Acting, Not Reacting: True Proactivity

We cannot always control events and circumstances or stop the reorganization and upheaval going on around us. What we can do is be aware of and anticipate change and choose to act in ways that increase our chances of success in the future. So far, I've discussed helping clients anticipate changes and cope more easily with unexpected changes. To be truly proactive, a person needs to act on change *before* it happens so as to get into position to take advantage of opportunities that will arise from change. Here are some questions designed to help clients take a more proactive approach:

- What change is likely to occur soon?

- How will this change affect me?

- Am I prepared?

- What can I do to be more prepared?

The next section will guide you through a process to maximize your clients' ability to use a proactive approach to change. Review the risk-taking tips from the productivity chapter to guide you when coaching your clients to adjust behaviors and try new ways of doing things.

FULFILLS CAREER AND LIFE GOALS

To capitalize on opportunities, people must use their future-watching skills to anticipate upcoming change. As well, they must be able to link future trends to personal opportunities. This can be accomplished by setting career and life goals, taking risks to facilitate personal and professional development, and engaging in self-promotion.

Sets Career and Life Goals

Anticipating change is helpful only when you can act to take advantage of it. To capitalize on change, your clients need to align upcoming organizational changes with their personal career and life roles.

DETECT & DESCRIBE
Sets Career and Life Goals

. . . .

Don't see high performance

Evidence of a lack of career and life goals:

○ Being unable to articulate matters of personal importance

○ Being unable to describe work interests, skills, values, constraints, and preferences

○ Being unable to describe a desired lifestyle

○ Being unable to describe where, when, or what would be desirable to do

Do see high performance

Evidence of setting career and life goals:

○ Articulating personal identity and matters of personal importance

○ Describing work interests, skills, values, constraints, and preferences

○ Describing lifestyle interests and preferences

○ Describing a work or life goal that matches the self-assessment

Career and life goals vary considerably in scope and content from one person to another, as do the processes people use to set career and life goals. By exploring these differences, you will be better able to identify your clients' approaches and help them articulate and evaluate their goals. There is no one right way to set a goal and no one right type of career or life goal to set.

It may help to coach clients to think about this topic by linking goal setting to decision making. When clients are in the process of making a decision or choosing a course of action, have them think about what criteria or values are important to consider. This focus may help them see the practical side of setting career and life goals.

Once clients have their goals in mind, they are ready to position themselves for success. The following sections describe some differences in the ways people set goals and the types of goals they tend to set.

Work, Career, and Life Goals

Some clients see clear distinctions between their personal and professional life. These clients tend to compartmentalize work and play and have separate goals for each part of their life. Some may see work as a means to make money that will allow them to do other, personally meaningful, things. In cases such as these, work satisfaction may be more related to factors such as pay, hours, and benefits than to interest in the work tasks or making an important personal contribution through the type of work being done. The idea of career development is not a strong motivator for people with this outlook. Here is an example of a man who sees his work mainly as a source of income.

I HAVE A JOB, NOT A CAREER

An ISTP was being encouraged by his boss to seek challenge and personal development in his work. The boss was trying to help the ISTP identify growth opportunities available to him. The ISTP was frustrated by his boss's approach and commented that he already had a life outside work and that he just wanted to do his job and then go home to his life. He said he was interested in learning and would be glad to take any courses or accept experiences that would help him do his job better. However, he wasn't really excited about or focused on setting career goals other than doing his job well, getting paid, and then going home.

Other clients will seek personal expression in their work and will want to make a contribution to the world by engaging in work they find personally meaningful. They will seek opportunities to express themselves and will be deeply committed to developing personally and professionally as part of their self-expression.

Not only do people vary in how personally meaningful they want work to be, they also vary in how much separation they want between their work and personal life. Some are comfortable integrating the two, while others want them to be as far apart as possible. For example, a ranger working in a remote forest fire tower may stay there for several weeks or months at a time. That kind of work becomes a lifestyle. Many kinds of work have similar effects on personal life because of the type of activities, schedule, time commitment, location, or other demands they impose.

When working with your clients, help them assess what their desired lifestyle looks like. This will probably affect several important career parameters such as salary, hours, and location. Also explore with them whether they see work as a place for self-expression or as a means to an end. Career counselors and others in the helping professions tend to believe work should be personal, meaningful, and self-expressive. This doesn't mean that everyone sees work this way. Explore your biases. Someone you are helping may see work as a means to an end and that is OK. They will still benefit from setting some specific career goals. When helping them set goals, recognize that they may want to have a more practical and utilitarian focus than those who are seeking personal satisfaction. Take this into account—you will not have much success helping a practical, pragmatic, logical individual set goals if you approach the topic by focusing only on meaningful self-expression.

Professional, Personal, and Humanistic Goals

People also vary in how much they consider others when setting their goals. For example, family needs are sometimes a consideration, even a major influence, on work factors such as where and when work fits into the family schedule. Families also have an influence on financial needs. But family is not always a factor; some people have no one else to support, and others are in a position where they need not take responsibility for family demands.

This aspect of life and career goal setting can change dramatically. For example, the birth of a child, divorce from a spouse who was fulfilling a child care role, or recognition of the needs of aging parents may suddenly place demands on someone who had no family concerns up to that point. When working with your clients, you can explore whether personal situations such as these are affecting their life and/or work goals directly or indirectly. You may have some clients who are not interested in exploring this, preferring to keep their personal and professional life separate. In this case, acknowledge and respect their preference. It can still be useful to have them share any considerations they want to incorporate in their work world without delving into their personal situation.

In addition to family commitments, people often have community, religious, or humanistic goals that influence what they do at work. These goals may be clear and simple, such as not wanting to work on a certain day of the week; or they may be complex, such as seeking opportunities to engage in work that has a positive effect on the global environment. These broader personal and humanistic goals may also affect day-to-day choices. Explore these areas if your client is receptive. Discuss how these types of goals affect the type of work the client does.

Short-Term and Long-Term Goals

Another significant difference in how people set goals centers whether the goals are focused on a short-term or long-term time frame. Each focus has advantages and disadvantages and is associated with characteristic ways of thinking about situations. People who prefer short-term goals tend to be practical and specific. They see goals as most useful when they can be linked to immediate actions and results. Once one short-term goal is achieved, another goal can be set and reached. This provides a way to actualize goals in the here and now. Long-term goals, in contrast, are broader and less practical and immediate. Achieving them requires effort over a period of time. Long-term goals can set a direction but often do not directly imply or link to a specific immediate action.

When working with clients, you will probably find it easy to see whether they prefer short-term or long-term goals. Point out the advantages of their preference and use goals of their preferred type as a starting point. You may want to have the short-term goal setters expand their time frame. Start from where they are setting goals now and gradually help them see a bit farther into the future. Show them practical reasons and use real data and experiences to extrapolate into the future. If you are working with long-term goal setters, help them consider how they can make faster progress by listing steps and actions that need to be carried out to actualize the goal. This will help them see how realistic their goal is as well as how to approach it most effectively. Start in the future, with the long-term goal, and work your way back to the present.

PERFORMANCE PREFERENCES
Short-Term and Long-Term Goals: Sensing and Intuition

People with a preference for Sensing (S) tend to prefer to set immediate goals that they can obtain in the short term. Their goals are usually practical and useful.

People with a preference for Intuition (N) tend to prefer to set long-term, global goals. Setting these goals helps them set direction and choose criteria for decision making rather than accomplish a practical and useful immediate result.

Imaginative and Realistic Goals

Some clients can be very imaginative when setting goals. Their goals are grandiose and ambitious. Imaginative goals can be an inspirational starting point for a successful change. They can also be unrealistic and overly idealistic. Other clients will be careful to consider realities when setting goals. Like short-term goals, realistic goals are linked to practical aspects of the person's situation. These goals tend to be readily achievable. However, realistic goals may lack the inspiration that will provide the client with an opportunity to make a broader and perhaps more meaningful change. Depending on their preferences, you may need to help your clients imagine possibilities or consider realities.

Planned and Emergent Processes

Individuals also vary in how planned out their path toward their goals tends to be. Individuals who like to decide on next steps just in time use emergent processes. In other words, they wait to see what happens before they decide their next step. Once they collect the data from the first step, then they decide on what the best second step will be. People who work in this manner tend to set flexible goals. If you do not have a spontaneous work style yourself, you are likely to see this work style as disorganized. Other individuals tend to plan their actions ahead of time to work effectively toward their goal, often in a step-by-step manner. They will have a definite target and will work steadily toward it.

Each of these processes has advantages and disadvantages for setting and working toward goals. You will need to understand and accommodate your clients' preferred process. A client who has an emergent style may be resistant to a structured, planful goal-setting process and may be more interested in setting flexible goals that open rather than limit the options for the next steps. Once you have accepted this open-ended style you can also demonstrate ways to increase effectiveness by adding in some structure and benchmarks for progress toward goals. Work with clients who prefer more structure and planning to map a path forward toward goals. While acknowledging the usefulness of planning and benchmarking, you can also encourage them to allow some flexibility to deal with unexpected changes, surprises, and opportunities.

Goal Definition

All the variations in the ways people set goals and the types of goals they set reinforce how important it is to customize your interventions to accommodate a client's style. Keeping this in mind, here are some ideas to help you facilitate your clients' assessment of career and life goals. (Remember to acknowledge and appreciate the types of individual differences discussed in Chapter 1.)

Career goals can involve specific roles or general directions or areas of work your client is interested in moving toward. Different clients will express their career goals with differing degrees of specificity and differing time frames. Life goals, specific or general ideas relating to what the client would like life to include, may involve even greater diversity. Work within your clients' comfort zone initially to define and describe their goals—for the long or short term, planned or emergent, specific or general.

Help clients work toward making their goals as operational as possible. For example, if someone wants a healthier lifestyle, help them define what a healthy lifestyle looks like to them. They may define lifestyle by where they live, what they eat, how much exercise they get, their stress level, or a combination of these and other factors. Once they target what a healthy lifestyle looks like they can look for opportunities to improve that aspect of life. When helping people set career goals, consider what types of work will suit their work style, interests, values, lifestyle, and constraints. Consider using one of the published self-assessment tools designed to facilitate the process of setting career goals. Here are some questions that will help your clients think about and set their goals:

- What are you good at?

- What do you enjoy doing?

- What is really hard for you to do?

- What do you dislike doing?

- What skills do you enjoy using and developing?

- What activities do you enjoy that can generate income?

- What do you value?

- When, where, and how much do you want to work?

- Where do you want to live?

- What do you want to do in the time you spend outside of work?
- Do you have physical or psychological limitations to what you can (or want to) do?
- How much money do you need to make?
- How much money do you want to make?
- Do you want to make lifestyle changes?
- Will lifestyle changes affect the amount of money you need or want?
- What life roles are important to you?
- What needs do significant people in your life have that will influence your goal setting?
- Do you want to learn something new? How do you like to learn?

Once clients have a goal for what they want to do and where they want to be, you can help them start to position themselves for success.

Uses Self-Development and Self-Promotion to Capitalize on Opportunities

Having career and life goals is not enough on its own; people still need to take action to achieve their goals. It takes a combination of self-development and self-promotion to capitalize on opportunities.

Self-Development

Self-development is most effective when it is an ongoing process aligned with personal goals as well as with the trends and changes happening in the outside world. For example, someone whose goal is to excel at operating a particular type of equipment must be aware of potential changes in the industries that use the equipment. If a highly specialized piece of equipment is used in only one industry, the client will want to explore the stability and locations of work in that industry, and to review sources of information that will reveal the financial, political, and environmental factors influencing how much work is likely to be available. As well as researching the industry, the client will also want to explore the equipment itself. What specialized skills are needed to operate it? How does one get training and how much does the training cost? Is the training transferable from that specific piece of equipment to other types of

DETECT & DESCRIBE
Uses Self-Development and Self-Promotion to Capitalize on Opportunities

Don't see high performance	Do see high performance
Evidence that self-development is not targeted or promoted:	Evidence of developing and promoting to capitalize on opportunities:
○ Being unmotivated to learn and develop in new areas	○ Developing skills and knowledge in new areas
○ Being unwilling to try new behaviors	○ Engaging in new experiences to promote learning
○ Being unprepared to adjust to changes that affect the chosen field of endeavor	○ Aligning learning to changes in the chosen field of endeavor
○ Missing out on opportunities	○ Developing skills likely to be useful for future opportunities
○ Neglecting self-promotion or using inappropriate self-promotion	○ Using tactful and appropriate self-promotion

equipment? Does the industry have up-to-date equipment? If not, will companies be replacing the equipment soon, and if so will different training be required? Does it help to get work if the operator can carry out basic mechanical maintenance? What is the required training for that and how much does it cost? Does the equipment have on-board computer systems, and if so what expertise do you need to use the computer systems? These are some of the questions the client will need to answer before seeking work or taking training on a specific piece of equipment. It may also be useful to find out if less-specialized types of equipment might provide more work options and greater flexibility. The information gathered will need to be aligned with the client's work and life goals. For example, someone who is motivated to spend more time at home with family will want to research which type of equipment operating requires the least travel.

Your challenge is to help your clients ask the right questions and gather the right information so they can see the realities and trends that relate to their work and life goals. Using sufficient information and mindfulness, clients can anticipate and prepare for changes by developing skills and knowledge. For example, say a client is highly motivated to remain in an organization that is merging with another company or reorganizing its processes. In this example, if the company is introducing a new expert computer system, the client may get into position for the change by being the first to volunteer for training on the system. The training may provide a competitive edge when the change occurs. Even if that sort of attempt to stay in the organization doesn't work out, enterprising clients will have an additional skill to enhance their marketability.

There are always lots of things to learn. Your clients will benefit from using their mindfulness and futuristic thinking to carefully consider what learning and development opportunities will provide them with the best chance to meet their goals. Help them see the perspectives of employers, contract managers, buyers, and other people who have the authority to hire others to do work for them. Who will those people be looking for? What skills, knowledge, and experience will the best candidates for work have? What services and products can your clients supply that will be of benefit to those hiring? How can your clients prove they are best suited for the work they want to do?

When helping clients take advantage of development opportunities, consider how they prefer to develop as well as what they need and want to develop. There are a number of ways to gain skills and knowledge. Some of these are relatively formal and easily recognizable by organizations—things like courses, workshops, structured mentorship, and on-the-job training programs. Other ways of learning can be relatively informal but equally effective—reading, observing, self-teaching through exploration and practice, viewing videos, informal mentorship, Internet research. With clients who prefer informal ways of learning, ensure they are able to demonstrate their learning so others will recognize their expertise. This can be part of their self-promotion process.

Self-Promotion

Your first challenge when helping clients with self-promotion is to explore their attitudes toward this topic. Many people do not know how to promote themselves and are uncomfortable with the idea. Others will find self-promotion difficult. They may have negative stereotypes and envision

A QUESTION OF BALANCE
Generalist or Specialist

Being a generalist has both advantages and disadvantages. Generalists tend to know a little about a lot of things. They can engage in several broad types of work and move between different work opportunities fairly easily. However, they may not have the depth of knowledge, skills, or experience to obtain work that requires a highly developed specific skill set. Generalists may not always be as highly paid as specialists.

Being a specialist also has advantages and disadvantages. Specialists tend to have extensive knowledge on a few topics. They are usually limited to a smaller number of work options. They can be highly paid for the work they do, especially if few people have their specialized knowledge, skills, and experience. It may be somewhat hard for an out-of-work specialist to find a new place. This can be a problem if the work they are specialized in is not in high demand.

Some clients will naturally be drawn to generalize, others to specialize. As you work with your clients, discuss this topic. Encourage generalists to develop a reasonable depth of skills in several complementary areas. This will open more possibilities and can increase the amount of remuneration they receive. Encourage specialists to look for some diversity of applications in what they do, so they can avoid narrowing their work options too much. Specialists need to be especially tuned in to futurist thinking, since changes in their field can greatly affect their work options. Keeping up on cutting-edge changes in their area of specialty is crucial to their ongoing success.

self-promotion as bragging, arrogant, and self-centered. In that case, provide examples to illustrate how self-promotion can be carried out in a tactful manner. Show your clients the value of promoting themselves.

Self-promotion provides an opportunity for people to highlight and capitalize on their strengths. To find an optimal position within an organization, clients need to be able to promote their unique set of abilities. This self-promotion ensures they will be considered for opportunities and advancements that suit their talents. Once someone has identified their strengths, help them find ways to showcase their abilities within the organization.

A QUESTION OF BALANCE
Self-Promotion and Humility

People need to be able to promote themselves within the organization to maximize their options and opportunities. When people do not engage in self-promotion, others within the organization will not recognize their strengths.

However, when people are too quick to promote themselves or when they overplay their abilities, others may see them as arrogant or presumptuous. Your task is to help clients find the right balance between these extremes, so they make sure their assets are recognized without coming across as conceited or overconfident.

Because there is a range of over- and underpromotion, your first step is to work with clients to develop an accurate idea of how well they are currently sharing and explaining their assets. Once this is established, you can provide suggestions to help them refine the amount of positive self-information they are sharing.

If people are too blatant about self-promotion, you will need to help them tone down the way they present themselves. They may need to learn how to turn the conversation toward the interests and accomplishments of others. The discussion of communication in Chapter 4 has several suggestions for developing active listening that will come in handy in this process.

Here are some points you may want to share with clients about the usefulness of self-promotion:

Qualities to demonstrate

- Skills
- Experience
- Competence
- Achievements
- Commitment

Concepts to communicate

- Interests
- Goals
- Career direction
- Initiative
- Enthusiasm
- Potential to achieve more
- Availability
- Ideas

Before engaging in self-promotion, clients need to recognize their unique skills, characteristics, and contributions. Work with your clients to clarify what their strengths are. Use your knowledge of personality type and work competencies to explore what your clients are good at and what they enjoy doing. Include general points as well as specific skills and knowledge. For example, characteristics such as enthusiasm and initiative are as important as knowledge of particular equipment. Unfortunately, many people are not able to quickly identify their strengths. In the following example, an employment counselor recounts her experiences in this area.

WHAT ARE MY STRENGTHS?

When I ask people about their strengths, they often reply, "I don't know" or "I haven't thought about that." So I reframe the question to "Why would I want to hire you and not someone else?" Many people are still unsure and have difficulty answering. But even if they come up with something as vague as "I am a good worker," it's possible to use this as an introduction to self-promotion. It provides a way to help someone identify the strengths they offer to the workforce.

Your clients can self-promote by walking their talk. If they are enthusiastic and positive, others will see this in their interactions. Modeling high performance is an effective start to self-promotion. However, your clients will also need to talk about their competencies. Others may not be in a position to observe their accomplishments or may rely more on what they hear than on what they observe.

Effective self-promotion must suit the time, place, people, and situation. It is unwise for people to promote themselves in situations or at activities that are focused on recognizing or celebrating the accomplishments of someone else. In these situations turning the focus away from the honoree's contributions and accomplishments will seem inappropriate and competitive. Self-promotion is also unsuitable in conversations that are focused on someone else or something else. Using tact and patience, effective self-promoters do not try to turn the spotlight on themselves at the expense of anyone else. Rather, they wait for appropriate opportunities to share their expertise and enthusiasm. In a similar way, direct comparisons such as "I could do a much better job than she did" are apt to be counterproductive. They come across as complaining and competitive rather than as effective self-promotion. A more fitting alternative could be, "Perhaps we could consider using a different strategy for accomplishing this. I think it might work to. . . . " This approach still shares expertise, but loses the negative tone.

Have your clients become aware of and focus on the events in organizations, associations, or communities that recognize others regularly. Help them identify vehicles within the organization where they can promote themselves, such as newsletters, awards, or recognition programs. Encourage them to research how the people receiving recognition are chosen. These individuals may have nominated themselves or had others nominate them to be included in the competition for recognition. If your clients have contributed or achieved in an area being recognized, encourage them to enter these types of competitions and recognition processes. Help them present their accomplishments in a form that meets the criteria of the group. Such public recognition can be a valuable self-promotion tool. For example, many communities have small business awards. Winners can include a line stating "Small business of the year award" on their résumés, in their portfolios, and in other promotional material. In an organizational setting, recognition for achievement provides a vehicle by which the client's name and achievements become more recognizable.

Have your clients create some short promotional statements to use in discussions. Discuss possible interactions where it would be appropriate to share some of their successes. Some individuals will need to practice or hear others model self-promotion.

Your clients will also find it useful to promote themselves in general conversations. This type of self-promotion is most effective when it is

PERFORMANCE PREFERENCES
Self-Promotion: Extraversion and Introversion

People with a preference for Extraversion (E) often find it natural and comfortable to promote themselves. They can usually share their thoughts and think of things to say right away.

People with a preference for Introversion (I) often find it challenging to engage in self-promotion. They may find it helpful to engage in some behavioral rehearsal or role playing to become more comfortable in this area.

QUICK TIPS
Developing Proactivity

Throughout the chapter you have seen many aspects of proactivity and factors that influence whether someone will demonstrate proactivity effectively. Here is a quick overview of the main chapter points to help you assess what areas of intervention will be most applicable in your situation.

- Show clients how to look for patterns and trends.
- Encourage the effort to see situations from diverse perspectives.
- Encourage taking an outside-the-box look at things.
- Help clients anticipate rather than be blindsided by change.
- Teach clients to think like futurists.
- Provide clients with what they need in times of change.
- Ensure clients are aware of and deal with personal effects of change.
- Work toward situations where clients can exert more control over change.
- Help clients set career and life goals.
- Use development as a tool to position clients for success.
- Show clients how to capitalize on opportunities.
- Encourage clients to promote themselves appropriately.

brief, targeted, and tactful. Help your clients create appropriate comments to use when talking to others. For example, say your client has just written a set of procedures for the organization and is interested in doing more writing. When discussing a problem related to a certain task with one of the leaders of the organization, the client has the opportunity to say something along the lines of, "You might find it helpful to look at the procedures I have just written for that task. I tried to make them as clear and specific as possible. Let me know what you think." These statements point out the work the client is doing and opens the door for the leader to look at the product. Later the client might comment on enjoying the procedure writing and ask the leader if there are any upcoming writing projects that need help. With these statements, the client is demonstrating interest and availability.

TLC FOR ALL TYPES: PROACTIVITY

All types can demonstrate proactivity. Here are some of the special challenges of developing this competency that relate to personality preferences. As you choose an intervention, be sure to take the personality type of your client into consideration.

RESPONDERS (ESTP AND ESFP)

The Responders' greatest strength, and biggest weakness, in times of change is their immediate and practical focus. They are adaptable in the moment and are especially creative when solving practical problems. They tend to react to change by being highly flexible and reactive. When faced with changes, Responders seek practical ways to maneuver through and adapt to current situations.

Responders may not focus on future trends and may be less interested in long-term effects than in immediate action. When helping them cope with unexpected change, you may need to help them see a practical way forward. Show them how concrete, immediate changes will help them achieve long-term results. Use practical language and examples when describing changes and focus on immediate benefits and effects.

Responders prefer to learn and develop through experience. They are not highly motivated to make long-term plans and often follow an emergent rather than structured path forward. They need to see a practical reason to promote themselves.

Logical Responders (ESTP) need to see logical as well as practical reasons for change. They are usually quick to respond and adaptable, but they may become resistant if proposed changes appear illogical or too time consuming for the resulting benefit. Compassionate Responders (ESFP) need to see how changes will affect the people involved. They want practical information to help people deal with the immediate effects of a change.

EXPLORERS (ENTP AND ENFP)

The Explorers' greatest strength, and biggest weakness, in times of change is that they are already there. They tend to be highly proactive and change oriented, and will jump in and try something new and different. They enjoy generating possibilities, seeing trends, and anticipating the future. When working to implement change, Explorers may miss important facts, details, and steps in the change process. They may seek a total rather than partial change and may not be concerned about preserving what still works.

Explorers can be resistant to imposed change if it does not fit with their view of the future or if the change creates additional structure or limits freedom of action. It may help to show Explorers long-term effects and possibilities of this type of change. They will make more sense of change when they can organize data, details, and structure into a conceptual framework. Explorers like to develop and position themselves for opportunities and usually find it easy to align themselves with future possibilities and opportunities. They can promote themselves easily, although they may need to be careful not to promise the moon.

Logical Explorers (ENTP) need to see logical reasons for change and look for a coherent overall framework and vision behind a change. Compassionate Explorers (ENFP) are especially interested in how change will affect people. Good change, in the mind of a Compassionate Explorer, ensures that people's needs are being considered and creates opportunities for people to develop their potential.

EXPEDITORS (ESTJ AND ENTJ)

The Expeditors' greatest strength, and biggest weakness, in times of change is getting the job done. They constantly analyze how well things are being done and focus on seeing possibilities for improving the efficiency of processes. When faced with unexpected changes, they may be impatient about dealing with the emotional effects of change. Because of this, when planning change themselves, they may miss effects of changes on people. Help them see the personal as well as the logical side of the changes.

Expeditors like to have some control and prefer to be in a situation where they can structure and plan change themselves. When faced with options during change, Expeditors may seek closure and take action too quickly. When helping them deal with change, provide interim activities for them to do while change is being conceptualized and implemented. Show them logical reasons for the change and emphasize how efficiency will be increased. Expeditors seek competence and want to do their work well. They set structured goals and strive to achieve them. Expeditors are able to highlight their strengths but may have to watch out for being negative or complaining about standards and abilities of others. People may see their analytical comparisons of themselves to others as arrogant.

Practical Expeditors (ESTJ) want practical information about change. They want change to be implemented immediately so they can continue to carry out their work. Insightful Expeditors (ENTJ) look for information that will convince them there will be long-term positive impacts of change. They want the change to be carried out as logically as possible with the most efficient use of time and other resources.

CONTRIBUTORS (ESFJ AND ENFJ)

The Contributors' greatest strength, and biggest weakness, in times of change is becoming personally involved in the situation. They are interested in trends that will increase morale or make the workplace a more harmonious environment. Contributors want everyone to be involved and engaged in changes in a positive way. They may take the effects of change personally. They dislike working in settings where people are uncomfortable or unsure.

When helping Contributors cope with change, discuss feelings and offer support for transitions. Show them how change will help the people involved and help them see the logical as well as the personal side of the change. When setting goals, Contributors often focus on the needs of the people who are important to them as well as their personal needs. They may focus on the achievements of their work group and not want to promote themselves. They tend to speak of their achievements in terms of "we" rather than "I." Although this approach is not necessarily seen as negative, Contributors may need to take time to focus on defining and sharing their unique contributions to team achievements.

Practical Contributors (ESFJ) are interested in understanding how change will help people in a practical way. Insightful Contributors (ENFJ) want to see how change will help people develop their potential.

ASSIMILATORS (ISTJ AND ISFJ)

The Assimilators' greatest strength, and biggest weakness, in times of change is preserving the status quo. They prefer practical, well-thought-out, well-organized, incremental change. Assimilators want to preserve what works and are cynical of change that alters things when they are working well. They can be uncomfortable when they are doing something they have not done before.

Assimilators may find it difficult to see trends that are not linked to their current or past experiences. When working with Assimilators to help them anticipate change, be sure to include lots of data for them to extrapolate from. They may resist change if it is externally driven or presented without detail and structure. Assimilators may be immobilized if they don't have time to think the change through.

To help Assimilators manage change, provide data and specific tasks, timelines, and details of new realities. Provide opportunities for them to share their rich experiential data about what will and won't work. Allow time for them to reflect, accept, and plan to implement change. Assimilators like to set goals that are structured and specific. They will not willingly talk about their achievements. To help them develop self-promotion skills, tap into their areas of expertise.

Logical Assimilators (ISTJ) want to understand the logical reasons behind change. They want to see how the new reality is an improvement over the old one. Compassionate Assimilators (ISFJ) want to know exactly what is expected of them and others during the change. They want to ensure everyone is still able to carry out their roles without feeling awkward or displaced.

VISIONARIES (INTJ AND INFJ)

The Visionaries' greatest strength, and biggest weakness, in times of change is a long-term future focus. They want to visualize and conceptualize global and sweeping changes and need to see a complex, integrated, long-term plan. They tend to be natural future watchers and find it easy to predict change. However, when planning for change, Visionaries can get lost in models and possibilities and may not always consider the realities.

Visionaries can experience a conflict between their need to achieve results and their need to think about and plan for change. When helping them deal with change, involve them in creating a vision. Show them long-term, big-picture aspects of change and link changes to theoretical models or provide additional sources of information for them. Visionaries enjoy setting and working toward long-term goals. They are able to promote their visions and strategic approach, but may use abstract language and concepts. They may have difficulty promoting their skills and experiences and may need help to turn their conceptual approach into a more practical one.

Logical Visionaries (INTJ) look for models and frameworks to help them see the vision and logic underlying a change. They are analytical and want others to explain why the changes are being implemented and what the long-term consequences will be. Compassionate Visionaries (INFJ) also want to understand the long-term consequences of change, but they are more interested in understanding the broad effects of the changes on people involved in the process.

ANALYZERS (ISTP AND INTP)

The Analyzers' greatest strength, and biggest weakness, in times of change is analysis and skepticism. They are willing to adapt and flex as necessary and enjoy change that is sensible. When future watching, Analyzers naturally see logical links and identify likely consequences of actions. Analyzers may maneuver around, ignore, or avoid changes that don't seem logical. They also may detach or withdraw from situations they can't maneuver around and can become noncompliant if they don't buy into change.

To help them manage change, show the logic behind the change and how change will make things quicker or easier. Let them maneuver independently without too many procedures or roadblocks. Provide them with options and time to think about the changes. Analyzers' goals reflect their interest in doing things faster and more efficiently. Analyzers are not comfortable promoting themselves and think highlighting their strengths is stating the obvious.

Practical Analyzers (ISTP) need to see practical applications of change. They are not motivated to engage in change that has some nebulous future result. Insightful Analyzers (INTP) want to understand the long-term need for and benefits of a change. Both question and resist change that doesn't make logical sense.

ENHANCERS (ISFP AND INFP)

The Enhancers' greatest strength, and biggest weakness, in times of change is a need to see meaning in change. They are sensitive to and focused on the needs of individuals involved in the change. When future watching, they tend to focus on what the implications of change will be for the people involved. Enhancers adapt as necessary and enjoy change that validates or helps people. If change is not congruent with their values, they tend to be highly resistant. They may not share these concerns until they are very frustrated by changes.

When helping Enhancers manage change, provide opportunities to share concerns and deal with emotions and personal needs. Provide a meaningful part for them to play in the process. Help them see the logical as well as the personal side of the change. Enhancers set goals that consider the needs of others. They may have difficulty separating what is important to them personally from the needs of those who are important to them. Enhancers may find it difficult to promote themselves. They are more comfortable promoting others and emphasizing the contributions others have made to their own success.

Practical Enhancers (ISFP) are concerned about how people are treated when a change is being carried out. They want to help make the immediate change as smooth as possible. Insightful Enhancers (INFP) are concerned with the long-term effects of change on the people involved. They want to understand how the change will affect people's ability to achieve their potential.

Summary of the Five Workplace Competencies

Facilitating development is a multifaceted process. By building a relationship and following a customized development plan you can help individuals improve the basic competencies they need to be successful in the workplace. Here is a summary of the five basic workplace competencies and their components. Target your development plan to enhance these competencies. As a result you will facilitate the development of individuals who demonstrate high performance in the workplace.

SELF-RESPONSIBILITY

Shows Up Ready and Willing to Work

- Is realistically optimistic
- Energetic and alert
- Independently works toward goals

Takes Ownership

- Demonstrates personal accountability
- Maximizes effective use of personal assets

When people achieve expertise in the self-responsibility competency they hold themselves accountable for their performance. They are ready, willing and motivated to take responsibility for performing well.

COMMUNICATION

Listens Carefully

- Encourages others to express differing opinions
- Clarifies and acts on communications
- Incorporates corrective feedback

Shares Information Effectively

- Customizes messages to show purpose, planning, and precision
- Gives both positive and corrective feedback
- Resolves issues

When people achieve expertise in the communication competency they interact effectively with others. They are able to work in a team, listen and share information effectively, and resolve conflicts.

MINDFULNESS

Knows How to Learn

- Accesses and uses relevant or new information
- Critiques and evaluates information sources
- Integrates and transfers new information across situations

Knows How to Apply Thinking

- Systematically solves problems and makes informed decisions
- Consciously applies different modes of thinking

When people achieve expertise in the mindfulness competency they know how to learn. Mindful workers solve problems, make informed decisions, and adjust their thinking processes to maximize their effectiveness.

PRODUCTIVITY

Focuses on Obtaining Results

- Prioritizes, plans, and organizes time and tasks
- Persists on tasks

Achieves Exceptional Results

- Completes work to a high standard
- Continually improves work processes and exceeds standards

When people achieve expertise in the productivity competency they achieve exceptional results. They can be relied on to get the work done to a high standard.

PROACTIVITY

Anticipates and Adjusts to Change

- Looks for patterns and trends from diverse perspectives
- Adjusts behavior to accommodate change

Fulfills Career and Life Goals

- Sets career and life goals
- Uses self-development and self-promotion to capitalize on opportunities

When people achieve expertise in the proactivity competency they anticipate change and react quickly to unexpected change. They position themselves for success by setting goals and then developing and promoting themselves.

Developing these essential competencies will prepare twenty-first-century workers to meet the unique and complex challenges of our rapidly changing workplace.

References

Barger, N., and Kirby, L. K. *The Challenge of Change in Organizations*. Palo Alto, CA: Davies-Black Publishing, 1995.

Barr, L., and Barr, N. *The Leadership Equation*. Austin, TX: Eakin Press, 1989.

Bender, P. *Leadership from Within*. Toronto, ON: Stoddart Publishing, 1997.

Berens, L., and Isachsen, O. *A Quick Guide to Working Together with the Sixteen Types*. Huntington Beach, CA: Telos Publications, 1992.

Bridges, W. *Transitions: Making Sense of Life's Changes* (2nd ed.). New York: Perseus Publishing, 1980.

Bridges, W. *Managing Transitions: Making the Most of Change* (2nd ed.). New York: Perseus Publishing, 2003.

De Bono, E. *Six Thinking Hats*. London: Penguin Books, 1985.

Dubois, D. *Competency-Based Performance Improvement.* Amherst, MA: HRD Press, 1993.

Dunning, D. *Learning Your Way*. Red Deer, AB: Unlimited Learning Publications, 1998.

Dunning, D. *What's Your Type of Career?* Palo Alto, CA: Davies-Black Publishing, 2001.

Dunning, D. *Introduction to Type® and Communication*. Palo Alto, CA: CPP, Inc., 2003.

Fitzgerald, C., and Kirby, L. K. (Eds.). *Developing Leaders.* Palo Alto, CA: Davies-Black Publishing, 1997.

Hirsh, S. K., and Kummerow, J. M. *Introduction to Type® in Organizations* (3rd ed.). Palo Alto, CA: CPP, Inc., 1998.

Isachsen, O., and Berens, L. *Working Together: A Personality-Centered Approach to Management.* Coronado, CA: Neworld Management Press, 1988.

Kroeger, O., and Thuesen, J. *Type Talk at Work.* New York: Dell Publishing, 1992.

Myers, I. B., with Myers, P. B. *Gifts Differing: Understanding Personality Type.* Palo Alto, CA: Davies-Black Publishing, 1995.

Myers, I. B. *Introduction to Type®* (6th ed.). Palo Alto, CA: CPP, Inc., 1998.

Myers, I. B., McCaulley, M. H., Quenk, N. L., and Hammer, A. L. *MBTI®
Manual: A Guide to the Development and Use of the Myers-Briggs Type
Indicator®* (3rd ed.). Palo Alto, CA: CPP, Inc., 1998.

Myers, K. D., and Kirby, L. K. *Introduction to Type® Dynamics and Development: Exploring the Next Level of Type.* Palo Alto, CA: CPP, Inc., 1994.

Pearman, R. R., and Albritton, S. C. *I'm Not Crazy, I'm Just Not You.* Palo
Alto, CA: Davies-Black Publishing, 1997.

Quenk, N. L. *Was That Really Me? How Everyday Stress Brings Out Our Hid-
den Personality.* Palo Alto, CA: Davies-Black Publishing, 2002.

Robinson, D., and Robinson, J. *Performance Consulting*. San Francisco:
Berrett-Koehler Publishers, 1995.

Thomson, L. *Personality Type: An Owners Manual*. Boston: Shambhala Publications, 1998.

Index

ness by, 202; proactivity by, 271–272; productivity development in, 235; qualities and preferences of, 43; self-assessment by, 119; self-responsibility development in, 119; thinking modes used by, 202. *See also* Insightful Contributors; Practical Contributors

control, 111

creative thinking, 193, 195–196

credibility: building of, 8; self-disclosures and, 13

critical thinking, 176

criticizing, 61

decision making: alternatives for, 189–191; criteria for, 190–191; evaluation of, 191–192; learning gained from, 191; poor approach to, 185; problem solving and, 185; steps involved in, 189–192

Development Plan: challenging of unproductive behaviors and beliefs, 80–81; consequences for noncompletion of, 73; customizing of, 74; description of, 20–21; effectiveness of, 84–87; evaluation of, 86; form for, 52–55; implementation of, 75–87; intervention strategy, 73–75; questioning, 77–79; reinforcement of progress, 81; results of, 84–87; structured, 71–75; success measures for, 72–73

differences: appreciation of, 35–36; interventions adjusted to accommodate, 38–40

differing opinions, 125–132

distractions, 216

diverse perspectives, 241–254

eating habits, 102–103

e-mail: description of, 168, 172; management of, 211; responding to, 208

emergent processes, for achieving goals, 259–260

emotions, 145

empathic responses, 130–132

energy levels, 101–103

ENFJ. *See* Insightful Contributors

ENFP. *See* Compassionate Explorers

Enhancers: change by, 274–275; communication by, 160; description of, 35, 37; mindfulness by, 204; proactivity by, 274–275; productivity development in, 237; qualities and preferences of, 46–47; self-responsibility development in, 121; thinking modes used by, 204. *See also* Insightful Enhancers; Practical Enhancers

enthusiasm, 146

ENTJ. *See* Insightful Expeditors

ENTP. *See* Logical Explorers

error analysis, 170–171

ESFJ. *See* Practical Contributors

ESFP. *See* Compassionate Responders

ESTJ. *See* Practical Expeditors

ESTP. *See* Logical Responders

expectations: clarification of, 222–224; exceeding of, 229–231; review of, 229–230; setting of, 110; unclear, 67

Expeditors: change by, 271; communication by, 157; description of, 30–31, 37; mindfulness by, 201–202; proactivity by, 271; productivity development in, 234; qualities and preferences of, 42; self-assessments by, 118; self-responsibility development in, 118; thinking modes used by, 201–202. *See also* Insightful Expeditors; Practical Expeditors

expertise areas, 15–17

Explorers: change and, 270; communication by, 156–157; description of, 30, 37; mindfulness by, 201; proactivity by, 270; productivity development in, 233–234; qualities and pref-erences of, 41–42; self-assessments by, 118; self-responsibility development in, 117–118; thinking modes used by, 201. *See also* Compassionate Explorers; Logical Explorers